4/--

(8)

6-50

0/-/

The Cavalry Manual of
Horse Management

ALSO BY FREDERICK L. DEVEREUX, JR.:

Practical Navigation for the Yachtsman
Ride Your Pony Right
Horses: A First Book
Backyard Pony
Horseback Riding: A First Book
Famous American Horses
Jump Your Horse Right
Horse Problems and Problem Horses

The Cavalry Manual
of Horse Management

Frederick L. Devereux, Jr.

SOUTH BRUNSWICK AND NEW YORK: A. S. BARNES AND COMPANY
LONDON: THOMAS YOSELOFF LTD

© 1979 by A. S. Barnes and Co., Inc.

A. S. Barnes and Co., Inc.
Cranbury, New Jersey 08512

Thomas Yoseloff Ltd
Magdalen House
136-148 Tooley Street
London SE1 2TT, England

Library of Congress Cataloging in Publication Data

United States. Calvalry School, Fort Riley, Kan.
   The Cavalry manual of horse management.

   Revision of Animal management, which was issued
as v. 2, pt, 3, of Horsemanship and horsemastership,
published 1941-42.
   Includes index.
   1. Horses. I. Devereux, Frederick L., Jr., 1914–
II. United States. Cavalry School, Fort Riley, Kan.
Horsemanship and horsemastership, v. 2, pt. 3.
III. Title.
UE460.U54   1978   636.1   76-50183
ISBN 0-498-01947-0 (hardcover)
ISBN 0-498-02371-0 (paperback)

PRINTED IN THE UNITED STATES OF AMERICA

Contents

Preface

In the 1930s the United States Army Cavalry School at Fort Riley, Kansas, was the internationally acknowledged fountainhead of wisdom in the teaching of equitation and the management and care of horses. The official texts prepared by the school's Department of Horsemanship, and known as the *Horsemanship and Horsemastership* series, contained all the horse-related material for the year-long course that lieutenants were required to complete satisfactorily before being qualified for horse troop command. When the mounted service was disbanded and merged with the Armor after World War II the series went out of print, but the demand for the information contained therein has continued—literally hundreds of books encompassing all phases of horsemanship, and using the Cavalry texts as the basic reference, have been published in the last four decades. None, however, has as comprehensively covered the subject of horse management as did the original text, which was officially known as Volume II, Part Three, hence this revised work, edited for the civilian horseowner's requirement for an authoritative reference on all the phases of caring for a horse.

I have attempted to do as little revision as possible, consistent with the obvious need to update and, in some areas, to delete information. Some paragraphs have been rewritten in the interest of more detailed or clearer explanation. Where a major change has been made the authority for the change has been stated. I have made no change or addition that I was not morally certain would have been made by the Department of Horsemanship if that body were still functioning; for example the development of commercial feeds (as opposed to natural feeds) is a post-World War II introduction; certainly this topic would have been covered for the examination of its nutritional comparison with other feeds and I have therefore included this and other postwar developments that have withstood the test of time. By the same token certain practices have either become obsolete (such as the chapter on Transportation, which dealt almost exclusively with shipping by rail) or were solely confined to the military and of no earthly use to today's horse owner (for example, the system of neck branding by which the army identified its animals). To reprint the manual without editing for today's needs would simply have been to preserve a historical document. Interesting though that might have been, such was not my purpose.

One minor change that old troopers will immediately note is the somewhat altered title. To the army, animals were either horses or mules (except for the period of Jefferson Davis's service as Secretary of War when he introduced a camel corps to the Southwestern frontier). The original title, *Animal Management,* has therefore been changed to *Horse Management* as more appropriate and accurate.

Frederick L. Devereux, Jr.

Acknowledgments

For the necessary updating that this work required after being out of print since World War II I am indebted to several present or former members of the faculty at two of the famed colleges of Cornell University, the New York State College of Veterinary Medicine and the New York State College of Agriculture and Life Science. I greatly appreciate the full and complete cooperation of Doctors Donald D. Delehanty, Harold H. Hintz, N. Bruce Haynes, and Samuel W. Sabin. In particular my good friend and polo companero, Stephen J. Roberts D.V.M., paved the way for Cornell's invaluable cooperation and also reviewed my changes, additions, and clarifications of the original manual. Without Doctor Robert's cheerful and knowledgeable assistance and expertise I very probably would not have attempted this work.

The photographs and illustrations in the original edition, while accurate but barely adequate for the most part, reflected the prewar Army's penurious condition, and many were of a "make do" caliber. Cornell's talents and facilities were therefore sought for completely new art work except for a very few carryovers from the original edition. Jane Tutton provided the line drawings and Robert F. Smith the photographs, except as otherwise credited.

I thank General William H. Sterling Wright, one of the cavalry's most distinguished horsemen, for his introduction to this revision of the animal management reference that was his "bible" while a student at the Cavalry School as a junior officer of the 7th Cavalry. General James H. Polk, a fellow-cavalryman and recently commander of the United States Army in Europe, kindly provided his treasured copy of the original when the need arose for a spare to replace my worn-out edition. Colonel Joseph P. Cribbins, once the stable sergeant in the troop in which I served as a green lieutenant and now the army's helicopter expert, has forgotten more about a horse than most men will ever know; his advice over the years has contributed greatly to whatever knowledge I may possess.

Rhonda White competently typed the manuscript and deciphered my marginal notations with great patience.

Finally, I am grateful for the dedication and interest of the instructors at the Cavalry School and pay tribute to their professional competence that made my assignment as a student in the last prewar horsemanship class such a meaningful and rewarding experience.

Introduction

None of us who were so fortunate as to serve in the cavalry branch of our Army in the happy and uncomplicated days between the two World Wars will ever forget the enjoyable if rigorous schooling that all the junior officers underwent at the Cavalry School at Fort Riley, Kansas. It included, of course, a thorough grounding in troop leadership, tactics, communications, and supply—all most essential to the troop commanders of the mounted service. But to the young cavalry officer, the diadem, glory, and joy of that course of schooling in those halcyon days was our instruction in horsemanship and horsemastership. Many happy and strenuous hours under great officer instructors, graduates not only of our own Cavalry School but, in many cases, of the French, Italian, or Polish schools, now flood back in glorious memory.

Those hours spent in the riding halls, on cross-country gallops, on the point-to-point course, on the polo field, and in the dressage ring gave the young officer a vigor, mobility, and boldness of body, mind, and spirit that were later to bring victory to our nation and its allies in the lightning spearheads of our armored divisions across the north European plain. The days at Fort Riley, training young horses and learning from veterans, were golden and never to be forgotten. They produced great combat leaders and great Olympic riders.

In addition to the hours in the saddle were many classroom hours devoted to horsemastership or, in today's terms, horse management. Here veterinarians, farriers, animal nutritionists, and veteran stable sergeants impressed upon the young officer the absolute necessity of knowing how to keep the cavalry mount in sound and vigorous condition. Many hours again were spent in the operating theater of the veterinary hospital, the horseshoeing school, and in the forage sheds. Many a retired general can still recount in vivid detail how he, as a junior officer, singlehandedly shod some stony-footed brute of an artillery draft animal just in from months of barefooted freedom at pasture.

All the elements of our instruction, both mounted and in the classroom, were distilled in a textbook entitled *Horsemanship and Horsemastership.* Roughly one half of the book was devoted to equitation and the other half to horse management. It was comprehensive, authoritative, and to my mind is still, in its essentials, unsurpassed.

Since those happy days many writers, some of them graduates of the discipline, have produced excellent books on equitation and the best of them often followed the Cavalry School methods of training both horse and rider. What has not been done until publication of Colonel Devereux's present revised volume is the production of a comprehensive work on horse management for the lay reader that distills in concise yet sufficiently detailed form all that the finished horseman or horsewoman needs to know about the care, conditioning, and management of the horse.

Colonel Devereux is eminently qualified to edit such a book for the horseman, or woman, of today based on the old Cavalry School text. He is an outstanding product of the Cavalry School. Before the cavalry was dismounted and incorporated into the Armor branch he served in all grades from private to lieutenant colonel. He has instructed in equitation at West Point and has been an active judge of hunters, jumpers, and equitation as well as serving as steward at the American Horse Shows Association's leading fixtures. Having followed Fred over many a fence, I most heartily endorse his much-needed work and wish it good galloping over a fair country.

W.H.S. WRIGHT Lt. Gen., U.S.A. (Ret.)

The Cavalry Manual of
Horse Management

1

Anatomy and Physiology

The intelligent operation and care of any mechanism is based on a good working knowledge of its general structure and normal functions. The animal body may be considered as a complex machine of many parts, with each of these various parts normally functioning in a more or less definite manner. The science that treats of the form and structure of the animal body is known as *anatomy*. The science that treats of the normal functioning of the animal body is known as *physiology*. It is quite essential that the study of animal management include a basic knowledge of the anatomy and physiology of the horse in order that the student may more intelligently recognize the reasons upon which the fundamental principles of animal management are based. In this text the study of anatomy and physiology will be correlated as much as possible and limited to those parts of greatest essential interest.

The body of the horse is in general structure quite like the body of man; their chief differences are in the relative size and relationship of the various parts, and for these reasons the various structures of the horse will in many instances be compared with the similar parts of the human body. The body of the horse, like that of man, is made up of a *skeletal* system, a *muscular* system, a *digestive* system, a *respiratory* system, a *circulatory* system, a *nervous* system, a *urinary* system, a *reproductive* system, and an outer covering of skin and hair.

SKELETAL SYSTEM

The skeletal system includes the bones and the ligaments that bind bones together to form joints. The skeletal system gives the body form and rigidity, and forms cavities for the protection of vital organs. Bones and joints together form a complex system of levers and pulleys that, combined with the muscular system, gives the body power of motion. The relative size and relationship of position of

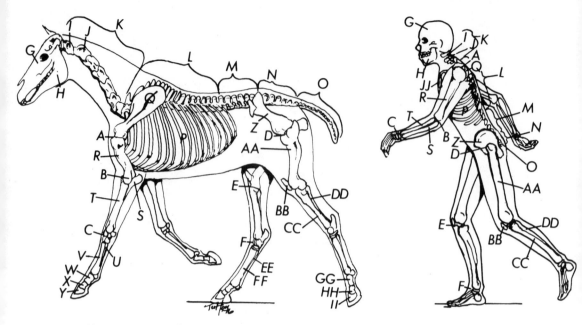

Skeletal System of Horse and Man Compared

Bones of Horse (Human Counterparts If Different Name)

A. Shoulder Joint
B. Elbow Joint
C. Knee Joint (Wrist Joint)
D. Hip Joint
E. Stifle Joint (Knee Joint)
F. Hock Joint (Ankle Joint)
G. Skull
H. Mandible
I. Atlas
J. Axis
K. Cervical Vertebrae
L. Thoracic Vertebrae
M. Lumbar Vertebrae
N. Sacral Vertebrae
O. Coccygeal Vertebrae
P. Ribs
Q. Scapula
R. Humerus

S. Ulna
T. Radius
U. Small Metacarpal or Splint ⎱ (Hand Bones)
V. Large Metacarpal or Cannon ⎰
W. First Phalanx or Long Pastern ⎫
X. Second Phalanx or Short Pastern ⎬ (Finger Bones)
Y. Third Phalanx or Coffin Bone ⎭
Z. Hip Bone
AA. Femur
BB. Patella
CC. Tibia
DD. Fibula
EE. Small Metatarsal or Splint ⎱ (Foot Bones)
FF. Large Metatarsal or Cannon ⎰
GG. First Phalanx or Long Pastern ⎫
HH. Second Phalanx or Short Pastern ⎬ (Toe Bones)
II. Third Phalanx or Coffin Bone ⎭
JJ. (Sternum or Breastbone)

the bones determine the real form (or *conformation*) of the horse and his efficiency for any particular work. The *trunk* (or *axial skeleton*) consists of the *skull, spinal* (or *vertebral*) *column, ribs,* and *breast bone.* The *limbs* (or *appendicular skeleton*) support the body and furnish the levers of propulsion.

BONES. The skeleton of the horse is made up of about 205 bones.* In their living

Variations in the number of bones, particularly in the spinal column, depend on the breed. The Arabian, for example, has fewer vertebrae than the Thoroughbred. [Ed.]

16

state bones are composed of about one part of organic matter and two parts of inorganic mineral matter (largely lime salts). The bones, as seen in a mounted skeleton, have been freed of organic matter and are white and brittle, but living bone is about twice as strong as a green oak stick of the same size. Bones, according to their shape, are classified as *long, short, flat,* and *irregular.*

Long bones are found in the limbs, where they support the body weight and act as the levers of propulsion.

Short bones occur chiefly in the knee and hock, where they function in the dissipation of concussion.

Flat bones, such as the ribs, scapula, and some of the bones of the skull, help to enclose cavities containing vital organs.

Irregular bones are such bones as the vertebrae and some bones of the skull.

All bones are covered with a thin, tough membrane, *periosteum,* except at points of articulation where they are covered with *cartilage.* The *periosteum* is closely attached to the bone; it covers and protects the bone and influences the growth of bone to a certain extent. This latter function is of particular interest, for injury to this membrane often results in an abnormal bone growth called an *exotosis,* occurring at the point of injury. Bone growths such as splints, spavins, and ringbones are the frequent result of some form of injury to the periosteum. The bone is in part nourished by blood vessels in the periosteum, and there are many nerve endings in this membrane.

The articular, or joint, surfaces of bones are covered with a dense, very smooth, bluish-colored substance called *cartilage.* The cartilage diminishes the effects of concussion and provides a smooth joint surface offering a minimum of frictional resistance to movement.

BONES OF THE SKULL. There are thirty-four bones in the skull, and it is divided into two parts, the *cranium* and the *face.*

The bones of the cranium are all flat or irregular and surround the *cranial cavity,* which contains the brain. The cavity is relatively small considering the size of the animal.* The bones join each other in immovable joints. The bone forming what is known as the *poll* has an articulating surface where the head is jointed to the vertebral (or spinal) column. Together with the bones of the face, the cranial bones form the *orbital* and *nasal* cavities.

The bones of the face form the skeleton of the mouth and nasal cavities and include the more important bones of the upper and lower jaws known as the *maxillae* and *mandible* respectively. Each maxilla has six irregular cavities for the reception of the cheek (or *molar*) teeth. From the maxillae forward the face becomes narrower and terminates in the *premaxilla,* which contains cavities for the six upper *incisor* teeth. Enclosed in each maxilla is a cavity known as the *maxilary sinus,* which opens into the nasal passages. This sinus contains the roots of the three back molar teeth and at times becomes infected due to diseased teeth.

On an intelligence scale where man is rated at 100 the horse will be rated at approximately 14, or one-seventh of man's ability. This ratio corresponds roughly to the relative cranial cavity size when considered in relationship to total body size. [Ed.]

The *mandible,* or lower jaw, is hinged to the cranium on either side by a freely movable joint in front of and below the base of the ear. At its front extremity it has cavities for the six lower incisors. Back of the incisors is a space between the incisors and the six lower molars in each side of the mandible known as the *interdental* space. Injuries to the periosteum or possible fracture of the mandible may occur in the interdental space due to rough usage of the bit. The space between the branches of the lower jaw is occupied by the tongue and important salivary and lymph glands.

VERTEBRAL OR SPINAL COLUMN. The vertebral or spinal column may be regarded as the basis of the skeleton from which all other parts originate. It is composed of irregular-shaped bones together with ligaments and cartilage forming a column of bones from the base of the skull to the tip of the tail. Through the length of this column is an elongated cavity called the *spinal canal* containing the *spinal cord,* which is the main trunk line of nerves coming from the brain, lying in the cranial cavity. Through this more or less flexible column of bones the powerful impetus of propulsion originating in the hind legs is transmitted to the forequarters of the animal and, indirectly, it bears the weight of the rider and his equipment.

The bones of the vertebral column are divided into five regions:

The *cervical* or neck region contains seven cervical vertebrae. The first of these, the *atlas,* is jointed to the cranium by a hingelike joint permitting only extension and flexion of the head on the neck. The next cervical vertebra, the *axis,* is so jointed to the atlas that it permits rotation of the head and atlas on the remainder of the neck. The remaining five cervical vertebrae have no special names. The column of bones in this region is arranged, when viewed from the side, in an S-shaped curve. Lengthening and shortening of the neck is brought about by lessening or increasing this curvature. The cervical region is the most flexible part of the vertebral column and, from the viewpoint of the student of equitation, the possible movements of the head and neck are of great importance.

The *thoracic* region contains eighteen thoracic vertebrae. These form, in part, the upper wall of the chest cavity. Each vertebra has on either side an articulating surface for jointing to its corresponding pair of ribs. Each vertebra has on its upper surface a spine, or process of bone, called the *spinous process.* These processes vary, increasing in length from the first to the fourth and fifth, which are the longest and form the summit of the withers, and then decrease in length. Movement in this part of the vertebral column is somewhat limited.

The *lumbar* region contains six lumbar vertebrae (sometimes five, especially in the Arabian horse). This part of the spinal column forms the framework of the loin; movement here is much greater than in the thoracic portion.

The *sacral* region contains five sacral vertebrae. These five bones are fused together and may be considered to be one bone, the *sacrum,* the highest point of which forms the croup. The sacrum is jointed very securely to the hip bones on either side; through this joint the propulsive impulses from the hind legs are transmitted to the vertebral column.

The *coccygeal* region contains from fifteen to twenty-one coccygeal vertebrae and forms the bony column of the tail. The spinal canal is practically absent in this part of the vertebral column.

The vertebral formula* of the horse is C7 T18 L6 S5 Cy15-21.
The vertebral formula of man is C7 T12 L5 S5 Cy4.

BONY THORAX (Chest). The bony thorax is a large cavity formed by the thoracic vertebrae above, the ribs on the sides, and the *sternum* (breast bone) forming the floor. This cavity contains the heart and lungs, large blood vessels and nerves, and part of the trachea and esophagus. Depth of the chest cavity, with moderate width, is desirable.

RIBS. The horse has eighteen pairs of *ribs,* all of which are jointed to the thoracic vertebrae at their upper ends. The lower ends of the first eight pairs, called *true* or *sternal* ribs, are jointed by means of cartilage to the sternum or breast bone. The last ten pairs, called *asternal* or *false* ribs, are continued at their lower ends by extensions of cartilage that are bound together by elastic tissue. The shape and length of the ribs determine the contour of the chest. The ribs form the direct skeletal support of the saddle. (Man has but twelve pairs of ribs, seven sternal and five asternal.)

STERNUM. The *sternum,* or breast bone, is canoe-shaped and consists of seven or eight bony segments connected by cartilage. The sternum forms the floor of the thorax, and the front end forms the bony prominence on the midline of the breast.

BONES OF THE FORELEG. The bones of the foreleg, named from the top downward, are the *scapula, humerus, radius* and *ulna, carpal* bones, three *metacarpal* bones, *first phalanx, second phalanx, third phalanx,* and the *proximal* and *distal* (navicular) sesamoid bones.

The *scapula,* or shoulder blade, is a triangular flat bone in the region of the shoulder and lies on the side of the thorax. Along its upper border (the base of the triangle) is attached a thin, flat and flexible cartilagenous extension. When the leg is extended to the front, the edge of this cartilage often slips under the front of the bar of the saddle without injury to the shoulder blade. The direction of this bone is sloping downward and forward, the average enclosed angle between the long axis of this bone and the horizontal is about 50° to 55° in the riding type of horse. If the direction of this bone approaches the vertical the shoulder is said to be straight or upright, which is not favorable for length and freedom of the forward movement of the foreleg. The scapula is attached to the thorax only by muscles, there being no bony union with the sternum, ribs, or spinal column. (In man the scapula is jointed to the sternum through the *clavicle,* or collarbone, a bone that is entirely absent in the skeleton of the horse.) The lower end of the scapula is jointed to the humerus.

The *humerus* is the bone of the arm and extends downward and backward from the shoulder joint to the elbow joint. The enclosed angle between humerus and scapula is usually about 115°, causing the direction of the humerus to be governed

*Vertebral Formula: A method of expressing the number of bones in the vertebral (or spinal) column as distributed in the five regions. In this formula C indicates the cervical (neck) region, T the thoracic, L the lumbar, S the sacral, and Cy the coccygeal (tail bone). [Ed.]

by the slope of the scapula. The humerus is surrounded with heavy muscles and is attached to the wall of the thorax by muscle. Because of its muscular protection and position this bone is not often injured. (In man, the humerus or arm bone is much freer of the body and has a much greater range of movement in the shoulder joint.)

The *radius* is the bone of the forearm and, with the ulna and humerus, forms the elbow joint. The *ulna* is a short bone that is fused to the upper part of the radius and also protects above the end of the radius to form the point of the elbow. (In man the ulna is comparitively longer and extends, on the little finger side, with the radius to the wrist joint.) The long axis of the radius should be vertical.

The *carpal* (or knee) bones correspond to the wrist bones of man. There are seven or eight carpal bones arranged in two rows. The top row articulates with the lower end of the radius, and most of the movement of the knee joint is confined to this articulation. The top and bottom rows articulate with each other, and the bottom row also with the upper ends of the metacarpal bones. A great deal of concussion transmitted up the bony column from below is absorbed and dissipated by the carpal bones.

The horse has three *metacarpal* bones. The large middle metacarpal *(cannon bone)* extends from the knee to the fetlock and is sometimes known as the third matacarpal. Because of the great strength of this bone it is seldom fractured, although it is one of the most exposed bones of the skeleton. In its early evolutionary stage the horse was a five-toed animal, but during the development to his present form the two inner and two outer toes were lost and only the two *splint bones* (small metacarpals) persist as vestigal remains of the original second and fourth metacarpals. These small bones are located on the internal and external posterior borders of the large metacarpal; their upper ends articulate with the lower row of carpal bones. Since they are only about three-fourths as long as the large metacarpal they have no direct support at their lower end but, where in contact with the large metacarpal, they are closely bound to it by the strong *interosseous ligament.* Strains of this ligament result in the condition known as *splints.* After a horse is about seven years of age this ligament begins to ossify and, in old animals, the splint bones may become firmly fused to the cannon bone. The long axis of the cannon bone should be vertical.

The *first phalanx,* or long pastern bone, corresponds to the first bone of the long finger of man. The *second phalanx,* or short pastern bone, corresponds to the second bone of the long finger of man. The *third phalanx,* or coffin bone, corresponds to the bone in the tip of the long finger of man and is completely enclosed in the hoof (which is analagous with the fingernail of man). The general shape of the coffin bone is very similiar to the shape of the hoof.

The three phalanges have their long axes in prolongation of each other; their direction is downward and forward so that the enclosed angle with the horizontal is about $50°$ in the foreleg. If the phalangeal column of bones approaches the vertical the horse is said to have upright or stumpy pasterns; in such a case greater concussion is imparted directly to the bony column. Upright pasterns are often associated with a straight or upright shoulder. When the slope of the region is greater than average an undue amount of strain is thrown on the flexor tendons and suspensory ligament.

The *sesamoids* are two pyramidal-shaped bones that form a part of the fetlock joint and articulate with the posterior part of the lower end of the cannon bone. They lie embedded in ligaments and cartilage and form a bearing surface over which the flexor tendons lie.

The *distal sesamoid* (or navicular) bone is situated in back of the coffin bone and articulates with the lower end of the second phalanx. The deep flexor tendon plays over its lower surface. This point is the seat of navicular disease.

os coxae (Hip Bone). The *os coxae* or hip bone is a paired bone, and each unites with its fellow of the opposite side at the lowest point to form the floor of the pelvic cavity. Each hip bone above is firmly jointed to the sacrum. This girdle of bone is called the pelvic girdle and encloses the pelvic cavity. Each hip bone bears on its side a cavity where the femur, or first bone of the hind leg, is jointed to it. The outer front angle of the hip bone forms the point of the hip or haunch, which is often injured. The inner front angle, together with the sacrum, forms the point or summit of the croup. The back angle of the hip bone forms the point of the buttock. A long and flat (approaching the horizontal) pelvis is most suitable for speed and freedom of movement of the hind legs.

BONES OF THE HIND LEG. The bones of the hind leg, named from above downward, are the *femur, patella, tibia* and *fibula,* six or seven *tarsal* bones or bones of the hock, *large metatarsal* (cannon bone), two small *metatarsals* or splint bones, *first phalanx, second phalanx, third phalanx,* and the *proximal* and *distal* (navicular) *sesamoid* bones.

The *femur,* or bone of the thigh, corresponds to the thigh bone of man. At its upper end this bone articulates with the hip bone in the hip joint and extends downward, forward, and slightly outward to the stifle joint. Viewed from the side, the enclosed angle between the long axis of this bone and the horizontal is about 80°.

The *patella* is a small bone lying on the front of the stifle joint and articulating with the lower end of the femur. It corresponds to the kneecap of man.

The *tibia* is the second long bone of the hind leg and lies in the region known as the leg or gaskin. It extends from the stifle joint downward and backward to the hock joint, forming an enclosed angle of about 65° to 70°. A position approaching the vertical is more favorable for speed of movement than one of considerable slope. Along its inner surface this bone has but a thin protective covering of skin and other tissue and, because of its exposed position, is the most frequently fractured bone in the horse's skeleton. The tibia corresponds to the shin bone in man. The *fibula* in the horse is a small rudimentary bone about two-thirds as long as the tibia and is attached to the upper and outer surface of the tibia. In man, this bone as well as the tibia extends from the knee to the ankle.

The hock (or *tarsus*) of the horse, like the ankle of man, contains six or seven *tarsal* bones arranged in a manner similar to the carpal bones of the knee. The largest of these extends upward from the back of the joint and forms the bony prominence known as the point of the hock, and serves as the point of attachment of the powerful Achilles tendon.

The *metatarsal* bones correspond to the metacarpal bones of the foreleg. The hind cannon bone extends downward and slightly forward at an angle of about 87°. The hind cannon is about one-sixth longer than the fore cannon and is also more circular.

The *phalanges* and *sesamoids* of the hind leg are very similar to those of the foreleg except that the phalangeal axis is inclined to be slightly more upright.

JOINT OR ARTICULATION. A *joint* or *articulation* is the union of two or more bones or cartilages. Joints are classified into three types according to structure and mobility:

(1) *Immovable,* in which the opposed surfaces of bone are directly united by connective tissue or fused bone, permitting no movement (such as between the bones of the cranium).

(2) *Slightly movable,* where a pad of cartilage, adherent to both bones, is interposed between the bones and a slight amount of movement is possible due to the elesticity of the cartilage. Many of the joints between the vertebrae are of this character.

(3) *Freely movable,* when a joint cavity exists between the opposed surfaces. The joints of the legs are examples of this type.

Structure. The freely movable joints are the truest examples of joints. The ends of the bones entering into a freely movable joint are held in apposition by strong bands of tissue called *ligaments,* which pass from one bone to the other. Ligaments possess only a slight degree of elesticity, and have a limited blood supply, which causes them to heal very slowly, and often imperfectly, following an injury. In freely movable joints the ends of the bones are covered with smooth cartilage that absorbs concussion and provides a smooth bearing. The entire joint is enclosed in a fibrous sac, called the *joint capsule,* which assists the ligaments in holding the bones in position. Its inner surface is lined with a thin secreting membrane called the *synovial membrane,* which secretes a fluid called *synovia,* or joint water. Synovia is a clear, slightly yellowish fluid having the appearance and consistency of the white of a watery egg; the fluid serves to lubricate the joint in the same way that oil lubricates a bearing. Normally the amount secreted is limited to the actual amount necessary to prevent friction in the joint. However, when a joint becomes inflamed as a result of undue concussion or from other causes, the amount of synovial secretion is increased and results in a distension of the joint capsule. Where the capsule is not closely bound to the joint by the ligaments the distended capsule will pouch out under the skin as a soft swelling. A bog spavin is an example, as are also certain windgalls. Wounds over a joint are always likely to be dangerous, for they may have opened the joint cavity. When the joint cavity is opened the synovia flows from the wound and the synovial membrane is stimulated to secrete more than normal. This synovia pouring over the wound surface retards healing and the joint cavity becomes readily infected. An open joint is usually very painful and, in a great many instances, results in permanent disability of the animal even with the best possible care. The hock joint is most frequently opened by accidental injury.

JOINTS OF THE FORELEG. The joints of the foreleg, named in order from above downward, are the *shoulder,* formed by the scapula and humerus; the *elbow,*

22

formed by the humerus, radius, and ulna; the *knee,* formed by the radius, carpal bones, and the three metacarpal bones; the *fetlock,* formed by the cannon bone (large metacarpal), two sesamoid bones, and the first phalanx (long pastern) bone; the *pastern,* formed by the first and second phalanges (long and short pastern bones); and the *coffin,* formed by the second and third phalanges (short pastern and coffin bones) and the navicular bone.

JOINTS OF THE HIND LEG. The joints of the hind leg, named in order from above downward, are the *hip,* formed by the hip bone and femur; the *stifle,* formed by the femur, patella, and tibia; the *hock,* formed by the tibia, the tarsal (hock) bones, and the three metatarsal bones. The remaining joints of the hind leg are named and formed the same as the corresponding joints of the foreleg.

SUSPENSORY AND CHECK LIGAMENTS. In addition to the ligaments forming a part of the joints there are certain other important body ligaments. The *suspensory ligament* of the foreleg is a very strong, flat ligament arising from the back of the knee and upper end of the cannon bone and passing down the back of the leg in the groove between the splint bones. A short distance above the fetlock the ligament divides into two diverging rounded branches, each branch attaching to the upper and outer part of its corresponding sesamoid bone and then passing downward and forward around the front of the long pastern bone to join its fellow in a point of union with the extensor tendon, which attaches to the front of the coffin bone. From the lower part of the sesamoids, bands of ligaments pass downward and attach to the back of the long and short pastern bones. From the nature of attachment it is readily seen that the suspensory ligament is a remarkable slinglike apparatus by which the fetlock is supported, concussion diminished, and the pastern axis mechanically held in its sloping position. The *check ligament* is a strong, short ligament arising on the back of the upper end of the suspensory ligament just below the knee and passing downward and backward for a short distance to where it attaches to the *deep flexor tendon,* which, in turn, passes down the back of the leg to a point of attachment on the under surface of the coffin bone. When the muscle above is relaxed, it is easily seen that the action of the check ligament converts the part of the tendon below the check ligament into a functional ligament that assists the general action of the suspensory ligament.* The suspensory ligament is considerably more elastic than the binding ligaments of joints. By its supporting springlike action it absorbs a great deal of concussion. This ligament is most frequently injured in horses that do a great deal of their work at the gallop. The suspensory ligament in the hind leg is very similar to that of the foreleg, but the check ligament is much less perfectly developed.

PLANTAR LIGAMENT. The *plantar ligament* is a strong band of ligamentous tissue on the back of the hock bones. It extends from the point of the hock to the upper end of the cannon bone and, by its strong attachments to the small hock bones, braces the hock against the strong pull of the Achilles tendon. It is of

The structural interrelationship of the suspensory and check ligaments and the deep flexor tendon is largely responsible for the horse's ability to sleep standing up without enduring muscle fatigue. [Ed.]

23

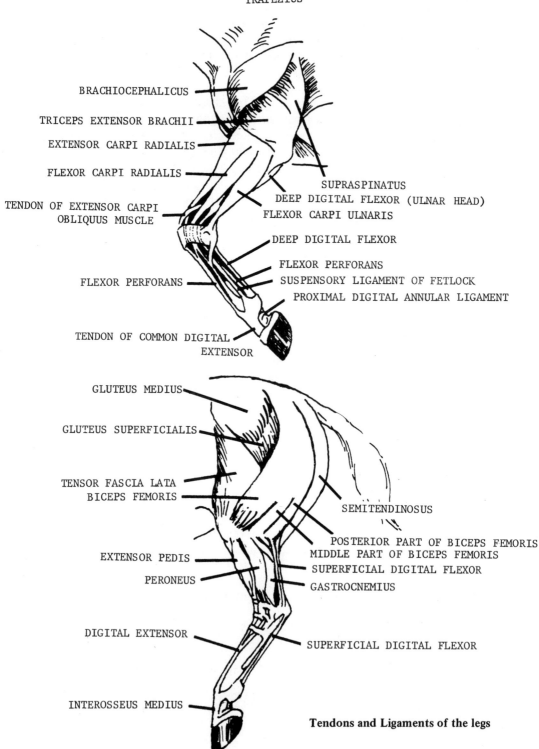

TRAPEZIUS

BRACHIOCEPHALICUS

TRICEPS EXTENSOR BRACHII

EXTENSOR CARPI RADIALIS

FLEXOR CARPI RADIALIS

TENDON OF EXTENSOR CARPI
OBLIQUUS MUSCLE

SUPRASPINATUS
DEEP DIGITAL FLEXOR (ULNAR HEAD)
FLEXOR CARPI ULNARIS

DEEP DIGITAL FLEXOR

FLEXOR PERFORANS
SUSPENSORY LIGAMENT OF FETLOCK
PROXIMAL DIGITAL ANNULAR LIGAMENT

FLEXOR PERFORANS

TENDON OF COMMON DIGITAL
EXTENSOR

GLUTEUS MEDIUS

GLUTEUS SUPERFICIALIS

TENSOR FASCIA LATA
BICEPS FEMORIS

SEMITENDINOSUS

POSTERIOR PART OF BICEPS FEMORIS
MIDDLE PART OF BICEPS FEMORIS
SUPERFICIAL DIGITAL FLEXOR
GASTROCNEMIUS

EXTENSOR PEDIS

PERONEUS

DIGITAL EXTENSOR

SUPERFICIAL DIGITAL FLEXOR

INTEROSSEUS MEDIUS

Tendons and Ligaments of the legs

24

particular importance because it is sometimes injured, resulting in the unsoundness known as *curb*.

LIGAMENTUM NUCHAE. The *ligamentum nuchae,* or ligament of the neck, is a fan-shaped ligament of very elastic tissue extending from the poll and upper surfaces of the cervical vertebrae to the longest spines of the thoracic vertebrae (the withers). It assists the muscles of the neck in maintaining the head and neck in position. It is of particular interest because the poll and withers are sometimes injured, resulting in the serious conditions of *poll evil* and *fistulous withers.*

MUSCULAR SYSTEM

Muscles are the active organs of motion and are characterized by their property of contracting or changing shape when stimulated. Muscles are red flesh, or lean meat, and make up about fifty percent of the total body weight. They are classified as *voluntary* and *involuntary.* Voluntary muscles are under the direct control of the will, such as the muscles of the legs. Involuntary muscles are those over which the will has no control, such as the muscles of the heart or stomach. The functions of muscles are to perform work and produce heat.

STRUCTURE AND ACTION OF MUSCLES. All voluntary muscles are composed of a *contractile* portion called the body or belly of the muscle, and a *noncontractile* continuation called the tendon, which is a fibrous continuation of one end of the body or contractile portion of the muscle. The contractile portion of the muscle is composed of many elongated muscle cells lying side by side lengthwise of the muscle that, when stimulated, becomes shorter and thicker. The tendon of a muscle is, in structure, quite similar to a ligament, and its function is to transmit the power of the muscle to some definite point of movement. The contractile portion has a large blood supply, but the blood supply of the denser tendons is rather limited.

The body of most muscles is attached to some bone and the point of attachment is called the *origin.* The tendon of the muscle may pass one or more joints and attach *(insertion)* to some other bone.

For almost every muscle or group of muscles having a certain general action there is another muscle or group whose action is the exact opposite; the most important examples are the *extensor* and *flexor* muscles of the legs. A muscle is an extensor when its action is to extend a joint and bring the bones into alignment. A muscle is a flexor when its action is to bend the joint. Some muscles, if their points of origin and insertion are separated by two or more joints, may act as a flexor of one joint and an extensor of another joint. Except to establish fixation and rigidity of a part, such opposed muscles do not act simultaneously in opposition to each other but rather act successively. There are hundreds of muscles in the body, but this text will consider only the general action of the important muscle groups.

TENDON SHEATHS AND BURSAE. Many muscles, especially those of the legs, have long tendons that pass one or more joints and undergo changes of direction or

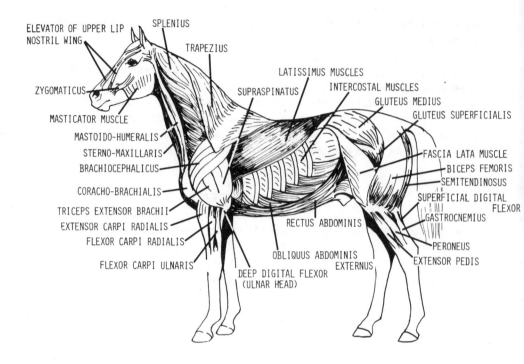

ELEVATOR OF UPPER LIP
NOSTRIL WING
SPLENIUS
TRAPEZIUS
LATISSIMUS MUSCLES
INTERCOSTAL MUSCLES
SUPRASPINATUS
GLUTEUS MEDIUS
GLUTEUS SUPERFICIALIS
ZYGOMATICUS
MASTICATOR MUSCLE
MASTOIDO-HUMERALIS
STERNO-MAXILLARIS
BRACHIOCEPHALICUS
CORACHO-BRACHIALIS
TRICEPS EXTENSOR BRACHII
EXTENSOR CARPI RADIALIS
FLEXOR CARPI RADIALIS
FLEXOR CARPI ULNARIS
DEEP DIGITAL FLEXOR
(ULNAR HEAD)
OBLIQUUS ABDOMINIS
EXTERNUS
RECTUS ABDOMINIS
FASCIA LATA MUSCLE
BICEPS FEMORIS
SEMITENDINOSUS
SUPERFICIAL DIGITAL
FLEXOR
GASTROCNEMIUS
PERONEUS
EXTENSOR PEDIS

Muscular System

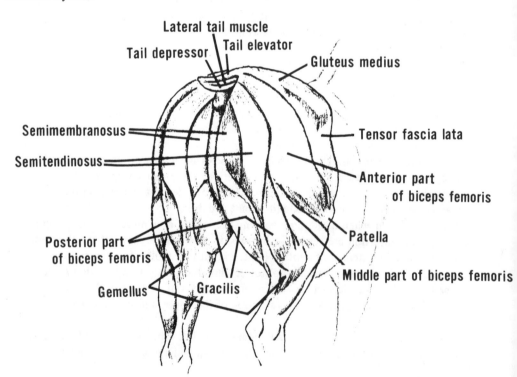

Lateral tail muscle
Tail depressor
Tail elevator
Gluteus medius
Semimembranosus
Tensor fascia lata
Semitendinosus
Anterior part
of biceps femoris
Posterior part
of biceps femoris
Patella
Gemellus
Gracilis
Middle part of biceps femoris

pass over body prominences before reaching their point of insertion. To avoid undue friction at these points, and to allow the muscle to act most efficiently, nature has supplied *tendon sheaths* and *tendon bursae* at various points of friction along the course of the tendon. A tendon sheath is a synovial sac through which a tendon passes; the inside of the sac secretes synovia and lubricates the tendon. A tendon bursa is a synovial sac that is interposed between the tendon and the surface over which it passes in a change of direction; it serves the same purpose as a tendon sheath but differs from it in that the tendon is not surrounded by a synovial sac. Tendon sheaths and bursae are found chiefly near joints. Due to chronic irritation from hard work or as a result of injury the amount of synovia secreted may be greatly increased and result in a distension of the sac characterized externally by a circumscribed puffy swelling. Such swellings are often seen above the fetlocks where they are called wind-puffs or windgalls. While seldom causing distinct lameness, they are evidence of a "second-handed" condition and indicate that the horse probably is a little stiffened and shortened in his gaits.

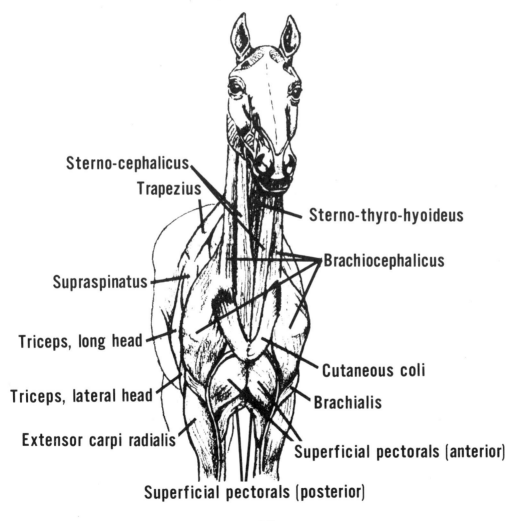

27

MUSCLES OF THE NECK AND ATTACHMENT OF THE FORELEG. The foreleg of the horse has no bony connection with the remainder of the skeleton. The foreleg is attached to the body by a very complex system of muscles that extends from the neck to the poll, thence upward to the withers, backward along the sides of the chest, and back and under the chest to meet at the sternum. The fore part of the horse is really suspended between two uprights, the forelegs, and by this elastic muscular sling a very efficient shock-absorbing mechanism is provided. Since the forelegs bear from nine to twenty percent more of the body weight than do the hind legs, it is easy to understand the importance of this muscular attachment, especially in the riding horse.

The long muscles extending from the region of the shoulder to the sides of the neck and to the head are of special interest to the student of equitation, for the manner of the horse's movement is profoundly influenced by their action. With the shoulders fixed these muscles cause movement of the head and neck; when the head and neck are fixed by opposing muscular action these muscles act to advance the shoulder. With the head and neck extended these muscles are most favorably placed for maximum extension of the shoulder and foreleg with a low and extended action. A high head carriage with shortening of the neck is most favorable for maximum elevation of the shoulder and foreleg, resulting in a higher and shortened stride. Much of the early training of a green horse is directly aimed at gaining suppleness and control of this group of muscles.

MUSCLES OF THE BACK, LOIN, AND CROUP. The triangular space on either side of the spines of the backbone in the region of the back and loins is filled with large muscles. The principal one of this group is the *longissimus dorsi,* the longest and largest muscle of the body. It extends from the posterior part of the loin along the back and down between the shoulder and thorax to the last cervical vertabra. These muscles, one on each side, are used extensively when the horse rears or elevates his hindquarters in kicking. Acting singly, the muscles flex the vertebral column laterally. In the thoracic region this muscular pad bears the weight of the saddle when the horse is ridden, and distributes the weight evenly to the supporting ribs. The croup and thighs are made up of groups of powerful muscles that are the chief source of propelling power.

MUSCLES AND TENDONS OF THE LOWER LEG. The extensor muscles of the foreleg attach mainly to the humerus and radius and lie on the front of the forearm. The *common digital extensor* originates on the lower end of the humerus and upper part of the radius. At the upper part of the knee this muscle continues as a tendon along the front of the knee, cannon, and pastern regions to its point of insertion on the upper end of the coffin bone. In the pastern region two branches of the suspensory ligament unite with the tendon. This muscle acts as an extensor of all joints below the elbow, but flexes the latter. Its tendon is seldom injured.

The *extensor of the knee* is a strong muscle attached to the humerus and lies on the front of the forearm. Its short, heavy tendon passes over the knee and attaches to the upper end of the cannon bone. It extends the knee joint and flexes the elbow. The tendon passes through a tendon sheath extending from the middle of the knee to about four inches above the knee. This region is often bruised in jumping horses, resulting in a synovial distension of the sheath commonly called "jumping knee"; while unsightly, it seldom causes lameness.

The flexor muscles of the foreleg lie on the back of the forearm and, like the extensors, originate on the humerus, ulna, and radius. The *superficial digital flexor* originates on the lower end of the humerus; its fleshy portion extends to the lower part of the forearm and from that point continues as a flattened tendon that passes down the back of the leg. Below the fetlock it divides into two branches that are inserted on either side of the upper end of the short pastern bone. This muscle flexes the knee, fetlock, and pastern. The tendon lies just under the skin on the back of the leg, and just in back of the deep flexor tendon.

The *deep digital flexor* originates with the superficial digital flexor. The body of the muscle lies on the back of the forearm and, from just about the knee, continues as the deep flexor tendon passing down the back of the leg in front of the superficial flexor tendon, passes between the branches of the latter, and continues to its point of insertion on the under surface of the coffin bone. This is the most powerful muscle of the foreleg. In the upper part of the cannon region the tendon is joined by the check ligament. Where the tendon passes over the back of the sessamoid bones at the fetlock joint it is enclosed in a tendon sheath that frequently becomes distended with synovia, causing windgalls or wind-puffs. This tendon also passes over a bursa, where it glides over the navicular bone near the coffin joint; injury to this bursa results in the condition known as *navicular disease.*

In the cannon region the two tendons appear to the eye as one large rounded tendon, but if the foot is raised and the structure examined with the fingers the separate tendons may be readily distinguished. These two muscles and their tendinous extensions, in addition to bringing about movements of the leg, also act as shock-absorbing mechanisms. The strains to which they are subjected seldom injure the bodies or bellies of the muscles but the tendons are not so exempt, particularly in the cannon region, and the resulting inflamed condition is known as *tendinitis.* Either or both tendons may be affected, the deep flexor more frequently than the superficial.

The general arrangement and action of the extensor and flexor tendons of the hind leg from the hock joint downward are almost identical with those of the foreleg. Tendinitis in the hind legs is uncommon because of the lesser amount of weight borne and concussion absorbed. Distension of the tendon sheath at, and just above, the fetlock often occurs, but the navicular bursa is rarely diseased. The navicular bursa of the hind leg, as in the foreleg, is sometimes opened by a nail penetrating from under the surface of the foot.

FATIGUE OF MUSCLES. Muscle fatigue follows continued work, principally due to the accumulation of waste products in the muscle cells. As soon as the wastes are removed by the blood and lymph, and a fresh supply of nutrition is brought to the muscles, a feeling of fitness again prevails. Hand-rubbing the legs of a horse is beneficial because the blood and lymph vessels are stimulated to increased activity in the removal of waste products, and it also causes the blood to circulate more freely. Fatigue may also be overcome, in part, by providing a feed of easily digested

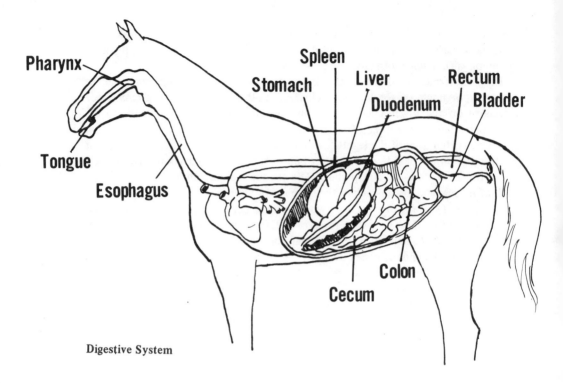

Digestive System

carbohydrates, which furnishes a maximum of energy.

A horse in soft condition and not accustomed to steady work fatigues much more easily than a hardened horse. This is due to the muscles being softer and possibly carrying an excess of fat. It should be remembered that there is a limit to continued muscular effort, and that harmful fatigue can be avoided only by working the horse at a moderate rate in order to keep the proper balance between the products of muscular activity and the ability of the blood to remove the waste material. An animal should never be worked until exhausted, if for no other reason than that it is not economical.

DIGESTIVE SYSTEM

The digestive system is really a muscular tube passing through the body and having two external openings, the mouth and the anus. This tube has a total length of about one hundred feet, looped on itself many times, dilated at intervals along its course, and provided with several accessory organs. The entire tube is lined with *mucous membrane,* a modified form of skin; this close relationship between the lining of the digestive tube and the covering of the body explains why digestive disturbances are often reflected in skin disturbances and vice versa. The digestive organs are the *mouth, pharynx, esophagus, stomach, small intestine, large intestine,* and *rectum.*

MOUTH. The mouth extends from the lips to the pharynx. It is bounded on the sides by the cheeks, above by the hard palate, and below by the tongue. Separating the mouth from the pharynx is the soft palate, a fleshy curtain suspended from the back part of the hard palate, which permits the passage of food and water from the mouth to the pharynx but prevents its passage in the opposite direction. The lips prehend (pick up) loose feed, which is passed into the mouth by the action of the tongue. When grazing, the feed is grasped with the incisor teeth. Feed is masticated, or ground, between the molar (cheek) teeth and mixed with the *saliva.* * The saliva is secreted into the mouth by the saliva glands, the largest of which is the *parotid,* lying below the ear and back jaw. The horse is, by nature, a slow eater and requires from fifteen to twenty minutes to eat a pound of hay and from five to ten minutes to eat a pound of grain. Hay, when properly masticated, absorbs approximately four times its weight of saliva, and oats a little more than its weight. The saliva moistens and lubricates the mass for swallowing and, as a digestive juice, acts on the sugars and starches. The ball of masticated feed, when ready for swallowing, is forced past the soft palate into the pharynx by the base of the tongue. Drinking is performed by drawing the tongue backward in the mouth and thus using it as the piston of a suction pump. A horse usually swallows slightly less than one-half pint at each gulp.** The ears are drawn forward at each swallow and drop back during the interval between swallows.

PHARYNX. The pharynx is a short and somewhat funnel-shaped muscular tube between the mouth and esophagus, and is also an air passage between the nasal cavities and the larynx. The muscular action of the pharynx forces the food into the esophagus. After entering the pharynx food or water cannot return to the mouth because of the traplike action of the soft palate; for the same reason, a horse cannot breathe through the mouth. Food or water returned from the pharynx passes out through the nostrils.

ESOPHAGUS. The esophagus is a muscular tube extending from the pharynx down the left side of the neck and through the thoracic cavity and diaphragm to the stomach. The swallow of food or water is forced down the esophagus to the stomach by a progressive wave of constriction of the circular muscles of the organ. In the horse this wave of constriction cannot move in the reverse direction and vomiting is therefore not possible. The return of food or water through the nostrils is almost a clear indication that the horse is choked because the esophagus is blocked by a mass of food.†

Normally a horse will generate about ten gallons of saliva in a twenty-four-hour period. [Ed.]

**Horses, by nature, drink slowly and tend to take a short rest interval after a very few gulps unless extremely thirsty. Since a horse requires about eight gallons of water per day under average conditions, he should not be pulled away from the watering point until he has indicated that he has drunk his fill. [Ed.]*

†Because the horse (unlike man and most other animals) is unable to regurgitate food from the stomach, digestive ailments resulting from several causes including overeating (gastric dilation) assume serious and sometimes fatal consequences. [Ed.]*

STOMACH. The stomach is a U-shaped muscular sac that lies in the front part of the abdominal cavity and close to the diaphragm. The esophageal and intenstinal openings are close together and, for this reason, water passes rather quickly through the stomach and small intestine at the first of the large intestines, the cecum (sometimes known as the water gut). Considering the size of the animal and the amount of food consumed, the stomach of the horse is relatively very small. The maximum capacity of the stomach is about four gallons, but it functions most efficiently when it does not contain more than two and a half gallons. These facts have a decided influence on our methods of feeding; the small size of the stomach makes it imperative that food be given in rather small amounts and at relatively frequent intervals. Overloading of the stomach not only lowers its efficiency as a digestive organ but, by pressure against the diaphragm, makes breathing more difficult. The food entering the stomach is arranged in layers, the end next to the small intestine filling first. The digestive process begins immediately upon receipt of food. No food leaves the stomach until that organ has been filled to about two-thirds of its capacity. While the horse continues to eat, the partially digested food passes out into the small intestine in a continuous stream; as a result, two or three times the capacity of the stomach may pass out during a bulky meal. The emptying process slows up only when the feeding stops; the stomach is never completely empty except after complete withholding of feed for one or two days. The contents of the stomach are squeezed and pressed by the muscular activity of the organ, but are never churned. The digestive juice secreted by the walls of the stomach is called gastric juice. This acid fluid contains the active enzyme called pepsin, which acts on the protein in the food. Some digested food is absorbed by the stomach but, as a whole, stomach digestion is partial preparatory digestion for more complete digestion in the intestines. The consumption of any considerable quantity of water during the period of stomach digestion tends to dissarrange the layering of food therein and causes as much as half of the contents to be washed into the small intestine. For this reason *the horse should be watered first and fed afterward* unless he is allowed free access to water during his meal. As food tends to leave the stomach in the order of its receipt, it is advisable to *feed some hay before feeding grain* so that the grain will be held longer in the stomach and undergo more complete digestion.

SMALL INTESTINE. The small intestine is a tube about seventy feet long and two inches in diameter, extending from the stomach to the cecum. Just after leaving the stomach it is arranged in a distinct U-shaped curve that seems to prevent food from returning to the stomach once it has entered the small intestine, and also tends to close the opening into the intestine when the stomach is overloaded with food. The small intestine lies in folds and coils near the left flank and is suspended from the region of the loin by an extensive fan-shaped membrane called the *mesentery*. The partially digested food in the small intestine is always quite fluid and seems to pass rather rapidly through this part of the digestive tract. Digestion is continued in the small intestine by the action of the bile and pancreatic juices, which are secreted by the liver and pancreas respectively. Some digested food is absorbed in the small intestine.

32

LARGE INTESTINE. The large intestine is divided into the *cecum, large colon, small colon, rectum,* and *anus.*

The *cecum* is a large, elongated sac extending from high in the right flank downward and forward to the region of the diaphragm. The openings from the small intestine and to the large colon are close together in the upper end of the organ. The cecum is sometimes known as the "water gut" for the reasons that water passes rather quickly to it and that its contents are always liquid. Digestion is continued in the cecum and some food is absorbed.

The *large colon* is about twelve feet long with a diameter of ten to twelve inches; it extends from the cecum to the small colon and is usually distended with food. The greater part of food digestion by the digestive juices and bacterial action takes place in this section of the digestive tract as well as the greater part of absorption of digested food.

The *small colon* is about ten feet long with a four-inch diameter and extends from the large colon to the rectum. The contents of the small colon are solid, and it is here that the balls of dung are formed.

The *rectum* is that part of the digestive tract about twelve inches in length, extending from the small colon through the pelvic cavity to the *anus,* the terminus of the digestive tract.

RESPIRATORY SYSTEM

ORGANS. The organs of respiration comprise the *nasal cavity, pharynx, larynx, trachea, bronchi,* and *lungs.* The lungs are the essential organs; all of the other parts simply act as passages for the air to and from them.

The *nasal cavity* is bounded by the facial bones, and begins at the nostrils, which are held open by cartilages; it is divided in half by the cartilaginous nasal septum. Each half is partially filled with thin, spiral, spongy bones that are covered with a very vascular mucous membrane; this serves to warm the inspired (inhaled) air. The *pharynx* is common to both the respiratory and digestive tracts (see page 31). The *larynx* is a short, tubelike organ situated between the pharynx and the trachea. It regulates the amount of air passing to and from the lungs and helps to prevent the inhalation of foreign bodies. It is the seat of a common disease of the horse known as "roaring," a paralysis of the muscles controlling the vocal cords. The *trachea* is a long tube connecting the larynx with the lungs and is located in the lower median border of the neck. It is composed of a series of cartilaginous rings held together by elastic fibrous material. The *bronchi* are branches of the trachea that connect with the lungs. They, in turn, branch into minute tubes that penetrate every part of the lung tissue.

The *lungs* are two in number and nearly fill the thoracic cavity. Lung tissue is pinkish in color and will float in water. The lung is made up of innumerable air cells having thin, elastic walls that contain capillaries of the pulmonary circulation; this elasticity of the lung tissue permits the organ to contract and expand in the act of respiration. *Heaves* is caused by a breaking down of the walls of some of the air cells with attendant loss of elasticity in that part of the lung.

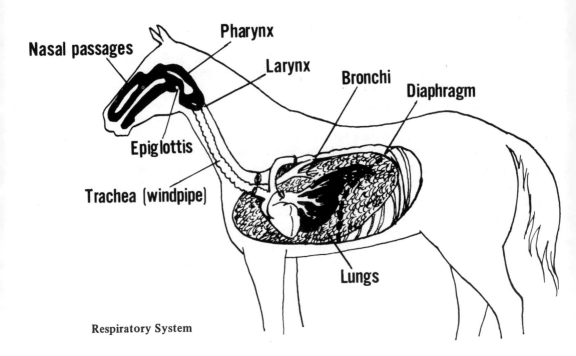

Respiratory System

THE PHYSIOLOGY OF RESPIRATION. Respiration is the act of breathing and is the most vital function in animals. It consists of an exchange of the oxygen in the air for the carbon dioxide in the blood, and an interchange of these gases between the blood and the body tissues. The former is external respiration and the latter is internal respiration. External respiration consists of two movements, inspiration and expiration. Inspiration is brought about by a contraction of the diaphragm and an outward rotation of the ribs. Expiration is effected by relaxation of this effort in combination with contraction of rib and abdominal muscles. The abdominal muscles are used extensively in labored breathing. Since the diaphragm plays such an important part in the respiration movement, it follows that distension of the digestive tract with bulky food materially interferes with normal breathing, especially when the animal is subjected to fast gaits. The lungs of the average horse contain one and a half cubic feet of air when freely distended. The normal horse at rest breathes from eight to sixteen times per minute, and inhales at each respiration approximately 250 cubic inches (four and a half percent of total capacity). A horse, while walking, nearly trebles the number of normal respirations, but the normal rate is regained in a very few minutes when the horse halts. If the animal breathes ten times per minute during repose the whole lung is ventilated in slightly more than one minute.* The amount of air required by the horse depends upon the extent of muscular work being performed. The following table shows the mean amount of expired air at the various gaits:

*The lungs of a horse at rest distend only about one-half as much as when fully distended at the gallop. [Ed.]

34

Gait	Cubic feet expired per hour
Repose	74.17
Walk	133.55
Trot	287.87
Canter	391.00
Gallop	849.10

CIRCULATORY SYSTEM

ORGANS. The organs concerned with the circulation of blood and lymph are the *heart, arteries, veins, capillaries, lymph vessels,* and *lymph glands.* The *heart,* the central organ of the system, is situated in the left half of the thorax, between the lungs and opposite the third to sixth ribs. In the ordinary-sized horse it weighs from seven to eight pounds. It is enclosed in a serofibrous sac, the *pericardium.* The heart is divided into four cavities by muscular walls and valves. The action of the heart is to receive the blood and to pump it out to the lungs and body tissues.

The *arteries* have rather thick elastic walls and carry the blood from the heart to the tissues of the body. The *veins* have much thinner walls, and carry the blood from the tissues to the heart. Many veins are equipped with valves (the veins of the leg are an excellent example) to prevent the blood from flowing backward. The *capillaries,* microscopic in size, function as connecting tubes between arteries and veins; the interchange of oxygen and food between the blood and tissues takes place through the walls of the capillaries. The *lymphatic* system supplements the functions of the venous system; lymph, a clear, yellowish, alkaline fluid, assists in carrying food from the digestive tract to the tissues and in transporting waste back to the bloodstream. *Lymph vessels* all converge to form one large duct that lies parallel to the aorta (main artery from the heart) and empties into one of the large veins near the heart. The *lymph* glands, which are connected to the lymph vessels, are located at strategic places along the vessels and act as filters for the lymph. The glands assume considerable importance in some diseases; strangles is one disease affecting these organs.

PHYSIOLOGY OF CIRCULATION. The heart movements are controlled by an intricate group of nerves. The heartbeat is the combined cycle of contraction and relaxation of the organ. In the normal horse at rest the heart beats from thirty-six to forty times per minute. The pulse rate is determined by counting the rate of pulsations in some artery that is easily palpated, for example, the artery at the angle of the lower jaw. Both the pressure and the rate of flow in the veins are very low compared with that in the arteries. The movement of blood in the veins is aided by the respiratory movements and muscular contractions, thus good circulation is made possible by exercise. While the left side of the heart carries on the body circulation, the right side pumps impure blood to the lungs to be purified before it returns to the left side of the heart; this is known as the *pulmonary circulation.*

THE BLOOD. The blood is a red alkaline fluid composed of blood plasma and red and white corpuscles. The white corpuscles are active agents in combating disease

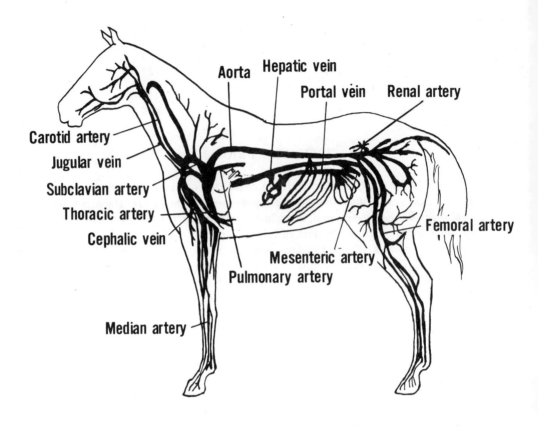

Circulatory System

germs in the body. The red corpuscles, which originate in the red bone marrow, liver, and spleen, carry oxygen from the lungs to the tissues. The blood carries food to the tissues, conveys waste away from the tissues, distributes heat, assists in regulating the temperature, and neutralizes or destroys bacterial invaders. Blood clots almost immediately when exposed to air. Blood accounts for about one-fourteenth of total body weight.

NERVOUS SYSTEM

The nervous system is made up of the *brain, spinal cord, ganglia,* and *nerves* and is the communication system of the body.

The *brain* and *spinal cord* are the most important parts of the system and form the *central nervous system,* which may be likened to the switchboard of a telephone system; it is the directing center that receives and dispatches nerve messages. The *brain* lies in the cranial cavity of the skull. Considering the size of the animal, the brain of the horse is small when compared with the relative brain size of other animals. Although relative brain size to size of body cannot be considered as an absolute indication of the degree of reasoning intelligence, there is, however, a distinct correlation. The horse is considered to occupy about a midway position in the scale of intelligence of the domesticated animals.*

The *spinal cord* extends from the brain back through the spinal canal of the vertebral column. The *ganglia* are secondary nerve centers located chiefly along the spinal cord, and may be likened to a subexchange in a telephone system; they receive and dispatch nerve impulses that do not of necessity have to reach the brain. Together with their communicating nerves they control the involuntary muscles, vital organs, and reflex actions.

The *nerves* are bands of white tissue emanating from the central nervous system and ganglia, and extending to all parts of the body; in general, they closely follow the course of the arteries. There are two kinds of nerves, those which convey sensation to the central nervous system and those which carry back the command impulses of the system. The nerves may be compared to the wire lines of a telephone system; the large nerves, like a telephone cable, contain many separate lines.

SKIN AND HAIR

SKIN. The skin is the covering tissue that acts as a protection to the surface of the body. Wherever the chance of injury is the greatest, the skin is the thickest; in those parts where sensibility is most required, it is the thinnest. The skin of the back, quarters, and legs are examples of the first type. An especially heavy protective covering is found on the back. In some horses, this covering is as much as one-quarter of an inch in thickness. The skin is very thin on the face and muzzle, inside the forearms and thighs, and on other parts not exposed to violence. In spite of this thinness, its strength is remarkable. It is highly sensitive because it is highly endowed with sensory nerve endings. Accessory organs of feeling are the tactile hairs on the muzzle and the eyelashes. The skin is easily irritated and the horse has the power of shaking the skin to relieve himself from slight irritations, such as flies. This is accomplished by the aid of the skin muscle *(panniculus carnosus)*, which is a thin, muscular layer lying directly underneath the skin and attached to it. In health, the skin feels pliable and elastic. The skin of the horse is black except on those parts of the body covered by white hair, where it is white or pinkish in color.

The skin is divided into two layers.

The *epidermis,* or outer portion, is nonvascular and contains the openings for the sweat and sebaceous glands and hair follicles.

The sebaceous glands are well distributed over the whole surface of the body and secrete an oily fluid. The oily fluid thus produced serves as a protective secretion against the disintegrating influence of water on the skin; keeps the skin supple; gives gloss to well-groomed skin; prevents penetration of rain; and saves, to some extent, undue loss of heat.

Involuntary muscle fibers are attached to the hair roots, which cause the hair to stand up when the horse is cold.

The *dermis,* or inner portion, is a vascular structure and is closely adherent to

The intelligence of the horse is considered to be less than that of the dog and more than that of the cow. [Ed.]

37

the underlying fat and skin muscles. It contains: the *nerve endings,* which give to the skin the sense of touch; the *hair follicles,* which grow the necessary hairs; the *sweat glands,* which discharge sweat directly on the surface of the skin. Sweat is a watery, salty, alkaline fluid of characteristic horselike odor. It serves to keep the skin moist, remove waste, and help regulate the body temperature by evaporation. It is not found to occur over the general surface of the body in any hairy animal other than the horse. The secretion of sweat is continuous. Certain parts of the skin sweat more readily than others. It appears first at the base of the ears, then the neck. The sides of the chest and back follow, and lastly, the hindquarters. No sweating takes place on the lower part of the legs. There are two kinds of sweating, viz., insensible, which evaporates as fast as it is formed, and sensible, which is visible fluid that collects on the skin when the secretion is rapid. The evaporation of sweat from the surface of the skin is a most important source of loss of body heat. Horses that have sweated freely show, when dry, a grayish covering of dried sweat on the hairs, resembling fine sand. Through sweating there is a loss of protein substance and of mineral matter, chiefly the chlorides. The loss thus produced accounts for the great reduction of vitality seen in some horses. It is, therefore, imperative that salt be included in the ration at all times, and especially during field service, to maintain proper salt balance in the body. Clipping of horses with long coats is desirable in order to prevent excessive sweating.

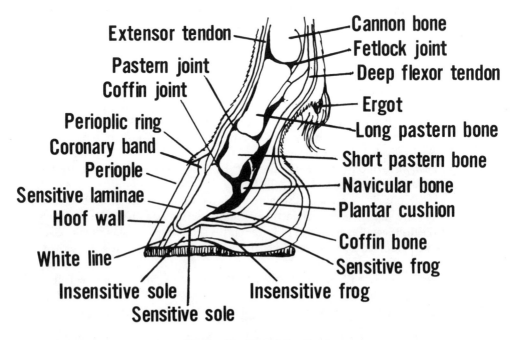

Median Section of the Foot

Sensible sweating usually results from work or exercise, but may appear as a result of nervousness or excitement. After hard work, horses that have been thoroughly groomed and dried sometimes break out in what is known as a second sweat. This usually indicates extreme fatigue or nervousness and that the horse has not been thoroughly cooled out. Patchy sweating, or sweating continuously in a certain localized area, is sometimes observed. The cause is not definitely known.

HAIR. Hair covers most of the skin except for the anal region, genitals, insides of thighs, and deep inside the ear. Even in these regions a few short hairs appear. Hair forms the clothing of the body, and its amount of growth is determined by the seasonal temperature. The permanent hair of the body is the hair of the mane and tail, eyelashes, long tactile hairs around the muzzle, and the long hair on the back of the fetlock. The permanent hair is not shed. The general body coat of hair is temporary and is shed twice yearly, spring and fall. The time of shedding is governed by weather conditions or temperature in which the horse is kept. The vitality of the horse seems to be somewhat lowered incident to shedding the coat. This is true particularly during the spring shedding, and at this time the skin is much more susceptible to eruptions, irritations, and infections. Mixed sparsely with the general body coat of hair, there will be found a few longer and more rapidly growing hairs that are known as "cat hairs." These hairs are most readily observed when appearing in the growth of the coat following clipping.

THE FOOT

PARTS OF THE FOOT. The horse's foot is composed of four general classes of structures:
The bones.
The elastic structures.
The sensitive structures. A layer of highly sensitive flesh or quick, the corium, covers the bony and elastic framework and grows the horny structure.
The horny structures. The box, or case of horn called the hoof, encloses and protects the other structures of the foot.

BONES OF THE PASTERN AND FOOT. The bones of the pastern and foot form a column extending downward from the fetlock joint into the hoof and are named as follows: the long pastern bone, the short pastern bone, the coffin bone, and the navicular bone.
The *long pastern bone* extends from the fetlock joint to the pastern joint. Its upper end joins, or articulates, with the lower end of the cannon bone, forming the fetlock joint. Its lower end articulates with the upper end of the short pastern bone, forming the pastern joint.
The *short pastern bone* follows the direction of the long pastern bone downward and forward and lies between the pastern and coffin joints, its lower end being within the hoof.
The *coffin bone* is of irregular shape, is situated within the hoof, and is similar to

39

the hoof in shape. The surface of the front and sides is known as the *wall surface.* It has a number of small openings for the passage of blood vessels and nerves and is roughened to give attachment to the *sensitive laminae* that cover it. On each side of this surface is a groove running forward to an opening, through which an artery and a nerve enter the bone and a vein leaves it. At the top of this surface, in front, is a projection called the *extensor process,* to which is attached the extensor tendon of the foot.

On each side of the coffin bone is an extension to the rear called the wing. The lateral cartilages are attached to the outer and upper borders of the wings, and the ends of the navicular bone are attached to the inner surfaces.

The lower surface of the coffin bone, called the *sole surface,* is concave, half-moon shaped, and smooth, except at the back part, which is roughened for the attachment of the deep flexor tendon.

The upper surface, called the *articular surface,* articulates with the short pastern bone and navicular bone and with them forms the coffin joint.

The *navicular bone* is of irregular shape. It is situated behind and below the short pastern bone and behind the coffin bone, forming a joint with both. The extremities of the bone are attached to the wings of the coffin bone. The lower surface is covered with cartilage, which forms a smooth surface for the movement of the deep flexor tendon. Because of its shape, the bone is frequently called the "shuttle bone."

ELASTIC STRUCTURES OF THE FOOT. All the structures of the foot, except the bones, are more or less elastic or springy, and yield when pressure is applied. Certain parts have a very high degree of elasticity, their special use being to overcome the effects of concussion or jar when the foot strikes the ground. These parts are the *lateral cartilages* and the *plantar cushion.*

The *lateral cartilages* are two large elastic plates of cartilage, one attached to the top of each wing of the coffin bone. They extend backward and upward so far that their borders may be felt under the skin above the coronet at the heels.

The *plantar cushion* is a very elastic, wedge-shaped pad. It fills up the space between the lateral cartilages on the sides, the frog below, and the deep flexor tendon. The point, or front part, of the plantar cushion extends forward to the ridge that separates the sole surface from the tendinous surface of the coffin bone, and lies just below the lower end of the deep flexor tendon. The base, or back part, is covered by the skin above the heels. When the frog comes in contact with the ground as the foot is planted, the plantar cushion acts as a buffer and prevents jar.

SENSITIVE STRUCTURES OF THE FOOT. Over the bones and elastic parts of the foot there is a complete covering of very sensitive flesh called the corium. From each part of this layer of flesh some portion of the hoof is secreted or grown. The sensitive structures are the *coronary band,* the *perioplic ring,* the *sensitive laminae,* the *sensitive sole,* and the *sensitive frog.*

The *coronary band* is a thick band of tough flesh, nearly an inch wide, extending entirely around the top of the hoof from one bulb to the other, and lying in a groove called the coronary groove on the inner surface of the wall at its upper border. The surface of the coronary band is covered with small, hairlike projections, called papillae, from which are grown the horny wall of the hoof.

The *perioplic ring* is a narrow band of flesh lying just above coronary band and separated from it by a faint groove in the wall. From the fine papillae on the surface of this ring, the delicate fibers grow that form the *periople* or varnishlike horn covering of the hoof that assists in the prevention of evaporation of moisture from the wall.

The *sensitive laminae*, or sensitive leaves, cover and are firmly attached to the wall surface of the coffin bone and to the lower part of the outer surface of the lateral cartilages. From these delicate leaves of flesh grow the *horny laminae*, or inside lining of the horny wall.

The *sensitive sole* covers the sole surface of the coffin bone, is covered with papillae, and grows the horny sole.

The *sensitive frog* covers the lower surface of the plantar cushion and from its papillae the horny frog is secreted.

THE HOOF. The *hoof* is the outer horny covering of the foot. It is divided into three general parts: the *wall, sole,* and *frog.* In the healthy foot these parts are firmly united.

The *wall,* except for the bar, extends from the edge of the hairline to the ground and is divided into the *toe, quarters,* and *buttresses.*

The *toe* is the front part of the wall. It is steeper in the hind foot than in the fore. The *quarter* extends backward on each side from the toe to the heel. The *buttress* is the back part of the heel and may be defined as the angle formed by the union of the wall and bar.

The *bar* is that part of the wall which extends inward and forward from the buttress to within an inch of the point of the frog. The hoof is thus made stronger by the ends of the wall extending inward to form the bars. The bars are weight carriers, and they also act directly on the wall to produce expansion when weight is placed on the frog.

The outer surface of the wall is covered by a thin, varnishlike coat of fine horn, called *periople.* The inner surface is covered with from five hundred to six hundred *horny laminae.* These are thin plates of horn running downward and forward. Between them are fissures into which dovetail the sensitive laminae. The horny laminae and sensitive laminae are firmly united. This union binds the wall of the hoof to the coffin bone and its cartilages, suspends the weight of the horse from the inner surface of the wall as in a sling, and thus prevents the bones from descending on the sole. On the upper border of the wall is the coronary groove in which lies the coronary band. The lower border is known as the *bearing surface.* It is the part that comes in contact with the ground in the unshod foot and to which the shoe is fitted in the shod foot.

The *horny sole* is a thick plate of horn that conforms with the sole surface of the coffin bone.

The upper surface is arched upward and is in union with the sensitive sole from which the horny sole grows. The lower surface is hollowed and is covered with scales or crusts of dead horn that gradually loosen and fall off.

41

The outer border of the sole is joined to the inner part of the lower border of the wall by a ring of soft horn called the *white line.* The shoeing nail should enter the white line.

The inner border is V-shaped and is in union with the bars, except where the sole joins the point of the frog. The sole protects the sensitive parts above.

The *frog* is a wedge-shaped mass filling the V-shaped space between the bars and sole and extending downward somewhat below the bars. The lower surface has two prominent ridges, separated behind by a depression called the *cleft,* and joining in front at the point of the frog. These ridges terminate behind in the *bulbs* of the frog. Between the sides of the frog and the bars are two depressions called the *commissures.*

The upper surface of the frog is the exact reverse of the lower. It has in the middle a ridge of horn called the *frog stay,* which assists in forming a firm union between the horny and sensitive frog.

The function of the frog is to assist the plantar cushion in absorbing the jar or concussion, to prevent slipping, and to produce expansion and contraction upon which the normal blood circulation in the foot depends. ·

DISSIPATION OF CONCUSSION. The concussion borne by the foot is lessened by a combination of functions of its varied structures. When the weight of the horse is transmitted down the bony column of the leg, the following things take place: Except possibly at the walk, the weight, or at least a considerable portion of the weight, is first received by the frog. The frog spreads and moves the bars outward, carrying the heels and the posterior part of the quarters outward. Simultaneously, the frog transmits the jar to the plantar cushion, which spreads and carries the lateral cartilages outward. The frog and plantar cushion, by virtue of their elasticity, receive the major portion of the concussion. At the same time the weight is initially borne by the wall and the bars. The end of the bony column is hung in a sling in the wall and bars by the dovetailing of the sensitive laminae into the horny laminae. As the weight comes downward, these leaves give way slightly and allow the coffin bone to approach the ground; this in turn causes the sole to be somewhat lowered. The arrangement of the deep flexor tendon under the navicular bone affords a means by which a portion of the shock is absorbed. The spreading movement of the elastic structures is known as *expansion.* When the weight is removed, these structures return to their normal positions. This is known as *contraction.*

BLOOD SUPPLY. The sensitive structures are highly vascular and filled with a network of veins. The arterial circulation is sufficient unto itself, but the venous circulation receives mechanical aid from the movements of the foot. When contraction takes place, the venous cavities fill with blood; later, during expansion, the blood is forced out of the veins. The movements of the foot materially aid in the circulation.

MOISTURE. The horn is made up of a network of tubules that are cemented together. The moisture is contained primarily in these tubules. It is derived internally from the blood supply and externally from moist standings and the soil.

The natural hardness of the horn and the periople on the wall tend to prevent undue evaporation. The wall is about one-fourth water, the sole one-third, and the frog one-half water.

2

Regions, Colors, Markings, and Measurement

In order to assure uniform phraseology the standard description and nomenclature of the various regions and markings of the horse are presented in the following paragraphs.*

REGIONS OF THE HORSE

1. *Lips*—upper and lower.
2. *Nostril.*
3. *Face.* From the muzzle to a line connecting the inner corners of the eyes. Bounded on the sides by lines from the outer corners of the eyes to the corresponding nostril.
4. *Eye.* Includes eyelids.
5. *Forehead.* From the upper border of the face to the poll. Bounded on the sides by a line from the inner corner of the eye to the base of the ear.
6. *Ears.*
7. *Poll.* The prominence between the ears.
8. *Throat.*
9. *Crest.* Upper border of neck bearing the mane.
10. *Neck.*
11. *Withers.*
12. *Shoulder.*
13. *Arm.*
14. *Breast.* A single region bounded by the neck, the region of the arm, and below by a horizontal line at the level of the elbow joint.

*Published in Army Regulations 40-2245. [Ed.]

44

15. *Elbow.* Corresponds to the ulna.
16. *Forearm.*
17. *Knee.* Corresponds to knee joint.
18. *Cannon.*
19. *Fetlock* or *fetlock joint.*
20. *Pastern.*
21. *Coronet.* Corresponds to coronary band.
22. *Hoof.*
23. *Back.*
24. *Costal Region* (region of ribs). Back border and lower border follow the line of the ends of the ribs.
25. *Loin.*
26. *Point of hip.*
27. *Flank.*
28. *Abdomen* or belly.
29. *Sheath.*
30. *Croup.*
31. *Thigh.*
32. *Stifle.* Corresponds to stifle joint.
33. *Tail.*
34. *Buttocks.*
35. *Gaskin* or leg.
36. *Hock.*
37. *Chestnut.* (Also on foreleg above knee.)
38. *Muzzle.* Includes lips, nostrils, and nose or space between the nostrils.

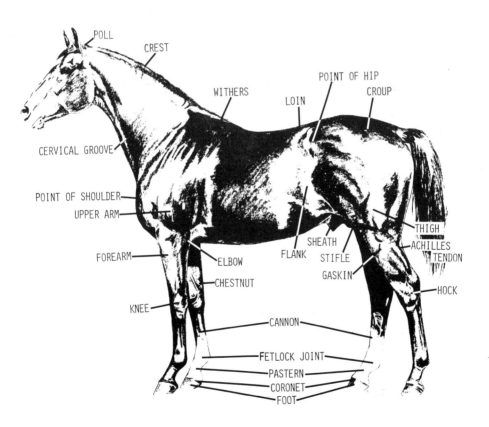

Points of the Horse

Intermaxillary space: The depression between the branches of the mandible or jaw.

Jaw: The branches of the jaw or mandible and including the sides of the head below the face and temple.

Temple: The area just back of the eye.

Interaxillary region: The space back of the breast and between the forelegs.

Axilla: The space between the foreleg and body.

Groin: The region between the inner surface of the hind leg and belly.

Dock: The anus and the hairless area in that vicinity.

Ergot: The small growth of horn appearing in the tuft of long hair on the back of the fetlock.

COLORS OF THE HORSE AND MULE. Herein are listed the most prominent and permanent characteristics by which an equine may be identified.

Black (blk) is applied to the coat of uniform black hairs.

Jet black (jet blk) is a black of a brilliant luster.

Rusty black (rusty blk) is the coat nearly black but lacking sufficient pigment to be termed black.

Chestnut (ch) is a medium golden color.

Light chestnut (lt ch) is a chestnut of yellowish tint.

Dark chestnut (dk ch) is a cinnamon shade bordering on brown.

Bay (b) is a reddish color of medium shade.

Light Bay (lt b) is a light red shade bordering on yellow.

Dark bay (dk b) is a dark red shade bordering on brown.

Brown (br) is the color of the coat almost rusty black and distinguished therefrom by the reddish coloration around the nostrils, axillae, elbows, and flanks.

Gray (gr) is applied to a coat of mixed white and dark-colored hairs, about equal in numbers.

Light gray (lt gr) is a shade of gray in which the white hairs predominate.

Dark gray (dk gr) is a dark shade of gray in which the dark hairs predominate.

Iron gray (ir gr) is a bluish shade of gray resembling a freshly broken piece of iron and includes the "blue" and "grayish-blue" coats.

Flea-bitten gray (fb gr) is a dark gray coat intermixed with small patches of whitish hairs.

Mouse (m) is an ashy gray shade resembling the color of the mouse.

White (w) is an absence of pigment.

Roan (r) is applied to a coat composed of red, white, and black hairs, usually red and white on body with black mane and tail.

Strawberry roan (st r) is a shade of roan in which the red hairs predominate.

Buckskin is applied to a coat of uniform yellowish-colored hairs.

Piebald (pb) is applied to the coat divided into patches of white and black only.

Pied black (p bl), *Pied bay* (p b), *Pied roan* (p r), are terms to be used to

46

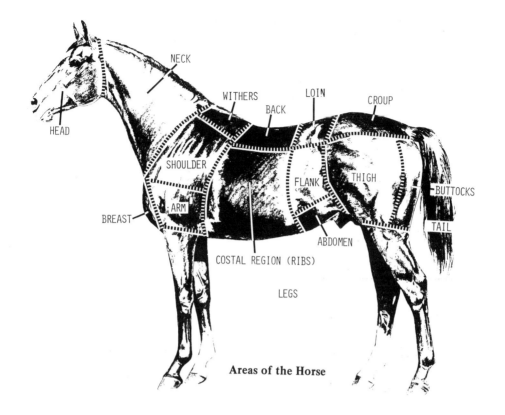

Areas of the Horse

designate the patched coats of white and black, white and bay, or white and roan. If the color other than white predominates, the term *pied* should follow the predominating color, as black pied (bl p), bay pied(b p), or roan pied (r p).

Dapple (d) is prefixed to the designation of any color when spots the size of a silver dollar, or thereabout, and lighter or darker, overlay the basic color.

MARKINGS OF HORSES AND MULES. The following are the principal white or other contrasting hair markings.

White hairs is a term used to designate a few white hairs on the forehead, at the junction of the neck and withers, on the shoulders, the coronet, or over the eyes.

Star designates a clearly defined area of white hairs on the forehead.

Race designates a narrow white stripe down the face, usually in the center, and further described as "short" when it does not reach the nose.

Snip designates a white mark between the nostrils.

Blaze designates a broad splash of white down the face. It is intermediate between a race and a white face.

White face means that the face is white from forehead to muzzle.

Silver mane and tail designates the reflection of white in these appendages.

White coronet or *white pastern* indicates that these regions are white.

Quarterstocking means that the white extends upward from the coronet and includes the fetlock.

Halfstocking means that the white has extended upward to midway between the fetlock and knee or hock.

Three-quarterstocking means that the white is well up the cannon region and approaching the knee or hock.

Fullstocking means that the white has reached or included the knee or hock.

Cowlick is a term applied to a tuft of hair presenting an inverse circular growth. Cowlicks are found on the forehead, breast, axillae, flank, on the lateral surface of the neck, between the ears, on the cheek, withers, internal surface of the thigh, and point of the buttocks. They are permanent distinguishing characteristics and are sometimes used in the identification of individual animals.

Black points means black mane, tail, and extremities.

Ray designates the dark line found along the back of some horses and many mules.

Cross designates the dark line over the withers from side to side.

Zebra marks designate the dark, horizontal stripes seen upon the forearm, the knee, and the back of the cannon region.

MEASURING ANIMALS. The *height* of a horse or mule is expressed in hands and inches. A hand is four inches. Place the horse on a level surface with all four feet properly placed and bearing weight. The head and neck should be in the position of normal carriage. The perpendicular distance from the highest point of the withers (center of the arch) to the ground is then measured with a stick that is graduated in hands and inches. The crossbar must rest firmly on the withers and the upright must be perpendicular.

The *girth measurement* is the circumference of the body measured at the juncture of the withers and back and is expressed in inches. Size in girth measurement is desirable as it indicates heart and lung space and is usually an indication of endurance. A well-conformed horse of riding type that is sixteen hands in height should have a girth measurement of about seventy-three inches.

The "bone" measurement of a horse is the circumference of the middle of the fore cannon region and is expressed in inches. The cannon region should be developed proportionately to the mass that it supports. Immediately below the knee there is a ligamentous ring by which the tendons are bound down and secured. If the accessory carpal bone on the back of the knee is not prominent, this ring is small, the region is constricted, and the horse is said to be *tied-in* below the knee. This can be most easily judged by comparing the front and rear borders of the cannon region as viewed from the side. In the normal cannon of good conformation these two borders appear to be parallel. When the condition of *tied-in* exists, the lines seem to converge as they approach the knee. Every horseman recognizes it as a most serious defect because bone and tendon troubles are far more likely. Tendons that are sharp, clean, and placed well back from the cannon bone, giving what is known as a "flat" cannon, are better indications of good measurement in this region than the size of the bone itself. Measurement will usually vary between 7¼ inches and 8½ inches in riding horses between 15/0 and 16/0 in height. Seven inches is a small bone measurement in any horse over 14/2, and 9 inches is an exceptional measurement even in a 17/0 horse. This measurement of the hind cannon is from one-half to one inch greater than the fore cannon.

48

3

Age Estimation

The average duration of life of the horse is about twenty years. A horse of this age might be considered comparatively as old as a man of sixty years. The percentage of animals that attain this age is relatively small due to the considerable numbers destroyed because of physical disability. Stallions and mares reach the age of puberty and are capable of reproduction at about one-and-a-half years of age, but they are not bodily mature until about six years of age. Horses can be trained better and more easily, with fewer unsoundnesses developing, if their training begins at six or seven years of age, rather than at the immature ages of three to five years. The period of usefulness will average about ten to eleven years. The average horse begins to show quite well-defined indications of senility at seventeen years of age, but many horses, like certain men, stay young beyond their years. It has often been observed that horses ten years of age and older seem better able to withstand hardships than younger horses. As a rule, mares show the effect of advancing years to a lesser degree than geldings.

Every horseman should be sufficiently familiar with methods of age estimation so that he can, by examination of the teeth, make an approximate estimate of the animal's age. The changes in the shape of the muzzle and face, the appearance of gray hairs about the eyes and temples, the depressions above the eyes, and appearances of "wear" of the legs are all general indications of the changes incident to increasing age, but it is only by an examination of the teeth that a reasonably accurate estimate of age can be made. There are so many outside influences that may cause digressions from the accepted rules that, even though the practice is based on the anatomy of the teeth, the basic knowledge must be augmented by the diligent study of animals of various ages and from the various parts of the country. The art of estimating accurately the age of a horse is something that cannot be learned from a book, and can only be perfected by much practice and experience.

49

NUMBER AND KINDS OF TEETH. The horse has two complete sets of teeth during his life. The first set of teeth are known as *milk teeth,* or *temporary teeth,* and as the foal develops to maturity these are shed and replaced by the *permanent teeth.* The temporary teeth are easily distinguished from the permanent teeth by their small size, pearly color, distinct neck, and small fang. The permanent teeth are much larger, stronger, and darker in color, and have a large and strong fang.

The incisor teeth are twelve in number, six each in the upper and lower jaw in both the temporary and permanent sets of teeth. In estimating age our attention is almost entirely confined to the changes appearing in these teeth. Going either way from the midline outward, these teeth are known in order as *centrals, laterals,* and *corners.* The incisors erupt and are shed in pairs as indicated by their names.

In back of the incisor teeth in each jaw there is a space on either side extending back to the molar teeth. This space is free of teeth, except for a single pointed tooth known as the *canine* or *tush.* The entire space is known as the *interdental space,* and that part back of the canine is known as the *"bar".* The four canine teeth appear only as permanent teeth and are fully developed only in the male. A considerable number of mares have small, underdeveloped canine teeth, usually barely extending above the surface of the *gums.*

It is fortunate for man that this interdental space is found in the horse's mouth, otherwise there would be no place for the bit to rest. [Ed.]

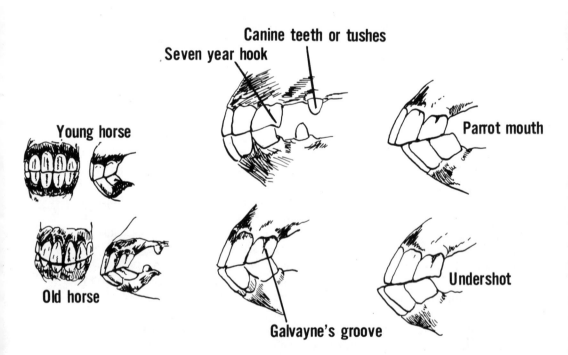

Angle of Incidence of Incisor Teeth

50

There are twenty-four *molar teeth* or grinders, six in each side of each jaw. The first three back of the interdental space are both temporary and permanent, but the last three appear as permanent teeth only.

At times a very small, pointed tooth, known as a "wolf tooth," may appear just in front of the first molar tooth. One may be present in front of each of the four first molars. There is no truth in the once-popular belief that these additional teeth often caused eye troubles or blindness.

ANATOMY OF THE INCISOR TEETH

Crown. Portion exposed above the gum.

Neck. Portion covered by the gum.

Fang. Portion imbedded in the alveolar cavity (bony).

Roots. Small projections on the end of the fang.

Table Surface. Grinding or contact surface.

Infundibulum. Inverted cone-shaped cavity formed by the invagination of the enamel from the table surface. The lower portion is filled with cement.

Cup. Upper unfilled portion of the infundibulum.

Pulp Cavity. A cavity within the fang of the tooth containing the nerves and blood vessels. In the young tooth this cavity extends upward to above the lower end of the infundibulum. As the horse ages this cavity fills at its upper end with tooth substance of a lighter color. When the tooth wears down to this level, this filled-in tooth substance appears on the table surface as a yellow line called the *dental star.* It is located in front of the inner enamel ring of the infundibulum.

WEAR OF INCISOR TEETH. After the horse is five years of age estimation of the age is based primarily on the changes in the appearance of the incisor teeth due to the progressive wearing away of the table surfaces. To compensate for the wearing away of a tooth at its table surface the gums and bony socket walls progressively recede and expose more of the tooth. The entire tooth has reached its maximum size about two years after it has erupted. After that time, the tooth is continually diminishing in size as it wears away on its table surface.

As the tooth begins to wear, the enamel wears off the table surface leaving two rings of enamel, the outer ring surrounding the tooth and the inner ring surrounding the infundibulum. The shape of the inner ring is oblong at this time, and the cup is deep. As the tooth wears down the cup becomes shallow and finally disappears; and the infundibulum becomes smaller and more nearly round, and approaches the back border of the booth. The surface of the filled portion of the pulp cavity appears as a yellow line, the dental star, in front of the inner enamel ring. The table surface becomes progressively narrower from side to side and wider from front to rear as the age increases. The shape changes from oval to more or less triangular. As a general rule, the cup disappears about three years after the eruption of the tooth.

As the tooth wears away on its table surface, the gums and bone surrounding the

51

tooth recede, exposing more of the tooth to wear. These changes cause the appearance of the crown or exposed portion of the tooth to change greatly as the tooth becomes older. When the tooth first comes into wear, its crown is short and broad from side to side, and the sides of adjacent teeth are nearly parallel to each other and in contact. As age increases, the crown becomes narrower and longer. The exposed portion of the tooth is decidedly narrower at the gum margin than at the table surface. In aged horses, adjacent teeth may have a distinct space between them throughout their length. In the young mouth, the opposing incisors meet each other at an angle approaching 180 degrees. The angle of meeting of the teeth is known as the *angle of incidence.* As the animal becomes older, this angle becomes more acute until in the aged horse the angle may be less than a right angle.

PRINCIPAL MEANS OF AGE ESTIMATION.
    Eruption of temporary teeth.
    Loss of the temporary teeth and their replacement by permanent teeth.
    Shape and disappearance of the cups.
    Appearance and position of the dental star.
    Shape, position, and disappearance of the enamel ring of the infundibulum.
    Shape of the table surfaces and crowns of the teeth.
    Length of the crown.
    Angle of incidence.
    Galvayne's groove is a groove that appears at the gum margin of the upper corner incisor at about ten years of age, extends halfway down the tooth at fifteen years, and reaches the table margin at twenty years.
    The seven-year notch usually appears on the upper corner incisor, where it incompletely overlaps the lower corner incisor. This notch usually persists for a variable number of years after its appearance.

PROCEDURE IN ESTIMATING THE AGE. The horse is approached quietly from the left side, and the lips parted with the thumb and forefinger, jaws closed. The angle of incidence and the length and size of the crowns are noted first. In case the animal is under five years of age, the progress of eruption, the loss of the temporary teeth, and the eruption of the permanent teeth can be determined without opening the mouth. After the examiner has obtained all the information possible by these means, the mouth is opened and the age further determined by examination of the cups, infundibula, and table surfaces. The lower incisors present much more constant guides to the age than the uppers, although consideration of Galvayne's groove, the seven-year notch, the angle of incidence, and, at times, the eruption of the upper permanent teeth, are equally important. In fact, before making a final estimate all "marks" should be examined and averaged.

APPEARANCE OF TEETH AT VARIOUS AGES. The development of the teeth of horses may be conveniently divided into periods based on the principal determining factors used in arriving at an estimate of the approximate age. The eruption and loss of teeth, the disappearance of cups, the changes in shape of table surfaces, and the length of crowns, are all variable guides. In this text for example, when the central permanent teeth are said to erupt at two-and-a-half years, it should be understood that *approximately* two-and-a-half years of age is meant. When a tooth is said to erupt it should be understood that the teeth of each pair do not always erupt simultaneously, and that the process of eruption is in effect until the tooth comes into wear on one border at least.

First Period (From Birth to Two-and-a-half Years).

At two to four days, the temporary central incisors erupt.

At six weeks, the temporary lateral incisors are well through the gums.

At ten months, the temporary corner incisors are well through and are in wear at about sixteen to eighteen months.

From one-and-a-half to two-and-a-half years, the exact age is difficult to ascertain, except by consideration of the degree of wear of the temporary teeth.

Second Period (From Two-and-a-half to Five Years).

At about two-and-a-half years, the temporary centrals are loose.

At two-and-a-half years, the permanent centrals erupt.

At three-and-a-half to four years, the permanent laterals erupt.

At four-and-a-half to five years, the permanent corners and the canines erupt.

NOTE: If the permanent incisor does not erupt directly beneath the temporary incisor, the temporary incisor may not be shed immediately but may remain in the jaw for some time. The permanent incisors often erupt in back of the temporary incisors.

At five years, the corners have short crowns and do not come in contact on their back corners. They have large, deep cups. The cups of the centrals are becoming shallow. A horse is said to have a full mouth at five years of age.

Third Period (From Six to Nine Years). Age is now estimated principally by changes in the size and shape of the cups of the lower incisors, and by the cups disappearing at quite regular intervals beginning with the centrals.

At six years, the table surface of the corners come into wear all around and the cups in the centrals disappear.

At seven years, the cups in the laterals are shallow or have disappeared. The seven-year notch appears on the upper corner incisor in most horses.

At eight years, the corner cup is shallow and rounded but may remain as a shallow cup until about eleven years of age. The central is triangular in shape, with the apex at the back of the tooth. The enamel ring in the central is back of the center of the table surface, and the dental star usually appears in front of the enamel ring as a rather long, faint yellow transverse line.

At nine years, the enamel ring or infundibulum is triangular and well toward the back of the tooth in the centrals and becoming triangular in the laterals. Galvayne's groove may appear in the upper corners. The crowns of the teeth are longer and the angle of incidence is noticeably narrowing. The dental star appears in the laterals.

Fourth Period (Aged). After nine years of age, the accurate estimation of age becomes more difficult because the changes in the appearance of the tooth become less constant.

At ten to twelve years, Galvayne's groove is distinct and the teeth are becoming more triangular. The enamel rings are becoming smaller, circular in shape, and approaching the back border of the table surface. The dental star, which is now narrower but more distinct, occupies a more nearly central position.

Usually between thirteen and seventeen years of age, the enamel rings disappear successively from the centrals, laterals, and corners. The exact time of their disappearance is variable. Galvayne's groove is moving down the upper corner incisor. At fifteen years of age it extends halfway from the gum margin to the table surface. The crowns are longer and narrower and the angle of incidence is more acute.

From seventeen to twenty years of age, the enamel rings have entirely disappeared. The dental star is large and distinct and occupies the central position of the table surface. The angle of incidence is pronounced. At twenty years, Galvayne's groove extends the length of the tooth. The table surfaces of the teeth are flattened from side to side and rectangular in shape. At about twenty years, there is quite noticeable spacing between adjacent teeth at the level of the table surface.

Beyond twenty years, the preceding changes become more pronounced, except that the crowns become shorter. Galvayne's groove begins to disappear at the gum margin at slightly past twenty years, and has entirely disappeared at about thirty years.

DENTAL VARIATIONS AND ABNORMALITIES. At times horses will be found that have certain dental variations or abnormalities that influence the wear of the teeth and make age estimation more difficult.

Parrot Mouth. A condition in which, due to the length of the upper jaw, the upper incisors overhang and do not properly oppose the lower incisors. In such cases the upper incisors are often very long and the wear of the lower incisors is uneven and irregular.

Undershot Jaw. Exactly the opposite of the preceding condition.

Cribbers. In horses that are cribbers or windsuckers, the outer edges of the table surfaces of both the upper and lower incisors are beveled, due to gnawing on hard objects. The beveling of the upper incisors is usually more pronounced.

Sand Mouth. If a horse grazes extensively on sandy pastures, the incisor teeth may wear away more rapidly than normal, causing the age as estimated by the teeth to be greater than the animal's actual age.

Bishoped Teeth. For the purpose of deception, an unscrupulous dealer may sometimes alter the normal appearance of the teeth by drilling, filing, and staining in such a way as to make the teeth look like those of a younger horse. This nefarious practice, known as bishoping, is believed to have derived its name from a horse dealer named Bishop.

4

Conformation and Judging

The word *conformation* as applied to animals refers to the structure of the parts as regards their external form or outline and the arrangement and relationship of the various parts as a whole. Good conformation of a part of a region implies that the part is so constructed that it is best mechanically adapted for the performance of its intended function. The term *good conformation,* as applied to the animal as a whole, implies that his component parts are of good conformation, and that these parts are so arranged and of such relative size and strength with relation to each other that the animal is best adapted to perform the particular work for which he is intended.

It is obvious that conformation is an index of utility and that any serious deviation from the essential points of good conformation can but lead to unsoundness or imperfect performance when the animal is put to work. From an aesthetic standpoint, good conformation may not always infer a body of beauty within the artist's conception of beauty, but good conformation cannot exist without harmonious arrangement, and symmetry or good proportion is the basis of useful beauty. What may be considered as perfect conformation in a horse for some particular use may be imperfect conformation in a horse intended for a radically different type of work. Within certain individual parts, the criterion of good conformation may be identical for both purposes; but in other unit parts, there may be wide differences. As an example, a large, clear, soft, and kindly eye is desirable in both the massive draft horse and the race horse, but the short, wide, sloping, and heavily muscled croup of the former would be very ill-suited for purposes of speed. This leads us to the matter of "type," which in horses may be defined as a division or group based upon the general purpose of the horse. The general types are *draft, driving* or *light* and *heavy harness* types, and *riding* type. Within each of these general types there are several less distinct subdivisions as to type. In the riding type we find the military riding type, the hunter, the polo horse,

and the racehorse, yet the distinction as to conformation is often rather indefinite.*
In this text we are primarily concerned with the riding type. The discussion of
conformation will be confined chiefly to the riding type and more especially to the
military riding type. As will be learned later, each general type is represented by
several breeds, as are also some of the secondary types.

From our consideration of conformation it is apparent that a *good horse* is one
with many good points, few indifferent points, and no bad points. Any number of
good points cannot compensate for one really bad point. The body as a whole can
be no stronger than its weakest part, although we cannot lose sight of the fact that
nature does much to compensate for deficiencies and we must always accept some
undesirable with the good. Perfection is always to be sought but is seldom attained.

HEAD. The head should be small in the riding horse. A large head acts like a heavy
weight at the end of a long lever, and has a tendency to make the horse heavy in
hand, although much depends on the obliquity or otherwise of its setting upon the
neck. A small and well-formed head is usually a sign of good breeding, although a
large but lean and well-shaped head is often found in well-bred horses.

The *ears* should be relatively small, pointed, set well apart, and not high on the
head. When the horse is alert and at attention the ears should be carried evenly
erect. *Flop ears* or *lop ears* frequently go with underbreeding and are often
associated with a phlegmatic, dull, stubborn, or indifferent temperament. The
forehead should be broad and flat. A bulging or narrow forehead is undesirable,
especially a bulging between the eyes.

The *eyes* should be large, bright, clear, kindly, and set far apart. A horse with a
small eye rather deeply set is said to be *pig-eyed.* Eyes that are very prominent are
apt to be strongly convexed and are often associated with nearsightedness and the
habit of shying.

The *face* should be of moderate length, lean, and finely chiseled, especially just
below the eyes. The face as viewed from the side should be straight or very slightly
concaved. A horse with a convex face is said to be *Roman-nosed,* while one with a
strongly concave face is said to be *dish-faced.* Both of these are undesirable for
obvious reasons.

The *nostrils* should be thin, mobile, and of ample size. The *lips* should be thin
but of moderate size and firmly and neatly held. The lips should be free from
coarse hairs other than the natural tactile hairs.

The *jaw* should be broad, flat, and well-muscled. The depth from the forehead to
the angle of the jaw should be great. Normally, this distance is equal to one-half the
total length of the head. The space between the angles of the jaw should be wide to
give plenty of room for the air and food passages that pass through this region.

The juncture of the head and neck should be lean and muscular and possess
definition without weakness, coarseness, or a meaty appearance. The most pleasing
carriage of the head is one in which the long axis of the head is carried at an angle
of about forty-five degrees to the horizontal when the horse is at attention without
restraint.

*The military riding type more closely resembles the Thoroughbred conformation
than that of the other breeds. [Ed.]*

NECK. The neck should be relatively long and of a thickness commensurate with its length. In the riding type, the neck can hardly be too long if its substance is developed proportionately. A thin and spindly neck indicates immaturity, general weakness, or want of vigor. The topline of the neck should present a slight dip in front of the withers and then a slightly convex curving line flowing into the poll. When the topline of the neck is distinctly concave, the horse is said to have a *ewe-neck,* or his neck is "on upside down," especially if the underline is curved downward. A horse with such a neck is likely to carry the head unduly high, especially the muzzle, and is often referred to as a *star-gazer.* When the topline of the neck is strongly arched, the horse is said to be *heavy-crested* or *bull-necked.* This defect appears in necks that are too short and heavy, and result in a horse likely to "bore on the bit." The underline of the neck should be nearly straight from the point where it flows out of the smooth curve of the throat to where it curves slightly downward to blend smoothly with the breast. The neck should be lean along its lower border with the outline of the trachea and large veins standing out sharply. The neck should be carried at a good angle, which in natural carriage is slightly less than forty-five degrees to horizontal. There is no part of the horse's body that has greater influence on the way of going than the length, shape, and carriage of the neck.

(A) Narrow chest; toed out (B) Good conformation (C) Pigeon toed or toed in

  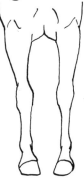

WITHERS. The withers should be moderately high and neither too thin nor bulky with muscle. There can be no objection to high withers if the shape is such that injury by the saddle can be avoided. Good height of withers goes with a good length of neck and shoulders, both of which are desirable. Too low and flat or meaty withers are spoken of as *mutton-withers.* The convexity of the topline of the withers should not be too acute but flow smoothly into the line of the back. The withers must not carry so far back as to interfere with proper placement of the saddle. The withers increase in comparative height until the horse reaches full maturity. A young or nearly mature horse with low withers will often develop much higher and better withers when put to work and trained.

SHOULDER. The shoulder can hardly be too long or too sloping, and it should be

57

well, but not bulkily, muscled. A thick shoulder gives the horse a constrained and lumbering action. A long and sloping shoulder is most advantageous for the mechanical action of the muscles and bones in the elevation and forward movement of the foreleg. A long and sloping shoulder puts plenty of horse in front of the rider. The action is good and the horse is pleasant to ride. A short and upright shoulder shortens the action, stiffens the gait of the forelegs, and places the rider forward where he unduly weights the forehand.

ARM AND ELBOW. The arm should be short and muscular and inclined toward a vertical. rather than a horizontal position. The elbow should be large, long and clean, and stand prominent and clear of the chest.

FOREARM. The forearm should be long and broad when viewed from the side, with the width continuing well into the knee. The forearm should be well-muscled, with the muscling extending well down. The direction of the forearm should be vertical when viewed from any side.

KNEE. The knee should be straight, broad, deep, and angular or well defined with no suggestion of roundness. The front of the knee should be broad and flat with the flattened surface facing toward the front as much as possible instead of too obliquely outward. The bone forming the prominence on the back of the knee should be large and prominent, for only by good development in this part is breadth in the lower forearm or width in the upper cannon region possible.

CANNON. The cannon should be short and strong. As seen from the front, the cannon bone should be of good width and well formed at its ends to enter into the knee and fetlock joints. Viewed from the side, the cannon region is broad and flat. Breadth is gained by the amount of separation of the tendons from the bones and by their size, rather than by front to rear diameter of the cannon bone itself. The tendon outlines should be clear and sharp. The back line of the tendon should be parallel to the front line of the cannon bone, or at the most should but very slightly tend to converge as they approach the knee. If these lines noticeably converge, the horse is said to *tied-in*, a serious defect. The direction of the cannon should be vertical when viewed from any side and in a line of continuation of the forearm and cannon. If, when viewed from the side, the line of the forearm and cannon is bent backward at the knee, the horse is said to be *calf-kneed.* The terms *knock-kneed* and *bowlegged* are self-explanatory.

FETLOCK. The fetlock should be broad, deep, and angular, and not rounded in appearance. It should appear broad when viewed from the side. The joint should be clean and well defined, with no tendency to appear puffy or meaty. A well-bred horse of the riding type will usually have only a small amount of long, coarse hair on the back of the fetlock.

PASTERN. The pastern should be of moderate length. Very long pasterns are weak and likely to be too sloping, placing a great deal of strain on the tendons. If, due to

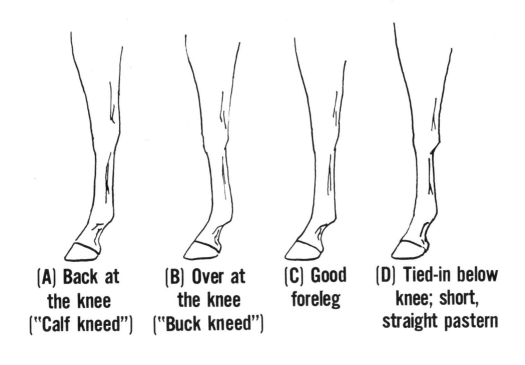

(A) Back at the knee ("Calf kneed")

(B) Over at the knee ("Buck kneed")

(C) Good foreleg

(D) Tied-in below knee; short, straight pastern

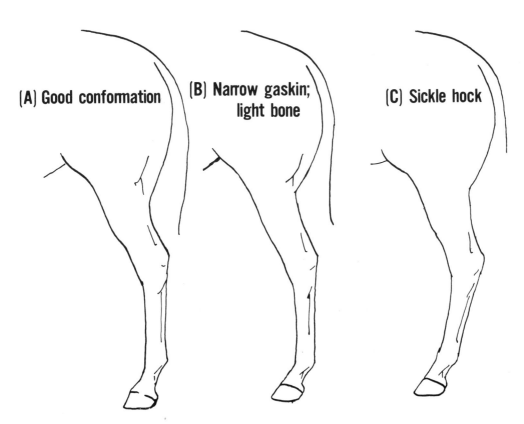

(A) Good conformation

(B) Narrow gaskin; light bone

(C) Sickle hock

59

very sloping or weak pasterns, the fetlock is depressed and the pasterns assume a horizontal position as the foot bears weight, the horse is said to be *coon-footed.* If the pasterns are short, they will be upright and the horse is said to have *stumpy pasterns.* Such a pastern conformation is usually associated with a short and upright shoulder. In addition to giving the horse a short, stiff, and stilted gait, this conformation increases the possibility of joint injury because of the increased concussion absorbed in the bony column. The normal slope of the fore pastern to horizontal is about fifty to fifty-five degrees.*

FOOT. The size of the foot should be in proportion to the size of the horse. In small feet, the horn of the hoof is often brittle, the base of support is insufficient, and the size is inadequate to absorb the concussion properly. If the foot is unduly large the gait is awkward, and clumsy, and stumbling and interfering are likely to occur. The heels should be broad and of moderate height. Low, weak heels are always a source of trouble. The hoof or foot should never be narrow and elongated like the foot of the mule. The sole should have a moderate degree of concavity, and the frog should be prominent and elastic.

When viewed from the front, a vertical line dropped from the point of the shoulder should bisect all the regions of the leg. If the midline of the toe is outside of this line, the horse is *toed-out* or *splayfooted.* If the opposite is true, he is *toed-in* or *pigeon-toed.* The former *wings in* and interferes, while the latter *wings out* or *paddles.* Both are defective, but the former is more serious. In the normal standing position the space between the forefeet should approximate that between the forelegs at the body, and is about equal to the width of the foot itself. If the feet are placed closer together, the animal is said to stand *base-narrow,* or *base-wide* if the opposite is true. If the forefeet are so placed that the legs are directed downward and forward, the horse stands *camped,* while if they are downward and backward, they are said to *stand under.* Most horses not at attention, or if cold, incline to *stand under,* but if there is soreness in the tendons or feet they may stand *camped.*

BACK. The back should be straight and not too long. Greater strength goes with straightness and shortness, but some degree of length is necessary for suppleness and speed. A horse with a short back is apt to overreach if the legs are inclined to be long. The back should be well muscled for strength and for the cushioning effect of the muscles between the saddle and the underlying bones. If the topline of the back and loin is strongly arched, the horse is said to have a *roachback* or a *hogback.* Such a back is strong, but it causes the saddle to slide forward onto the withers and is often associated with a crooked hind leg and a too-sloping croup. A hollowed or *sway-back* is weak and always becomes more accentuated with weight carrying and age.

CHEST. The chest should be of moderate breadth and cannot be too deep; ample

The ideal shoulder slope for a riding horse is also between 50° and 55°. When the slope angle of shoulder and pastern (extended through the hoof) both correspond, the result is the best possible relationship between form and function. [Ed.]

room must be provided for the vital organs of breathing and circulation. A deficient chest also means a deficient belly. The ribs should have good curvature and great length. Strong curvature without length makes the animal *barrel-chested*. A horse with such a conformation lacks lung-expansion capacity and length of shoulder, while the too-wide chest places the shoulders far apart and makes the gait wobbly and rolling. The ribs should have stronger curvature back of the saddle and rib out well back toward the flanks. A horse that lacks curvature of his back ribs is said to be *slab-sided* and will be lacking in belly, stamina, and easy-keeping qualities. In the riding horse of good conformation, the distance from the summit of the withers to the underline at the girth is approximately equal to the distance from the underline to the middle of the pastern region.

LOIN. The loin should be of moderate length, broad, and well muscled. It should be straight or slightly arched but never concave. A moderately long loin, if sufficiently wide and well muscled, is desirable for speed and suppleness, but length and small size will make the horse weak in this part and *long-coupled*.

BELLY. The belly should be large but not pendulous. The size of the belly is very largely determined by the length and spread of the back ribs. A belly of good size is an indication of stamina and easy-keeping qualities. The horse with a small belly and an underline that cuts sharply upward is said to be *herring-gutted* or *shad-bellied*. The *flank* should be narrow and well let down.

CROUP. The croup should be of good length and of moderate width and slope. A long, rather narrow, and flat croup is mechanically best adapted for speed, while the rather short, wide, sloping, and heavily muscled croup is best suited for draft purposes. The weight-carrying military horse lies between these extremes but approaches more closely the former. The absolute length of the croup is the measurement of the line from the point of the hip to the point of the buttock. The slope of the croup is determined by the inclination of this line to horizontal. The topline of the croup should carry back well. If the croup is very sloping the horse is said to have a *goose rump* or a *rainy-day croup*. The points of the hips should be defined but not unduly prominent or "ragged." Prominent buttocks, which indicate length of pelvis and croup from the hip joint backward, are much to be desired.

THIGH. The femur, or thigh bone, should be relatively short and directed forward, downward, and outward, so that in motion the stifle joint will be free and unimpeded in its range of movement. If the stifles are turned inward, the points of the hocks will turn outward. The thighs should be heavily muscled and separated between their inner surfaces by just sufficient space to prevent serious friction. If the space is wide and extends high between the thighs the horse is said to be *split up behind*.

LEG. The tibia, or bone of the leg, should be proportionately long. It extends downward and backward to enter the hock at an angle of sixty-five to seventy degrees to the horizontal. The nearer the leg and gaskin approach the vertical

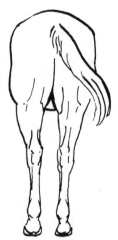

(A) Good conformation

(B) Hips ragged and odd; "split up;" leg undeveloped

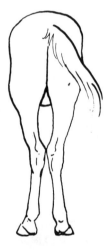

(C) Cow hocks

(D) Bowed hocks

position, the straighter will be the appearance of the hind legs. Length from hip to hock and straightness of the hind legs are factors that make for speed and give the form of conformation that the horseman speaks of as *well-let-down hocks*. A horse with very straight hind legs, while usually capable of speed, may have some difficulty in readily engaging the legs forward under the body to check forward movement or to execute about movements on the hindquarters. The lower part of the leg, or part known as the gaskin, when viewed from the side, should be as broad and strong as possible, muscled well down, and the Achilles' tendon or "hamstring" clear and prominent. Width in this region is made possible by the point of the hock being long and prominent. If the leg and gaskin are deficient in muscling, the leg has a cut-in appearance on its back line and the horse is *cat-hammed.*

HOCK. The hock should be clean and well defined, giving the appearance of great strength. The bones entering into the joint should be large and prominent, yet the region should present definition and leanness with no appearance of roughness or puffiness. The os calcis, or point of the hock, should be long and prominent. The back line of the hock in profile should be a straight line from almost the summit of the point of the hock to the fetlock joint. The lower part of the hock must have great width and breadth and meet an equally strong hind cannon. If this region is deficient, the horse is said to be *tied-in below the hocks.* If the points of the hocks are turned in toward each other, the horse is *cow-hocked* and is likely to *wing in* behind and interfere.

CANNON. The same general qualities of conformation are desired for the hind cannon as described for the fore cannon. Differing from the fore cannon, the hind cannon is not quite vertical, but its direction is downward and forward. The forward direction should be *very slight.* If the cannon is considerably inclined, it makes the hind legs appear crooked and the horse is said to be *sickle-hocked.* This conformation renders the hock more susceptible to strain. Such a conformation is sometimes spoken of as a *curby-shaped* hock because it is more susceptible to the unsoundness known as *curb.* The hind cannons are about one-sixth longer than the fore and show from one-half to one inch greater bone measurement.

FETLOCKS, PASTERNS, AND FEET. The same desirable qualities are looked for in the hind fetlocks, pasterns, and feet as were described for the corresponding regions of the foreleg. The hind feet normally tend to toe out slightly, but the degree should not be sufficient to cause interfering. A horse seldom toes in behind, but it is a defect of conformation and is almost always associated with an outward bowing the hind legs and a turning outward of the points of the hocks. The hind pasterns have slightly less slope than the fore.

METHODS OF JUDGING. Conformation judging may be confined to the judging of a single part or region, the judging of a single animal, or the judging of several animals in comparison or completion. The competent judge must first have a definite and clear mental picture of what constitutes perfect conformation of each individual part or region. Having a clear picture of perfection in each part, he must next have a mental picture of the perfectly combined parts as assembled to form his ideal for the type that is being judged.

The student of conformation should begin with the study of the various regions as individual parts. This is best accomplished by the study of many different horses selected to show clearly the perfections and defects in the various regions. He should familiarize himself with how they may best be observed.

The next step is to study selected horses and score the individual parts and the horse as a whole by the use of a score card. The scorecard drills the student in following a routine in his method of examination and serves as a check list to bring each individual region to his attention. The scorecard also teaches the student to consider the general relative values of the various regions. It gives each part a numerical value which serves as a basis for evaluating the merits of that individual part, but can only indicate relative values in a general way. Its main use is one of instruction and not for practical comparative judging of a group of horses. It is quity possible that the numerical rating of a horse with several minor defects might be lower than another with perfection in all but one vital part, yet obviously the former is the more useful horse. The numerical rating may lead the judge into a maze of figures in which he loses sight of the real value of the horse as a whole. The entry under the heading "reasons" is of far greater importance than the actual numerical rating.

The scorecard method of judging conformation is little used in the show ring because it is too time-consuming. The job of the show-ring judge is to pick the best horses, and the job should be done accurately but without trying delay. The judge should be so well schooled in his perception of the good qualities and defects that he can quickly evaluate each individual horse. He should then consider only the outstanding horses, compare their merits and defects, and make his final selection of the winners.

CONFORMATION JUDGING

Ed. note: The ratings given below are condensed from the extensive card which students at The Cavalry School were required to use. The percentages assigned to evaluate the various parts of the horse are intended to give a general idea of the relative importance of the various factors making up the total conformation of a horse and to provide familiarization, by practice in judging different horses, with the points and their desirable qualities.

GENERAL APPEARANCE (rate Excellent, Good or Bad)

FORM: _____

QUALITY: _____

TEMPERAMENT: _____

GAITS (rate Excellent, Good or Bad)

WALK: _____

TROT: _____

GALLOP: _____

POINTS

HEAD	Maximum Percentage
Ears	1.0
Forehead	1.5
Eyes	1.5
Face	.5
Muzzle	1.5
Jaw	1.0
Total	7.0

NECK

Shape	2.5
Set on	2.5
Total	5.0

FOREQUARTERS

Shoulders	5.0
Arms	1.0
Elbows	1.0
Forearms	3.0
Knees	3.0
Cannon	2.5
Fetlocks	1.5
Pasterns	2.0
Feet	5.0
Legs, general shape and direction	4.0
Total	28.0

BARREL	Maximum Percentage
Withers	4.0
Chest	3.0
Ribs	3.0
Back	5.0
Loin	5.0
Flanks	2.5
Belly	2.5
Total	25.0

HINDQUARTERS

Hips	3.0
Croup	3.0
Tail	1.0
Buttocks	3.5
Thighs	3.5
Stifles	1.0
Gaskins	3.0
Hocks	4.0
Cannons	2.0
Fetlocks	1.5
Pasterns	1.5
Feet	4.0
Legs, general shape and direction	4.0
Total	35.0
GRAND TOTAL	100.0

5

Physical Examination of Animals
for Soundness

The physical examination of horses and mules is strictly a professional procedure. Every horseman should, however, be conversant with the proper procedure and be able to recognize the more common unsoundnesses, defects, and blemishes. The detection of an abnormal or pathological condition requires a thorough knowledge of what constitutes the normal anatomy and appearance. The physical examination procedure must follow a definite routine, or many important things will be overlooked.

DEFINITIONS OF COMMONLY USED TERMS.

A Sound Animal. One without any pathological (diseased) deviation from the normal. Few animals are free from unsoundness.

A Serviceably Sound Animal. One in which the pathological deviations present do not interfere with its serviceability; for example, small splint, wind-puff, or small white spot on the cornea.

An Unsoundness. Any pathological (diseased) deviation from the normal.

An Unsound Animal. One having an unsoundness that interferes with its serviceability; for example, spavin causing lameness, or the loss of sight in one eye.

CLASSIFICATION OF UNSOUNDNESSES.

Congenital Unsoundness. A pathological condition that the animal possesses at birth; for example, hernia, cryptorchid, or hydrocephalus.

Hereditary Unsoundness. A hereditary unsoundness is a pathological condition appearing subsequent to birth, developing as the result of some inherent weakness or poor structural quality of the tissues or structures involved, and having a

66

tendency or predisposition to be transmitted from the sire or dam to the offspring. The tendency toward the development of the unsoundness, rather than the unsoundness itself, is inherited. This type of unsoundness should disqualify an animal for breeding purposes. Bone spavin, ringbone, curb, and roaring are considered hereditary unsoundnesses when their presence is associated with tissue weaknesses or structural defects of a predisposing character.

An Acquired Unsoundness. A pathological condition not caused by prenatal influences. It occurs subsequent to birth, and generally as a result of usage. This condition does not disqualify an animal for breeding purposes. Examples: Fistula of the withers, poll evil, or bowed tendons.

A Defect. A deviation from the normal, either pathological or structural. It may or may not interfere with the serviceability of the animal.

A Pathological Defect. Any pathological deviation from the normal. It may or may not interfere with the serviceability of the animal (synonymous with an unsoundness). Examples: Ringbone and high splint.

A Structural Defect. One that is classified as a congenital deformity other than pathological (synonymous with a defect of conformation). An animal with such a defect should not be used for breeding purposes. These conditions predispose such an animal to unsoundness. Examples: Badly formed legs (sickle hocks, calf knees, or buck knees).

A Blemish. Any apparent trace of depreciation having its seat in the skin or in the subjacent tissues, and not interfering with the serviceability of the animal. This trace need not be persistent. Examples: Wire cuts, saddle scars, and collar marks.

*A Vice.** An acquired habit that may interfere with the usefulness of the animal. Examples: Weaving, cribbing, and halter pulling.

METHOD OF INSPECTION. The complete examination for soundness consists of three phases as follows:
Observation of the animal in his stall.
Examination of the horse in hand on the halter.
Observation in motion and after exercise.
Observation in the stall is made principally to observe evidences of vice, such as weaving, halter pulling, stall kicking, wind sucking, and cribbing. Crampiness, stringhalt, spavin lameness, slight lameness, and general stiffness are often most easily noticed when the horse is moved in his stall, or while being taken from the stall. The usual dark background of the stall provides a good setting for the detection of certain eye troubles if the horse's head is turned toward the source of light.

Cavalry doctrine to the contrary, not all authorities agree that all vices should be classified as unsoundnesses. Veterinarians generally distinguish between the two, considering a vice to be a bad habit or an undesirable mental trait, whereas an unsoundness is considered to be a physical aberration. Many noninjurious habits, such as shying or exhibiting herd-bound tendencies, are often referred to as merely bad manners rather than vices. [Ed.]

The examination made in hand on the halter should be conducted in a good light and on a level and smooth surface. This part of the examination should be searching and systematic in conduct. The order of examining the various regions should be the same as that in judging the conformation of the various parts, and the unsoundnesses to be looked for are listed on page 66 in substantially this order. The examination as conducted should be largely a visual one and the sense of touch used only to confirm, if necessary, what the eyes have seen, or to complete the examination for such a condition as sidebone. The trained eye can detect an abnormality, or asymmetry of parts, that the sense of touch may fail to disclose. Much close-in examination and handling of the parts will cause the examiner to lose the full picture of the horse and will almost invariably result in his overlooking some important region or defect. Such tactics can usually be taken as an indication of the inexperience of the examiner. Any routine of examination is satisfactory as long as it is complete and is *rigidly adhered to.* Certain positions of the examiner with reference to the horse are most advantageous for the ready detection of each of the various unsoundnesses, and the route must so combine these that the examination may be made with a minimum of lost motion.

After completing the preceding part of the examination, the horse is observed in motion for lameness, irregularities of gait, and wind. The methods of conducting this part of the examination and unsoundnesses revealed by it, will be described later.

COMMON STABLE VICES.

Wind Sucking. A practice in which the horse assumes a position with upper teeth bearing on the manager or other projecting object, flexes the head on the neck, and proceeds to suck wind into his stomach. This is accompanied by a long grunting sound. Windsuckers are difficult to keep in condition.

Cribbing. A vice in which the edge of the manger or any other projection is grasped between the teeth and gradually bitten away. The habit results in a characteristic beveling of the front margins of the teeth, although the rounded wear from an iron feedbox may produce much the same appearance in the teeth. Wind sucking and cribbing are usually associated, although a horse may be subject to one and not the other. The habit is not confined to the stable, but may be practiced whenever the opportunity offers. A smooth-finished stall in which there is nothing to offer a tooth-hold, or the use of a strap fitted sufficiently close about the throat to compress the larynx when the head is flexed, but causing the horse no discomfort when not indulging in the vice, are the usual means of preventing the horse from practicing the habit.

Weaving. A rhythmical shifting of the weight of the forehand from one forefoot to the other in much the same manner as is displayed by a bear in captivity. As a rule, enforced idleness is an active cause. It has been suggested that horses tied with chain halter shanks have acquired this habit in order to rattle the chains.

Kicking. Horses kick with various motives, such as maliciousness, playfulness, or willful attempts to injure either companions or attendants. A great many horses that never manifest an inclination to kick elsewhere acquire the habit of kicking in the stable. Mares are kickers more frequently than are geldings. Some horses kick only at feeding time, thus giving vent to their impatience. A true stable-kicker appears to have no other excuse than the satisfaction of kicking. Padding the stall with salvaged mattresses will prevent the horse from injuring himself and will very often stop the habit, because it seems that many animals kick the side of the stall for no other reason than to hear the sound produced. Hobbling the two hind feet, or even shackling one to a weight, is sometimes resorted to, but such practices are often attended with more serious danger than is the original offense.

Tail Rubbing. The presence of animal parasites, neglect of the dock region, or a dirty sheath are the more common causes of tail rubbing. The last-named cause is probably the most frequent. Once acquired, however, the practice is often persisted in, even after the correction of the conditions that originally induced it. If thorough grooming fails to stop it, the horse may have to be put into a specially constructed box stall provided with a fender arranged at such a level that the horse cannot rub his tail against it or any other part of the stall. Still better is a stall wall built about the height of the horse, with an upward and outward slope from the floor so that the horse, with his heels against the wall, cannot reach it to rub his tail. Shields and bandages may be employed, but they are liable to injure the hair of the tail.

Halter Pulling. Confirmed halter pullers are best secured by placing ropes or chains across the stall behind them. The habit may be broken in the earlier stages by a slip noose about the flank, the rope being carried forward between the front legs, through the halter ring, and then fastened securely to the manger bar. After pulling back and tightening the noose about his flank, the horse usually takes greater care to keep the rope slack. Another method often successful is to pass the free end of the tie rope from the halter through the manger tie ring and secure it to a hobble placed on one fore pastern.

Bad Habits. Horses are most liable to fall into bad habits during periods of idleness. A regular daily routine, therefore, of either moderate exercise or work, and a ration that is not too stimulating, are the best safeguards against their acquiring bad habits.

DEFINITION AND DESCRIPTION OF THE MORE COMMON UNSOUND-NESSES.

Regions of the Head and Neck.

Infected Sinus is an acquired unsoundness characterized by an infection of a sinus of the head with pus-producing germs. It is manifested by a bulging of the face or lower part of the forehead and an offensive nasal discharge. The most common cause is a diseased molar tooth.

Periodic Ophthalmia (Moon Blindness). An acute or chronic disease of the whole eye that recurs at more or less frequent intervals and that often results in total blindness after several attacks. Each attack comes on suddenly and lasts one to three weeks. During the attack, the eye is swollen, the cornea is white or cloudy, tears flow freely, and the eyelids are closed to keep out light. One or two attacks

69

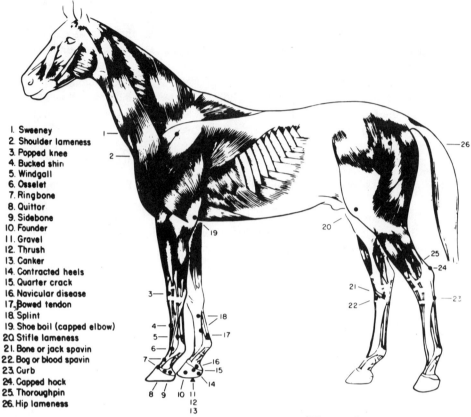

1. Sweeney
2. Shoulder lameness
3. Popped knee
4. Bucked shin
5. Windgall
6. Osselet
7. Ringbone
8. Quittor
9. Sidebone
10. Founder
11. Gravel
12. Thrush
13. Canker
14. Contracted heels
15. Quarter crack
16. Navicular disease
17. Bowed tendon
18. Splint
19. Shoe boil (capped elbow)
20. Stifle lameness
21. Bone or jack spavin
22. Bog or blood spavin
23. Curb
24. Capped hock
25. Thoroughpin
26. Hip lameness

Locations of Unsoundness

generally leave the cornea or lens cloudy, and the eye is known as a "blue eye." The cause is unknown, but it is safest to consider the disease contagious. Several attacks invariably result in a cataract, followed by total blindness. A cataract is an opacity of the crystalline lens and is seen as a white object in the pupil. An eye that has had several attacks of periodic opthalmia is smaller than normal, and the upper lid is often slightly elevated in the center and appears wrinkled.

Feather (Scar on the Cornea). A white scar on the transparent cornea. It is not a serious defect unless the scar interferes with the vision.

The examination of the eyes should not be made in direct sunlight. Stand the animal in a partially darkened aisleway or stall with his head toward the source of light. Compare both eyes and be deliberate in the examination. If it is suspected that vision is impaired, place a thick towel over one eye and then lead the horse over a bale of hay or some other obstacle. Repeat with the other eye. Testing the vision by feinting at the eye with a finger is deceptive because the horse may feel the movement of air, or one may touch a tactile hair and cause the animal to move the head.

Paralyzed Lips. An acquired unsoundness characterized by a pendulous condition of the lips that interferes with the act of prehension. It is caused generally by an injury to the nerves controlling the lip muscles.

70

Lop Ears. A congenital or acquired deformity in which the muscles of the ears are weak or partially paralyzed. It is often associated with a degree of deafness. Young Thoroughbreds frequently have drooping ears, but they usually become erect when the animal reaches maturity.

Fistula of the Poll (Poll Evil). An acquired unsoundness characterized by a swelling in the region of the poll and the atlas and axis. This swelling abscesses and often discharges pus through one or more openings. It is caused by an injury to the ligamentum nuchae at or near its attachment to the poll.

Wry Neck (Torticollis). An acquired unsoundness characterized by a chronic contraction of the muscles on one side of the neck and manifested by a lateral curvature of the neck. It often results from an animal becoming cast in a stall and lying with the neck twisted for several hours. It is seldom permanent.

Collapsed Trachea. An acquired unsoundness caused by a fracture or cutting of one or more of the cartilaginous rings of the trachea. It is manifested by a depression that can be felt by passing the hand along the trachea and lower border of the neck.

Regions of the Withers, Shoulder, and Foreleg.

Fistula of the Withers. An acquired unsoundness characterized by a diffuse swelling of the region of the withers and the formation of an abscess that may discharge pus through one or more openings. It is caused by an injury or an infection of the ligamentum nuchae in this region and often involves the tops of the spinous processes of the thoracic vertebrae. The pus generally burrows between the layers of shoulder and neck muscles. It is an extremely difficult condition to treat. Even when the infection is completely overcome, the resultant scar tissue may leave the animal stiff in the shoulders.

Sweeny. An acquired unsoundness characterized by an atrophy of one or more of the muscles covering the shoulder blade. It is generally caused by an injury to the large nerve of these muscles, where it passes over the front border of the middle third of the scapula. The condition is seen more often in draft animals. Sometimes it is secondary to some disease or injury that causes the animal to refrain from use of the muscles, hence the wasting away from disuse.

Shoe Boil (Capped Elbow). An acquired unsoundness characterized by a serious or fibrous enlargement on the point of the elbow. It is caused by bruising with a long-heeled shoe when lying down, or by lack of sufficient bedding to prevent the elbow from being in contact with the hard floor of the stall. The forward slipping of the forefeet on a slippery stall floor while the horse is attempting to arise often bruises the point of the elbow and causes a shoe boil.

Hygroma. An acquired unsoundness characterized by a soft, fluctuating enlargement on the front surface of the knee. It is caused by a contusion resulting from a fall, striking a hurdle, or pawing against the manger. When acute, it generally causes lameness. It often becomes chronic; the swelling organizes into a cyst and the lameness disappears. Often referred to as *jumper's knee.*

Broken Knee. An acquired unsoundness characterized by a bony enlargement on the front surface of the knee. It is a serious defect because it is generally associated

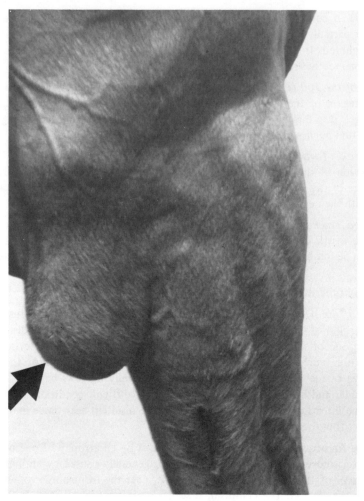

Shoe Boil: Right Foreleg

with some degree of inflammation and stiffness of the knee joint. It should not be confused with fibrous growths, which are soft and movable. The latter are only scars resulting from injuries to the skin and the underlying soft tissues. Examination of an animal with swellings around the knee should include flexing of the joint by folding the foot back against the elbow.

Knee Sprung (Over in the Knee). An unsoundness in which the knee is continually flexed to a certain degree. It is associated with a temporary or permanent shortening of the flexor tendons, which is caused by a tendon injury or an inflammation of the knee joint. Young foals, which are frequently knee sprung, will usually straighten up with proper care. In mature horses and particularly old horses that develop the unsoundness as the result of hard use, the condition is usually permanent and incurable. A tied-in condition below the knee predisposes to inflammation and a shortening of the flexor tendon.

72

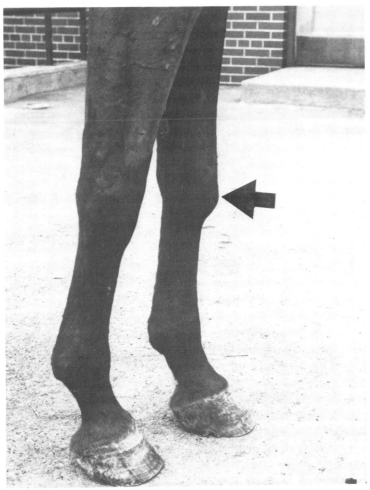

Popped Knee (Carpitis) *Usually associated with fractures of the lower carpal bones.* *[Ed.]*

Bowed Tendon (Chronic Tendinitis). An acquired unsoundness characterized by a chronic thickening the flexor tendons or the suspensory ligament in the cannon region. It is the result of one or more acute inflammations of the tendons or the ligament and is a serious defect.

Bucked Shin. An acquired unsoundness characterized by a bony enlargement that is most apparent on the front surface of the cannon bone. The condition is the result of an extensive periostitis of the cannon bone ("sore shins") caused by concussion in the bony column. Sore shins are quite prevalent among young racehorses that are raced on hard tracks. The bony enlargement that may be present after the subsidence of inflammation seldom causes lameness. The condition is rarely observed in army horses inasmuch as horses that have been raced are seldom purchased for military use.

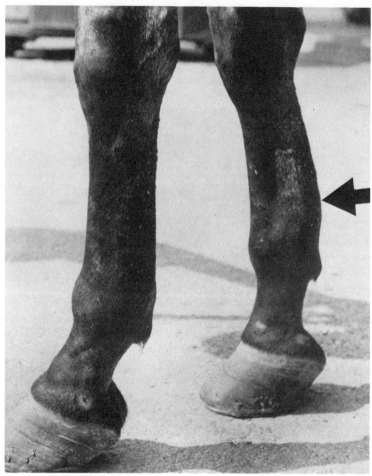

Bowed Tendon: Right Foreleg *Actually somewhat of a misnomer, since the injury is to the tendon sheath rather than to the tendon. [Ed.]*

Splint. An acquired unsoundness characterized by a localized bony enlargement along the groove formed by the union of the splint and cannon bones. Splints may be classified as high, low, forward, and back. They may cause lameness when just forming, when fully developed and located high enough to interfere with the articular surfaces of the lower row of carpal bones and the cannon bone, or when situated far enough back to irritate the flexor tendons or suspensory ligament. Those located well forward or low seldom cause any lameness. Splints seldom develop on animals over ten years of age, and usually appear before the horse is seven years old. When the growth has formed, the lameness generally subsides. Poor conformation (tied-in or light cannons), concussion, work on hard roads, fast work on irregular ground, and unequal distribution of weight on the bony column caused by faulty conformation or poor shoeing, are the most common causes.

74

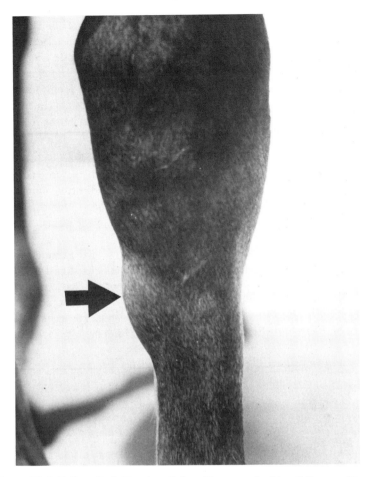

Large High Splint: Left Foreleg, Below Knees on Inside of Cannon Bone

Wind-puffs (Windgalls). An acquired unsoundness characterized by distension of the synovial bursae in the region of the fetlock joint. They are an indication of hard usage but are not a serious defect, since they seldom cause lameness.

Enlarged Sesamoids (Sesamoiditis). An acquired unsoundness characterized by a bony enlargement on the back surface of the fetlock joint. The enlargement is caused by a chronic inflammation of the mass of cartilage that surrounds the sesamoid bones. This inflammation causes the cartilage to ossify, resulting in a roughening of the smooth articular surface and the groove for the flexor tendons. This is a serious defect, and lameness caused by it is practically incurable.

Ringbone. An acquired unsoundness characterized by a bony enlargement in the pastern region. The bony growth may appear on the long pastern bone, the short pastern bone, or both. It is sometimes classified as high or low depending on whether it is above or below the pastern joint. The enlargement may appear on the front, sides, or back of the region. In the more severe cases the exostoses may completely ring the bone. It is the result of inflammation of the periosteum and bone and is caused by sprains, blows, wounds, concussion, or other injury. Small and weak pasterns, particularly those which are short and upright or stumpy, are frequently involved. When occurring in horses of this type, ringbone should be considered hereditary unless evidence to the contrary is forthcoming. Not all ringbones cause permanent lameness; however, in most cases the lameness is severe and permanent, often becoming progressively more incapacitating in spite of any form of treatment.

Sidebone. A hereditary or acquired unsoundness characterized by ossification of the lateral cartilage and manifested by a bulging of both the coronary band and hoof wall over the affected cartilage. Inasmuch as the ossification almost invariably begins deep down in the foot where the cartilage is attached to the coffin bone, it is impossible to prove its existence during the early stages of the disease except by the use of the X ray. The extent of a more complete ossification can be determined by raising the foot and pressing down on the cartilage with the thumb. The normal cartilage is soft, elastic, and thin, while a diseased one is hard, inelastic, and thick. Inherited tendency to the disease and a short, upright pastern are the chief predisposing causes. Concussion, improper balancing of the foot, and shoeing with high heal calks are the chief exciting causes. The condition affects the forefeet almost exclusively, and the outer cartilage is involved more frequently than the inner.

Quittor. An acquired unsoundness characterized by infection and necrosis of the lateral cartilage, thickening of the area, and discharge of pus from one or more openings in the region of the coronet immediately over the affected cartilage. It is caused by deep wounds, such as calk wounds, which become infected and injure the cartilage.

Quarter Crack. An acquired unsoundness characterized by a fracture of the wall at the quarter, extending from the coronary band downward a variable distance. Lameness is caused by pinching of the sensitive laminae in the crevice and a resultant inflammation of the surrounding laminae. The principal causes are contracted heels, dry feet, improper balancing of the feet, concussion, and fast work on hard roads. The condition is seldom found in the hind feet.

Toe Crack. An acquired unsoundness characterized by a fracture of the wall at the toe, extending from the coronary band downward a variable distance. The causes are the same as for a quarter crack. Small fissures in the wall that extend upward from the ground surface are called sand cracks. They result from improper nailing and a dry, brittle condition of the horn. Although not serious, they indicate a poor quality of horn. This may result in breaking away of the lower edge of the wall and insecure nailing.

Seedy Toe. An acquired unsoundness characterized by a separation of the wall and sole near the toe and manifested by a bulging of the wall over the affected part. The separation may extend up between the wall and the coffin bone.

Navicular Bursitis (Coffin-joint Lameness, Navicular Disease). A hereditary or acquired unsoundness characterized by an inflammation of the navicular bursa or

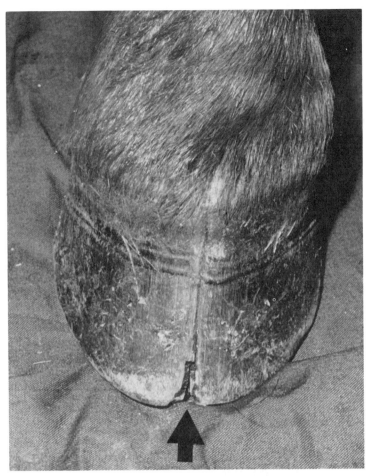

Severe Toe Crack *Originating from a defect or injury at the coronary band. [Ed.]*

bone. In a chronic state, it extends to the surrounding structures. Both forefeet may be affected, but it is rare that the hind feet are involved. Unquestionably many horses are born with a predisposition to the disease, and some are affected as foals. Concussion from high action, straight shoulders and pasterns, and much work on hard ground are the principal exciting causes. Lameness, stumbling, and stilted gaits are the most prominent symptoms. The affected foot is often contracted or boxlike, but it may be well formed and appear normal in every respect. It is difficult to diagnose except by close study and by a process of elimination.

Dropped Sole. An acquired unsoundness characterized by a flattening of the sole and chronic lameness. It is caused by a downward rotation of the toe of the coffin bone as a result of chronic laminitis. The chronic inflammation of the sensitive laminae causes them to separate from the horny laminae, thereby permitting the coffin bone to rotate downward because of the pull of the deep flexor tendon. The

77

resultant pressure on the sole causes it to lower and become flattened or even convex. The wall of such a foot is generally wavy and often concave at the toe, as viewed from the side.

Regions of the Body.

Hernia (Rupture). A congenital or acquired unsoundness characterized by an opening in the abdominal wall and by a protrusion of a portion of some abdominal organ through the opening into a pouch under the skin. Abdominal hernias in horses and mules generally occur at the umbilicus or navel.

Scars. Scars on the back or withers of such nature that they are likely to become injured by the saddle should always be considered as unsoundness rather than blemishes.

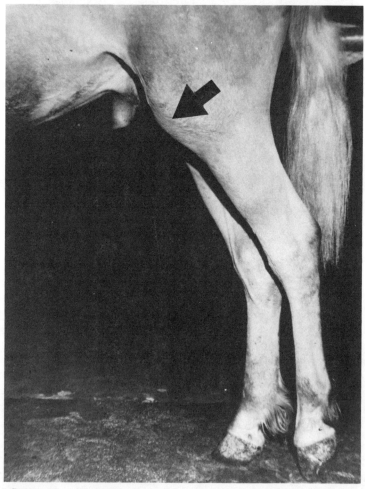

Gonitis *Commonly referred to as the condition of being stifled, this is a semidislocation of the patella that immobilizes the stifle joint, usually causing it to protrude. [Ed.]*

78

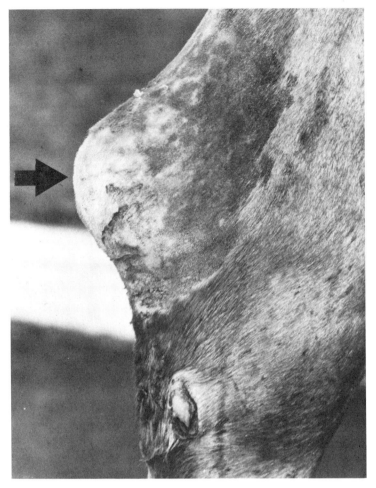

Capped Hock: Right Hind Leg *Caused by external injury. [Ed.]*

Region of the Hind Leg.

Knocked-down Hip (Hipped). An acquired unsoundness characterized by a fracture of the external angle of the hip bone. It is manifested by the point of the affected hip being lower than the normal one. The fracture may be caused by a fall, by running through a narrow doorway, or by striking against a tree or post. The fractured end is pulled downward by the strong muscular attachment and gives the hips an unsymmetrical appearance. The condition is best seen when standing directly in back of the animal.

Gonitis. An acquired unsoundness characterized by an inflammation of the structures forming the stifle joint. It is manifested by a characteristic pouching, pendent swelling about the joint, and a lameness in which the toe is usually dragged.

79

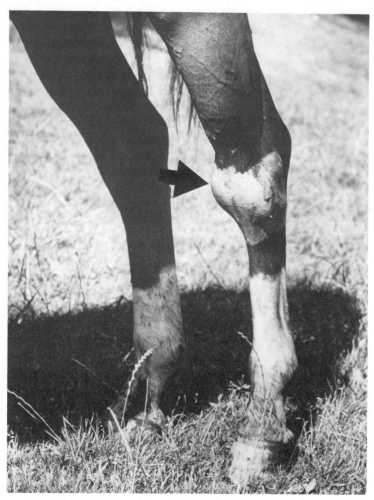

Very Large Bog (or Blood) Spavin *A distension of the joint capsule of the hock.* *[Ed.]*

Stringhalt (Springhalt). An unsoundness, the cause of which has never been conclusively demonstrated. Many theories have been expounded, such as heredity, disease of the sciatic nerve, contraction of various muscles, and diseases of the foot. It occurs more frequently in old animals. It does not necessarily render an animal unserviceable. It is manifested by a spasmodic flexion of the hock, and is most markedly evinced when the subject is first taken from the stable or caused to back.

Capped Hock. An acquired unsoundness characterized by a serious or fibrous enlargement on the point of the hock. It is often caused by bruises due to stable kicking or falling, and seldom causes lameness.

Bone Spavin (Jack). A hereditary or acquired unsoundness characterized by a bony enlargement on the inside and lower portions of the hock joint. The principal

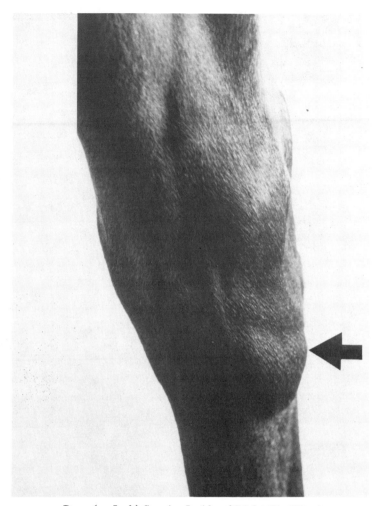

Bone (or Jack) Spavin: Inside of Right Hind Hock

predisposing causes are a faulty conformation of heavy, muscular hips; small, weak, crooked hock joints; and a predisposition to bony growths. The exciting causes are sprain and concussion. The lameness is caused by a roughening of the articular surfaces of the lower hock bones. The visible exostosis is best seen from a point near the shoulder on the same side as the affected leg. The examiner should compare both hocks from the same relative positions. Many animals have spavins and suffer no lameness therefrom, but the defect constitutes a continual liability and should be considered as a potential source of lameness.

Bog Spavin. An acquired unsoundness characterized by a distension of the joint capsule of the hock joint. The principal exciting causes are strain and concussion in the hock joint. The distension is seen at the inner and upper portion of the front of the hock. It does not cause lameness, except occasionally in the acute stages of the distension. It is seen most frequently in horses with rather straight hocks.

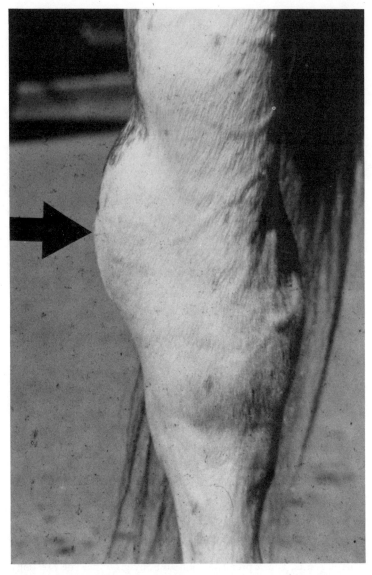

Thoroughpin: Right Hind Leg *A distension of the sheath of the deep digital extensor tendon. [Ed.]*

Thoroughpin. An acquired or hereditary unsoundness characterized by a distension of the synovial sheath of the deep flexor tendon. This is manifested by fluctuating swelling on both sides just in front of the point of the hock and beneath the tendon of Achilles. Small thoroughpins show a bulging on the outside only and are common to coarse animals that have worked hard. The condition seldom causes lameness unless an excessive strain causes an acute distension of the sheath.

Curb. A hereditary or acquired unsoundness characterized by a chronic thickening

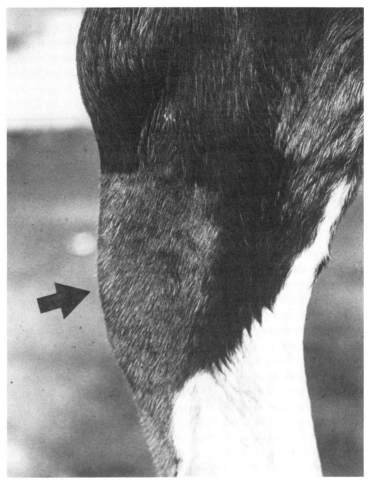

Curb: Right Hind Leg *Caused by severe tendon strain. [Ed.]*

of the flexor tendon sheath and plantar ligament on the back border of the hock. Viewed from the side, the back line of a curby hock appears rounded instead of straight. The size varies considerably, but it is always conspicuous when the leg is viewed in profile. It is more commonly found on sickle hocks and weak, tied-in hocks, and is itself an indication of weakness of the joints. It seldom causes lameness, except during the early and acute stage.

Respiratory Organs (Wind). To test the wind, have the animal ridden or driven at an extended gallop until the breathing is quite accelerated, then have him stopped abruptly in front of you so that you may hear the air rush through the air passages. To make sure that both nasal passages are functioning, hold the hand tightly over first one nostril and then the other and note whether the air passes readily through the opposite nostril.

Roaring (Whistling). A hereditary or acquired unsoundness characterized by a paralysis of the nerves and a relaxation of the muscles of the vocal cords, which has caused the cords on one or both sides of the larynx to hang loosely in the lumen of the organ. A roaring, whistling sound is produced when air is drawn *into* the lungs. The sound may not be noticeable when the animal is at rest, but is apparent when the animal is moved at a canter or gallop. The condition is the result of hereditary influence in most cases but can result from debilitating diseases, such as influenza and pneumonia. It occurs more frequently in the riding or galloping type of horse, especially in large animals.

Roaring is characterized by a more or less shrill whistling sound at each inhalation. The sound produced may be lessened or entirely prevented by plugging one nostril. Advantage is sometimes taken of this fact by unscrupulous dealers.

Heaves. An acquired or hereditary unsoundness characterized by a breaking down of the walls of a portion of the air cells in the lungs and a resultant loss of elasticity of the lung tissue. It is manifested by a peculiar manner of breathing during exertion. In bad cases, when the horse is at rest, this peculiar breathing may be due to an extra contraction of the flank muscles subsequent to the normal contraction that takes place during expiration of the air. The condition is often associated with an affection of the heart and a lack of stamina. Pneumonia, severe exertion of horses not in condition, and the feeding of dusty hay may cause this condition.

LAMENESS. Lameness is a symptom of an ailment or affection and is not to be considered in itself as a disease. It is the manifestation of a structural or junctional disorder of some part of the locomotory apparatus and is characterized by a limping or halting gait. Any affection, therefore, that causes pain that is increased by the bearing of weight upon the affected member or by the moving of such distressed part, or which mechanically interferes with the movement of any part, results in an irregularity of locomotion known as lameness. The degree of lameness, though variable in different instances, is in most cases proportionate to the amount of pain caused by movement. This fact serves as a helpful indicator in the matter of establishing a diagnosis and giving the prognosis. This is especially true in cases that are somewhat unusual in character.

Types of Lameness. There are three types of lameness recognized as follows:

Supporting-leg lameness is the most common. The greatest pain is evidenced as the full weight is borne either in motion or at rest. Diseases of the foot, the lower joints and their ligaments, and the supporting structures of the leg are characterized by this type of lameness.

Swinging-leg lameness is characterized by the movement of the limb in its extension or flexion causing the greatest pain. Diseases of the shoulder, elbow joints, or the muscles of extension and flexion, are characterized by this type of lameness.

Mixed lameness is manifested by the symptoms of both of the other types of lameness. This is generally characteristic of true joint lameness.

The manner of manifestation of lameness is as follows:

Lameness in a Foreleg. In the case of a supporting-leg lameness of the left foreleg, for example, the contact with the ground is lighter and of shorter duration than

84

that of the unimpaired right, and the beat or sound of contact of the diseased member is less distinct. At the moment of contact of the left foot, the head is approaching the *summit* of an upward gesture or movement of the head and neck, which was begun while the diseased member was in flight. This gesture, by force of inertia, decreases somewhat the weight and concussion borne by the diseased left leg. The head is lowered as the sound right foot contacts the ground and the horse seems to nod. Note that the head is in its lowest position as the sound foot is in contact. The diseased left foot is carried well forward in flight and planted well in advance of the point of contact of the right foot, but the right foot is planted soon after passing the point of contact of the left. In other words the length of the step (distance the foot is advanced beyond the point of contact of the opposite foot) of the diseased leg is lengthened and that of the sound leg is shortened.

In the case of a swinging-leg lameness of the left foreleg, the manifestations would be almost the exact opposite of those outlined above and practically the same as those of a supporting-leg lameness of the right foreleg.

Lameness in a Hind Leg. In the case of a supporting-leg lameness of the left hind leg, for example, the manifestations are the same as in the case of a similar lameness in the left fore, except that in the head gesture the head is approaching its *lowest* position at the moment the left hind foot strikes the ground, and at the same time the croup is being elevated. The croup is lowered as the sound right hind foot strikes the ground. As in the case of lameness in the foreleg, the gesture or movement of the head and neck is used to lighten the contact on the diseased member. In the case of a swinging-leg lameness of the left hind leg, the manifestations would be the opposite of those just stated.

Diagnosis of the Cause of Lameness. Obviously, it is absolutely necessary to locate the cause before any rational treatment can be instituted. In fact, the diagnosis is often far more difficult than the treatment. In many cases the cause is perfectly obvious, such as an acute tendinitis or a bad quarter crack that is bleeding. In a large percentage of the cases it requires, however, a careful and painstaking examination, coupled with a most thorough knowledge of the parts. A routine examination should proceed somewhat as follows:

Obtain a complete history of the case.

Stand off and watch the animal at rest. Note the posture, the shoeing, evidence of pain, and look for wounds or swelling.

Have the animal walked and trotted up and down grade on both soft and hard footing. Observe the motion of the head, neck, and each hip. Note the length of the steps, the manner in which the legs are moved when extended and flexed, and the length of time each foot is on the ground. This examination should lead to a determination of the lame leg, the type of lameness, and its degree of severity.

Next, make a detailed examination of the leg starting at the foot and working up. The forelegs are far more frequently the seat of lameness than are the hind legs. Fully sixty percent of all lameness in front is caused by injury or disease of the foot; in ninety-five percent of all cases the cause is found from the knee down. Shoulder lameness is rare. The cause of a large percentage of lameness in the hind leg is found in the hock joint; other causes are located largely in the foot, pastern, and fetlock. The possibility of each region is eliminated as one works up from the foot. If there is still doubt, the foot is examined again. The examination must not be started with a preconceived prejudice toward finding the cause at some particular place, but must be approached with an open mind. The diagnosis of lameness is one of the most difficult tasks and requires a most thorough knowledge of anatomy, physiology, and gaits, as well as a sound and logical manner of procedure.

6

Feeds and Feeding: Forage Inspection

Within rather recent years the chemist, the physiologist, and the scientific animal husbandman, working together, have learned many facts concerning the proper feeding of animals. The chemist has determined the basic food constituents of plants utilized for animal food. The physiologist and physiological chemist have determined the animals' requirement of the different food constituents under varying conditions, and the efficiency of the animal organism in the utilization of these foods. With these facts at hand, the compounding of rations from various forms of plant foods becomes but a mathematical computation. The scientific feeder then tests the ration so compounded and by slight variation is usually able to meet the actual feeding requirements. The chief value of this method of determining an animal ration lies in the fact that we can select those feeds most advantageously priced. The scientific methods of feeding have, to a very great extent, replaced the trial and error methods in use since animals were first domesticated. However, practical feeding experience is still highly important. For a thorough understanding of the method of computing rations, it is necessary that we possess some knowledge of the basic principles involved.

THE ANIMAL BODY AND ITS FOOD REQUIREMENTS

The animal body grows, moves, generates heat, and reproduces. These are four of its basic functions. All of these functions are but manifestations of energy in one form or another. The total of the world's energy seems to have but one source, the sun. Whether that energy is latent or kinetic; whether it is stored as fat, sugar, or protein within the animal body or deep in the earth's crust as coal or petroleum; and whether it appears as heat or man-made light, or in any other form, it came from the sun and was made available for earthly use only by the growth of plants.

87

Animal bodies do not, except to a very limited degree, have the power to utilize directly the sun's energy, nor has man yet constructed any device for the practical direct use of the energy of sunlight. The animal body must be nourished by plant tissues or by animal tissues that have been built from plant tissue.

The animal body is composed of but a small group of the many elements found in nature. The elements found in the body in quantity are carbon; hydrogen, one of the elements occurring in water; oxygen, found free in the air and in water; and nitrogen, an air gas. In much smaller quantities we find sulphur, iron, calcium, phosphorus, chlorine, fluorine, silica, manganese, potassium, sodium, and copper. Aside from water, which comprises about fifty percent of the body, the most important part of animal tissue is *protein*, which amounts to ten to twenty percent of the body weight. Protein is composed of carbon, hydrogen, oxygen, nitrogen, and sulphur or phosphorus. The muscles, nerves, and internal organs are largely protein. *Fats,* which are composed of carbon, hydrogen, and oxygen, are the reserve food of the body. They form the fatty tissues and occur mixed with other tissues, such as muscles. The amount of fat may vary from but a small part of nearly fifty percent of the body weight. *Carbohydrates,* which are also made up of carbon, hydrogen, and oxygen, but in different proportions, form a small part of the animal body. The *mineral elements,* occurring chiefly in bone but to some extent in other tissues, account for over four percent of the body weight.

The body requires food for:

Growth.

Repair of worn-out body tissue.

Fuel to maintain body temperature.

Energy for vital body functions of heart, lungs, and digestion.

Energy for the production of movement or external work.

At least half of the food requirements are for the first three factors listed, or for maintenance.

Protein is required for body growth and repair of worn-out tissues, and minerals are needed for the bones. Carbohydrates and fats are required for the production of heat and energy, or to be stored as fat or sugar as an energy-food reserve. Protein can be used by the body as a source of heat and energy, but such utilization of expensive protein is both uneconomical and inefficient.

In addition to the well-known food compounds (proteins, carbohydrates, and fats), investigations in recent years have shown that *vitamins and minerals* also are essential for the proper growth and health of animals. Vitamins do not themselves contribute to the energy supply of the body, but facilitate utilization of the proteins, carbohydrates, fats, and minerals. A well-balanced ration of dry feed supplemented by occasional grazing will, as a rule, meet the vitamin requirements of mature horses. Growing foals require an ample supply of calcium, phosphorus, and vitamin D to enable them to develop sound, strong bones. Pregnant and nursing mares have a higher calcium-phosphorus requirement than do other mature horses. Vitamin D deficiency in foals may be avoided by feeding an ounce of cod-liver oil daily, or an equivalent amount of vitamin D concentrate. Legume hays, bone meal, and ground limestone are excellent sources of calcium and phosphorus. If sufficient minerals are not supplied by the regular concentrates and roughages in the ration, they may be supplied by allowing access to a mineral mixture of ground limestone and bone meal. A calcium-deficient diet for mature horses may at times be the cause of bone disease or obscure lameness. Nonleguminous hay grown on calcium-deficient soil is sometimes the source of a calcium deficiency in the diet, and for this reason the inclusion of some alfalfa or other legume hay in the ration is desirable, especially during the winter months.

An animal's body may be likened to a gasoline engine that has been strangely endowed with the power of replacing its own worn-out parts. For fuel it uses food, and by its process of digestion breaks down the protein, carbohydrates, and fats and absorbs them into the body, where they are used to repair the worn-out tissues and to produce heat and muscular energy. Like the exhaust gases of an engine, the indigestible matter and body waste products are thrown off. Heat and energy are produced within the body by a process of oxidation or burning at a low temperature. Like the gasoline engine, the more work the body is called upon to perform, the less efficient it becomes, the more fuel it requires, and the greater is the wear upon and the greater repair needed by its working parts. Proportionally, the demand for food for repair increases more rapidly than the demand for fuel for energy. In any food, a definite ratio exists between the nutritive value of the tissue-building or repair part of the food (proteins) and the heat- and energy-producing part of the food (carbohydrates and fats). This is spoken of as the *nutritive ratio*. The ratio is said to be narrow when the amount of digestible protein approaches the amount of combined digestible carbohydrates and fats, and wide when the amount of energy-producing compounds is several times that of proteins. Fats are two and a fourth times as valuable as carbohydrates as a source of energy.

$$\text{Nutritive ration} = \frac{\text{carbohydrates} + (2.25 \times \text{fats})}{\text{protein}}$$

or

Protein: Carbohydrates plus (2.25 x fats)

The nutritive ratio should be between 1 to 11 for horses at rest and 1 to 7 or less for horses at fast, hard work. The nutritive ratio of oats is 1 to 6.6, and timothy hay 1 to 15.2.

COMPOSITION OF PLANTS

Knowing in general the composition of the animal body, it is obvious that its food requirements must include proteins, carbohydrates, fats, minerals, water, and vitamins. The source of this food, directly and indirectly, is plant life, because plant tissues contain the same group of organic compounds (proteins, fats, carbohydrates, and vitamins), but in slightly different form and in different proportions.

Plant tissue differs in general composition from animal tissue in that carbohydrates, rather than proteins, make up the major portion of its substance. In their dried state most plants average thirty to eighty percent carbohydrates. Because of the relatively small amount of protein in plants, *nitrogenous* or protein feeds command higher prices than carbohydrate feeds. Except for a few of the oily seeds (flax, cotton, peanut), most plant tissue is much poorer in fat content than is animal tissue.

After water, the most important requirement of plants is carbon dioxide. It is absorbed by the leaves from the air and is the plant's source of carbon and oxygen. Nitrogen is taken as nitrogen compounds (nitrates) from the soil. The mineral substances, such as sulphur, phosphorus, calcium are taken from the soil through the roots. Within the plant, these simple compounds are converted in some mysterious way to plant proteins, carbohydrates, and fats by the combined action of the green coloring matter of the plant (chlorophyll) and the energy of the sun's rays. This is a form of chemical reaction in which sun energy is absorbed and held latent to be freed later to warm our bodies, provide muscular energy, or turn the wheels of industry. It is the plan of Nature that plants shall use the energy of the sun to build, from the inorganic compounds of the earth and air, the organic compounds so necessary for animal life. After its span of existence, the animal body reverts to the inorganic compounds of the earth and again becomes plant food.

DETERMINATION OF FEEDING VALUE

The food value of any feed is probably best measured in terms of the amount and proportion of the digestible nutrients (protein, carbohydrates, and fats) it supplies; however, its palatibility, bulk, mineral content, vitamin content, and net energy value are factors that also should be considered. Research workers have determined these values for almost all feeds, and have tabulated them in simple tables that make it possible to readily select the appropriate feed or feeds for inclusion in the desired ration. The table at the end of this paragraph shows the feeding values of the more common horse feeds. Upon examination of this table, it will be noted that, as regards the digestible nutrients, only the digestible protein and total digestible nutrients are shown. The digestible protein represents the tissue-building nutrient, and the difference between this figure and that for total digestible nutrients represents the combined heat- and energy-producing nutrients.

			MINERALS				
FEED	Total dry matter	Dig. protein	Total dig. nutrients	Nutritive ratio	Calcium	Phosphorus	Vitamins*	Net energy per 100 pounds
CONCENTRATES	%	%	%	1:	%	%		Therms***
Oats	91.1	9.4	71.5	6.6	0.09	0.33	BEg	64.9
Dent Corn	88.5	7.4	83.7	10.3	0.01	0.28	ABEg	82.3
Wheat bran	90.6	13.1	70.2	4.4	0.12	1.32	BEg	59.7
Barley	90.4	9.3	78.7	7.5	0.05	0.38	BEg	70.5
Kaffir corn	86.6	9.1	80.1	7.8	0.04	0.30		75.2
Linseed meal O. P.	91.3	30.6	78.2	1.6	0.33	0.86	e	76.9
Cottonseed meal 43%	93.5	35.0	75.5	1.2	0.24	1.11		74.2
Rice, rough	86.6	6.3	69.1	10.0		0.21	BE	62.7
Rice bran	91.1	8.8	67.7	6.7	0.08	1.36	BE	60.0
Wheat	89.6	11.6	84.0	6.2	0.03	0.43	BEg	84.7
Rye	90.0	10.3	80.1	6.8	0.04	0.37	BEg	72.1
Soybeans	90.2	32.8	86.2	1.6	0.20	0.60	Bg	84.7
Molasses, cane	74.1	0.9	56.6	61.9	0.56	0.06	BE	55.6
Bone meal, steamed					32.61	15.17		
DRY ROUGHAGES	%	%	%	1:	%	%		Therms
Alfalfa hay	90.4	10.6	50.3	3.7	1.43	0.21	ADEGb	41.5
Clover hay	88.2	7.0	51.9	6.4	1.21	0.18	ADEGb	42.8
Lespedeza hay	89.1	9.2	52.2	4.7	0.99	0.19	ADEGb	43.1
Prairie hay	90.4	2.6	49.2	17.9	0.49	0.10	AEbdg	36.9
Timothy hay	88.7	2.9	46.9	15.2	0.27	0.16	AEbdg	35.2
Johnson grass	90.1	2.9	50.3	16.3	0.87	0.26	AEbdg	37.7
Oat hay	88.0	4.5	46.3	9.3	0.22	0.17		34.7
Wheat hay	89.0	3.2	46.5	13.5	0.18	0.21		32.6
Grass hay	89.0	3.5	51.7	13.8	0.48	0.17	AEbdg	36.2
Corn stover**	90.6	2.2	52.2	22.7	0.46	0.09	abd	27.0
Oat straw	89.6	0.9	44.1	48.0	0.36	0.13		23.3
Wheat straw	90.1	0.8	35.7	43.6	0.22	0.07		10.0
Rice straw	92.5	0.9	39.4	42.8	0.19	0.07		
GREEN ROUGHAGES	%	%	%	1:	%	%		Therms
Alfalfa	25.4	3.4	14.7	3.3	0.40	0.06	ACEGb	12.8
Bermuda grass	34.2	2.8	25.0	7.9		0.07	ACEGb	
Blue grass	24.8	4.4	17.7	3.0	0.12	0.09	ACEGb	15.4
Carrots	11.9	0.8	9.6	11.0	0.06	0.06	ACb	9.6
Grasses, mixed	29.7	3.6	20.2	4.6		0.09	ACEGb	

From—*Feeds and Feeding,* Morrison, 20th Ed.

*A capital letter in this column indicates that the feed is at least a good source of the vitamin designated by the letter shown. A small letter indicates an appreciable amount.

**Corn stalks, excluding the grain. [Ed.]

***Units of heat equal to 100,000 British Thermal Units (B.T.U's). [Ed.]

FACTORS INFLUENCING DIGESTIBILITY AND FEEDING VALUES. The following factors influence the digestibility of the feed and the feeding value.

Quality. The table of feeding values given on page 91 is based on feeds of average quality. However, there are wide variations in quality that can be determined only by intelligent inspection. The grades described later in this chapter reflect the quality of the food.

Quantity. Insufficient feed, particularly bulky feed, causes loss of condition and general debility, and predisposes an animal to devastating diseases. Food in excess of the body needs is wasteful and harmful. It overtaxes the digestive organs and may cause either diarrhea due to irritation or colic due to constipation. It has been found that an animal digests and assimilates his feed most efficiently when fed a maintenance ration, and that as the ration is increased, the wastage increases.

Combination of Feeds. Horses and mules cannot thrive on concentrated foods; bulk is absolutely essential if the digestive tract is to be properly distended and digestion unimpaired. Excessive amounts of proteins or fats and carbohydrates decrease the digestibility of the whole ration.

Water. The nutrients of the feed must be in solution before they can be absorbed. During work, sweating and other physiological functions greatly deplete the water content of the body tissues. To compensate for this loss, water is drawn from the digestive tract. A deficiency of water in the digestive tract not only affects digestion, but is liable to affect the general health of the animal by causing such diseases as colic and debility. A horse can survive for a considerable time on water alone, but succumbs in a few days if deprived of water.

Work. Slow work usually does not affect digestion. This probably accounts for the fact that draft horses are easier to keep fat then riding horses. Fast and fatiguing work retards digestion. It causes a loss of tone in the digestive apparatus and reduces secretion because of the withdrawal of blood from the viscera to meet the more immediate demands of the body muscles. If horses are called upon to do hard, fast work after a full feed, the breathing is interfered with, the feed is not properly digested, and severe digestive disturbances may result. It is necessary to bear in mind that animals require several hours a day to eat and digest their feed; and for this reason, most of the feed should be given at the evening meal after a reasonable period of rest. Kind treatment, comfortable stalls, and regular hours of feeding increase the efficiency of digestion.

Preparation of Feed. Grinding, cracking, or rolling grain increases digestibility only in the case of hard seeds, such as barley, wheat, millet, and rice. It is, however, beneficial in the case of other grains for feeding young foals and animals that are unable to chew their feed properly. The feeding value of oats is increased about six percent by crushing when fed to healthy horses with good teeth, and undoubtedly much more for young horses or horses with defective teeth. Because of its hardness, barley is sometimes soaked in water for several hours before feeding. The chopping of hay does not increase its digestibility except insofar as it promotes more thorough mastication when fed with grain. Numerous and careful trials have shown that the cooking of either grain or roughage increases neither its digestibility nor its nutritive value, and it may even decrease the digestibility of the proteins.

Health of the Animal. It naturally follows that healthy animals are better able to digest feed than those suffering from disease, and special care must, therefore, be given the diet of the latter. When animals with sharp or diseased teeth cannot masticate properly, it is necessary to correct these conditions in order to obtain the full value of the feed.

PREPARATION OF A RATION. A *ration* is the feed allowed for an animal during a day of twenty-four hours, whether it is fed at one time or in portions at different times.*

A *balanced ration* is one that furnishes the several food compounds—protein, carbohydrates, fats, minerals, and vitamins—in such amounts and proportion as will properly nourish a given animal for twenty-four hours.

Feeding experiments and experience have shown that a one-thousand-pound horse has the daily food requirements shown in the following table.

DAILY REQUIREMENTS PER ANIMAL

Nature of Work	Dry Matter	Dig. Protein	Total Dig. Nutrients	Nutritive Ratio	Net Energy
	lbs.	lbs.	lbs.	1:	Therms
Idle	13.0-18.0	0.6-0.8	7.0-9.0	10-12	5.6-7.2
Light Work	15.0-20.0	0.8-1.0	9.0-11.0	9-11	7.5-9.1
Medium Work . . .	16.0-21.0	1.0-1.2	11.0-13.0	9-11	9.4-11.1
Hard Work	18.0-22.0	1.2-1.4	13.0-18.0	9-11	11.3-13.9

Knowing the feeding values of feeds and the animal's requirements, we may compute a trial ration and determine whether or not it meets the requirements. In preparing a trial ration, we first apply the old rule of thumb that a horse at moderate work requires about one pound of grain and about one-and-a-half pounds of hay for each one hundred pounds of body weight. Thus a one-thousand-pound horse would require about ten pounds of grain and about fourteen pounds of hay. This is the ration allowance for a light horse. It contains about twenty pounds of total dry matter. Assuming that we use oats and timothy hay, we refer to the table of feeding values on page 91 and compute the feeding value of our tentative ration. Our computation will show that the ration has a feeding value as follows:

The army recognized three classifications of ration: garrison ration, issued at permanent posts and in semipermanent camps; the field ration, issued where stabling facilities could not be maintained, as on the march or on maneuvers, and the emergency ration. Of these, only the garrison ration is described herein. [Ed.]

FEEDING VALUES

Feed	Total dry matter	Dig. protein	Total dig. nutrients	Nutri-tive ratio	Cal-cium	Phos-phorus	Vitamins	Net energy
	lbs.	lbs.	lbs.	1:	lbs.	lbs.		Therms
10 lbs. Oats	9.1	0.9	7.2	6.6	0.01	0.03	BEg	6.5
14 lbs. Timothy	12.4	0.4	6.6	15.2	0.04	0.03	AEbdg	4.9
Total	21.5	1.3	13.8	9.6	0.05	0.06	ABEdg	11.4

Comparing this with the requirements for a one-thousand-pound horse at medium work, we find that our ration more than meets the requirements in every respect. In fact, it appears that our ration would be satisfactory for a horse of the same weight doing hard work. The amount of minerals seems adequate; however, the calcium-phosphorus ratio of 1:1.2 is slightly outside the optimum range of from 1:1 to 2:1. In other words, the ratio would be better from the standpoint of preventing bone diseases due to a calcium deficiency or mineral imbalance if it contained a higher proportion of calcium. The substitution of five pounds of alfalfa for a like amount of timothy hay would double the calcium content and only slightly increase the amount of phosphorus. The substitution of bran for a part of the oats, without feeding alfalfa, would result in an undesirable increase in the proportion of phosphorus. The supply of vitamins is probably adequate.

It is important from a cost standpoint, as well as for the health and efficiency of the animal, that the ration be balanced. Feeds rich in protein are usually the most expensive, and to feed a ration too high in protein not only greatly increases the cost but may actually impair the health of the animal. Many skin and digestive disorders in the horse result from a too-rich protein diet, especially when coupled with insufficient exercise. A ration that is too rich in protein is conducive to excessive sweating and urination. For the mature horse the amount of protein should be limited to the amount necessary to replace the wear in body tissues. The energy needed to perform work should be supplied by the more economical carbohydrates. In other words, the nutritive ratio should be as wide as possible and yet supply a sufficient amount of protein.

ALLOWANCES. The basic allowance prescribed for the ration is:

	Small Horses (Foreign stations)	Light Horses (1150 lbs. or less)	Heavy Horses (Over 1150 lbs.)	Mules
Grain	7 lbs.	10 lbs.	12½ lbs.	8 lbs.
Hay	14 lbs.	14 lbs.	15 lbs.	14 lbs.
Bedding ...	5 lbs.	5 lbs.	5 lbs.	5 lbs.
Salt	1/8 lbs.	1/8 lbs.	1/8 lbs.	1/8 lbs.

Basic Components of the Ration. It will be noted in the preceding table of basic

94

allowances for the ration that the general classes of components—grain, hay, and bedding—are listed, but the kinds of forage to comprise each component are not specifically prescribed. For more or less general use and for the purpose of establishing the ration cost, oats are considered the basic grain component; however, other grains may be authorized for use. Bran and linseed meal are supplied at all stations as regularly authorized substitutes for oats in the grain component. The substitution is not to exceed three pounds of bran for a like quantity of grain, and one-half pound of linseed meal for one pound of grain is authorized. The hay issued shall be one of several equivalent classes or grades of hay. The same applies in the case of the bedding component. Since the list of authorized hays and bedding material is rather extensive and frequently revised, it is not included in this text.

Variations of the kinds or amounts of components must be planned well in advance of their effective dates and provided for by timely requisition. In general, it is believed that more advantage should be taken for variation of the ration in both kinds and amounts of components. It creates a greater interest in the feeding of our animals, which will be reflected in their better condition. It appears logical that a horse that is being fed year after year on a straight ration of ten pounds of oats and fourteen pounds of nonleguminous hay, possibly produced on depleted soil, may not be receiving the necessary minerals and vitamins to keep him properly nourished and in the best possible health. The use of three to five pounds of alfalfa daily during the fall and winter months is probably the most economical insurance against malnutrition in horses. Corn, linseed meal, and molasses should also be considered. Corn combines well with alfalfa in a ration for winter feeding. The greater the variety of the components in the ration, the greater the probability of supplying the necessary elements for proper nutrition. The following are suggested variations of the ration:

	Light Horses (1150 lbs. or less)	Heavy Horses (Over 1150 lbs.)	Mules
Oats	8 lbs.	10 lbs.	5 lbs.
Alfalfa	5 lbs.	5 lbs.	5 lbs.
Hay (other than alfalfa) ...	9 lbs.	10 lbs.	9 lbs.
Oats	6 lbs.	6 lbs.	3 lbs.
Corn	2 lbs.	3 lbs.	2 lbs.
Alfalfa	5 lbs.	6 lbs.	6 lbs.
Hay (other than alfalfa) ...	9 lbs.	9 lbs.	8 lbs.
Crushed wheat ..	5 lbs.	6 lbs.	3 lbs.
Rolled barley ...	5 lbs.	6 lbs.	3 lbs.
Alfalfa	6 lbs.	6 lbs.	3 lbs.
Other hay	5 lbs.	5 lbs.	10 lbs.
Crushed wheat ..	5 lbs.	6 lbs.	3 lbs.
Corn	5 lbs.	6 lbs.	3 lbs.
Alfalfa	6 lbs.	6 lbs.	3 lbs.
Other hay	7 lbs.	7 lbs.	10 lbs.

OATS. No other grain is so keenly relished by horses of all classes and ages nor so prized by horsemen as the oat. It is the standard of excellence with which other concentrates are compared. Oats are the safest of all grains for the horse because the adherent hull affords enough bulk to prevent some of the errors in feeding that are common when more concentrated grains are fed.

Feeding of Oats. Oats may be safely fed in quantities up to sixteen pounds, but the average thousand-pound riding horse does not require over ten to twelve pounds per day. Horses when rested for more than two days at a time should not be given more than five pounds daily. Oats may be fed whole or crushed. Crushing ensures more thorough mastication and digestion. Care should be taken not to crush the grain too flat, since this results in a loss of a part of the flour.

Horses that eat hurriedly, either from natural greediness or from fear that their neighbors may rob them, swallow the grain without proper mastication. Bolting of oats is also a common cause of choke in horses. Mixing five to ten percent of dry bran or chopped hay with the oats prevents this to a considerable extent. Oats may be steamed or boiled. As a general rule, this is not recommended; it is usually more suitable to the needs of the hospital than to the organization stable. New oats should not be fed until a month after threshing.

CORN. Corn is less desirable than oats for riding horses because of its tendency to produce heat and fat. It is, therefore, best fed during the colder months of the year when there is a greater demand for heat-producing food to maintain the body temperature. Combined with oats and hay, as indicated on page 95, it forms a well-balanced ration.

Corn may be fed either shelled or on the cob. It should, when practicable, be fed on the cob rather than shelled, however. To feed shelled corn, mix with dry bran or oats, or both, to prevent bolting of the feed. When feeding ear corn, the feed consists of from six to twelve ears, depending on the size of the ears, the amount of work performed, and the individual animal. There is no advantage in crushing or grinding corn for horses and mules that have normal teeth.

The change from oats to corn should be made gradually, substituting about two pounds of corn for two pounds of oats each successive week. Later, as the animals become accustomed to the corn, the oats may be discontinued and the corn correspondingly increased.

BARLEY. Barley is a very good feed for horses and mules and may be safely substituted for oats and fed in the same quantities. The change from oats to barley should be gradual and extended over a period of at least two weeks. Barley may be fed whole, but because of its excessive hardness, it is usually crushed, or soaked in water for two or three hours before feeding.

It is not used extensively as a horse feed in North America, since oats are generally available, but it is used extensively in Asia, Asia Minor, and the southern part of Europe.

RYE. Rye is not regarded as a good forage. It ferments readily in the stomach and also frequently causes diarrhea. Rye forms a large portion of the diet of horses in

Denmark, Belgium, Sweden, and parts of Russia. As a horse feed it should not, except under pressure of necessity, be fed alone as a whole ration, but should be mixed with other bulkier feeds such as oats or bran. Whenever possible, it should be crushed or rolled before feeding.

WHEAT. Wheat alone is not a safe food for horses. If given to horses, only one or two pounds should be fed at first, and the amount gradually increased to a maximum of six pounds a day. Wheat should be combined with some bulky grain or mixed with bran, chaff, or chopped hay. It is desirable to roll or crush wheat before feeding.

BRAN.

Characteristics. Wheat bran is the coarse outer coating of the wheat kernel that is removed in the process of milling wheat for flour. The bran coating is the part of the kernel richest in minerals, vitamins, and protein. One hundred pounds of wheat will produce about ten pounds of bran. Good bran should be flaky, sweet, pleasant to the taste, practically free from middlings or floury appearance, and free from dirt or grit. Storage in damp places causes it to cake or mold readily, thereby rendering it unfit for use. Bran possesses four qualities that make it a valuable adjunct to the ration, namely: its bulk, palatability, nutritive value, and mildly laxative action. Its bulk, which is twice that of oats, makes it useful for mixing with grain to induce slower eating and more thorough mastication. It is relished by practically all horses, and in nutritive value is almost equal to oats. The mild laxative action of bran is due to certain chemical constituents (phytin and pentosans) and its fiber content. It is a good muscle builder and promotes digestion by adding bulk to the grain. It is particularly useful for growing foals, brood mares, horses that eat fast, and thin horses.

Bran is very rich in phosphorus (1.32 %) and very low in calcium (0.12 %). This fact should be borne in mind in preparing rations, and the mineral content of the ration should be kept balanced so that the calcium-phosphorus ratio is between 1:1 and 2:1. Bran is best combined in the ration with calcium-rich feeds such as the leguminous hays.

Feeding Bran. Bran may be fed dry or as a mash. When fed dry, up to two pounds daily are ordinarily incorporated into the grain mixture. The daily feeding of small amounts in this way is desirable if attention is given to the maintenance of a proper mineral balance. Rice bran may be fed in the same amounts as wheat bran. It has about the same feeding value but is less laxative. An occasional feed of bran in the form of a mash is relished by most horses and is quite beneficial. In this form bran has a more pronounced laxative action. Bran mashes are best given the night before a day or so of idleness or light exercise. A bran mash is made by placing two to four pounds of bran in a feedbox, sprinkling about a mess-kit spoonful of salt over the top, and then adding *boiling water* while stirring until the mixture is well dampened but not sloppy. Wrap the feedbox in a horse cover and allow to steam until cool enough to feed. The feedbox should always be cleaned as soon as the mash has been eaten.

LINSEED MEAL. Linseed meal is ground linseed cake. Linseed cake is the hard cake that remains after the linseed oil has been extruded from the ground flaxseed. Linseed meal is an excellent feeding supplement for animals that are run-down in condition. Its effect is slightly laxative and its use will improve the gloss of the coat. It is useful during the spring shedding. The allowance is one-half pound daily in lieu of one pound of grain. Since linseed meal is unpalatable to most horses, it should be mixed with other feed, such as oats and bran, so that it will be held well in the mixture. As a general rule, it should not be fed in larger amounts than one-half pound daily; a heaping tablespoonful mixed with the grain three times a day often is sufficient.

COTTONSEED MEAL. Cottonseed meal is the finely ground cottonseed cake that is the residue remaining after most of the hulls and lint have been removed and the cottonseed has been crushed, heated, and the oil pressed out. Cottonseed meal should be a light yellow in color. A dark color indicates the presence of ground hulls, which often are used as an adulterant.

Cottonseed meal is richer in protein than is linseed meal, but supplies slightly less total digestible nutrients.

Cottonseed meal is often used as a protein supplement in rations for horses and mules. The amounts generally fed are one to one-and-a-half pounds per day per animal. Up to two pounds for horses and up to three pounds for mules can be fed with satisfactory results. When cottonseed meal is added to a ration low in proteins, it improves the condition and appearance of the animals. Using it as a large part of the concentrates is not safe, since it may cause serious digestive disturbances because of its heavy nature. Also, it may be poisonous when fed in too large amounts. Wet, musty, or moldy meal should never be fed under any conditions. Since cottonseed meal is not particularly relished by horses, it should be mixed with better-liked feeds, such as oats and bran. It is best to feed not over one-quarter pound per head daily at first, and gradually increase the amount as the horses or mules become accustomed to it. It is not ordinarily authorized, but might be utilized in lieu of linseed meal when the latter is not available.

RICE. Rough rice (unhusked or paddy rice), when rolled, crushed, or coarsely ground, may be fed in quantities up to about one half of the grain ration. In emergency, it may be fed in quantities up to ten to fourteen pounds daily. It is rather indigestible for animals unaccustomed to its use, and for this reason crushing or rolling is desirable. It is fed quite extensively in parts of India, Burma, China, and other rice-growing countries.

GRAIN SORGHUMS. Grain sorghums are important grain crops in the central and southern parts of the western plains states, especially in Texas, Oklahoma, Kansas, New Mexico, Colorado, Nebraska, and South Dakota. Because the sorghums are heat-loving, and more drought-resistant than corn, they have taken its place in those areas which have too little rainfall for corn. The grain sorghums are important in India, China, Manchukuo, Africa, and parts of Asia Minor both as animal and human food. The grain sorghums comprise but one of the two general types of sorghums, the other being sweet sorghums. The juice of the grain sorghums is sour or but slightly sweet while that of the sweet sorghums (sorgos) is distinctly sweet. Sweet sorghums are grown as roughage crops and for the production of syrup. There are many varieties of grain sorghums and the plants vary from one-and-a-half to seven feet in height. The growing plant somewhat resembles corn, except that the seeds are borne in rather large loose seed heads at the top of the stalk. The general feeding value of grain sorghums is slightly less than that of corn. They may be fed in approximately the same amount as corn and under the same circumstances. Grain sorghums are less fattening than corn because they have a higher protein content. The seeds are rather small and hard and for the best results they should be crushed or coarsely ground for feeding horses; however, they may be fed whole. As they are somewhat constipating, they should be combined with feeds having a laxative effect, such as bran or alfalfa. The grains of the various varieties vary considerably in appearance.

Kaffir. Kaffir, sometimes incorrectly called kaffir corn, is one of the most important grain sorghums. The seed heads are long, erect, compact, and cylindrical. The seeds are small, egg-shaped, and generally white, blotched with red. One variety of kaffir has red seeds.

Milo. The seeds of milo are considerably larger than those of kaffir and the seed heads are larger, shorter, thicker, and less erect. The grain or seed is a half sphere. There are both white and yellow varieties of milo. The latter is the more important and is sometimes nearly an orange shade.

Feterita. The seeds are about the size of milo, but are chalky white and wrinkled on one side. The seed heads are erect.

Hegari. Hegari closely resembles kaffir in growth. The seeds are quite similar to feterita, but they are slightly smaller, bluish white, and smooth.

Kaoliang. Kaoliang is an important grain crop of northern China, where it is used for both humans and animals. The seeds have a triangular wedge shape and are brown.

Durra. Durra seeds are distinctly flattened. They are white or brown. Durra is known in India as *jowar* or *jowari.* It is important there, especially in the western Punjab, as a horse feed.

Other Varieties. Other less important varieties of grain sorghum are shallu, darso, shrock, sagrain, and atlas.

LEGUME SEEDS. Legume seeds, like the legume hays, are rich in protein. In general, legume seeds are not extensively used in the United States except in limited amounts as protein supplements for horses. In Europe and Asia, legume seeds are used extensively in horse feeding. The amounts fed to horses are variable. As a rule, legume seeds should not exceed one third of the concentrate mixture, especially if legume hays are included in the ration. Also, excessive amounts of legume seeds will cause digestive troubles due to their heavy nature. In emergencies, the legume seeds can be fed as the grain component of a ration provided that the horses are fed small amounts and the amounts gradually increased over a period of time. The most important legume seeds will be discussed individually as to their geographical distribution, uses, and feeding value.

Soybeans. Soybeans belong to the pea family and are native to eastern Asia. The principal producing areas are Manchukuo, Northern China, Japan, Russia, and the United States. In the United States, the soybean thrives well in the corn belt, particularly in the southern half of the corn belt and the northern half of the cotton belt. In China and Japan, soybeans are used as one of the chief grain components, while in the United States very little use has been made of soybeans as a concentrate for horses or mules, and it seems improbable that their use will increase. Some reports state that feeding a small amount of soybeans to horses in the spring seems to have the same effect as feeding linseed meal in making the hair smooth and sleek. Soybeans are the richest in protein of all the common seeds used for feed. In addition to their richness in protein, they contain a large percent of fat.

Field Peas. Field peas are raised chiefly in the northernmost states, Canada, and in certain sections of the western states where the climate is cool. Field peas are relished by stock and are an excellent feed. They are not as high in protein as other legume seeds but their total digestible nutrients are the same. They should ordinarily not be fed in greater amounts than one to three pounds mixed with other grains, but under necessity they might be fed in greater amounts as the sole grain component.

Horse Bean. The horse bean is used in England for feeding stock, especially horses. This legume seed grows fairly well in some parts of Canada, but not successfully in the United States, except in certain sections of California. Horse beans are similar in their uses and feeding values to field peas and may be fed in the same way.

Chick Peas. Chick peas, also called *gram* (Chenna), are grown from India to southern Europe and northern Africa. They are used often as the chief grain in India. As a general ration, it contains too large a proportion of protein to be suitable for an unlimited ration, and ten pounds daily is the most that should be given. The general method of feeding is to crush it sufficiently to split the husk and then mix it with other feed or with bran, either dry or slightly dampened, to ensure thorough mastication.

MOLASSES. Molasses and molasses feeds have been used for many years with good results. Its nutritive value is somewhat less than that of oats, and is due almost entirely to its sugar content. Molasses is relished by horses and it is of value as an appetizer. It is an exceptionally rich source of calcium. The undiluted molasses may be mixed with grain, or it may be diluted with one or more parts of water and sprinkled over the hay or grain. It may be most advantageously mixed with grain in amounts up to about ten percent of the mixture. The greatest disadvantage is the inevitable soiling of the coat and mangers with the sticky, fly-drawing liquid.

SALT. The horse and mule show great fondness for salt and thrive best when regularly supplied with it. It should always be available in the form of bulk (cake) or rock salt placed in or conveniently near the manger. It is better not to put salt in the feedbox, especially when rock salt or granulated salt is fed, because while eating grain the horse may eat more salt than is needed or is good for him. Feeding as brick salt in the manger is far preferable to placing it in an exposed container in the corral. The horse's need for salt is greatly influenced by the amount and character of his work, for a considerable amount is excreted in the sweat. A supply of salt adequate to replace that lost through sweating is an important factor in preventing heat exhaustion during hot weather. For this reason the need for salt while in the field is greater than in garrison. Feeding it regularly and in proper amounts is more difficult in the field. In the field it is best fed in the feed bag, either separately or mixed with the grain. A heaping tablespoonful should be given at least twice a week, and more frequently if the horses sweat considerably. When it is not mixed with feed, horses may safely be given all the salt that they will eat. The daily allowance of salt per animal is two ounces.

HAY. Hay is the harvested, cured, unthreshed herbage of forage plants having feed value. It is made either from the plants of the grass family or from legume plants and is frequently classified on this basis. However, some hay contains both grasses and legumes. Legume hays are protein-rich and for this reason they usually are more expensive than the hays produced from the grass plants. Most of the hay that is produced is used as loose hay on the farms where it is produced, while that marketed is always baled before shipment.

Hay is the natural diet of the horse. The horse in his natural state subsisted on the green and growing grass in summer and the naturally cured grasses in winter. Only under domestication has he had access to more than a very limited amount of concentrated feed in the form of seeds (grain). For these reasons, hay or other bulky feed is an absolute necessity if the horse is to digest his feed properly. No horse can long remain healthy if fed grain alone, irrespective of the amount fed. Should the supply of hay normally required for the daily ration be diminished it is extremely important that animals be grazed, or fed such roughage as can be gathered or produced locally. Oat straw is one of the better substitutes for hay. Any straw that is not spoiled may be used, but barley and rye straw are the least desirable because of the long beards. In the absence of other bulky feed, green or dried weeds or leaves may be fed to supply roughage.

In England, India, Australia, and some other countries, hay, sometimes straw, or straw and hay, is cut into short lengths with a chaffcutter and the product is known as chaff ("chop"). For shipment it is baled into small, compact bales. This method of preparing hay does not directly increase its digestibility or food value but it is said to reduce waste. Chaff is frequently mixed with the grain to ensure more thorough mastication. The *tibben* of Egypt and the *bhusa (bhoosa)* of India are broken straw from the threshing floor and are really forms of chaff. They are frequently used as horse feeds. Tibben was often the only roughage available for the horses of Allenby's divisions during the Egyptian campaign (1918).

FEEDING OR NONLEGUME HAYS. The so-called feeding or nonlegume hays are produced from the grass plants or grasses. The bulk of roughage ration for light horses doing fast work is ordinarily one of the hays of this type. The various kinds of hays of this type have approximately the same feeding value if of the same grade (quality).

Timothy Hay. Timothy hay, while not quite the equal of some other feeding hays in total nutrients (see page 91), was long recognized as the standard hay for feeding horses. Much of its popularity was due to its bright color, cleanness, and relative freedom from dust. It is still highly prized by many horsemen, although feeding experiments have shown that it is not superior to other feeding hays. It is produced in marketable quantities chiefly in the Middle Atlantic and East North Central groups of states and the state of Washington. Timothy is a native grass of the temperate regions of Europe and Asia where it is often known as herd's grass. In England it is frequently known as meadow cat's tail. This name is quite descriptive, since the long, rounded, and compact seed head has much of the appearance of a cat's tail. Clover, one of the legumes, thrives under the conditions of soil and climate suitable for timothy, and many meadows are seeded with both. Timothy-clover hay is a good hay for horses, provided the hay does not contain over fifty percent of clover.

Prairie Hay. Prairie hay, as it is known in North America, is hay made from the wild, perennial grasses that are indigenous to the virgin meadows of our prairie states. It is marketed chiefly from Kansas, Oklahoma, Texas, Nebraska, and the Dakotas. There are two general types of prairie hay—upland and midland. Upland prairie, which is produced on the higher ground, is the better type and constitutes the bulk of all prairie hay. Midland prairie hay, which is from lower prairies and bottom lands, is coarser and less nutritious. The Army does not buy midland prairie hay. Any sample of upland prairie hay will likely contain several different species of upland prairie grasses, but the bluestem and grama grasses usually form the bulk of the mixture. Big bluestem is probably the most common grass in upland prairie hay, and frequently the hay will be almost pure big bluestem. Since prairie grass is usually cut before full maturity, seedheads are seldom seen in the hay and specific identification of the grasses comprising the hay is difficult or impossible. Baled upland prairie hay can often be identified as such, particularly if it contains bluestem, by the fact that the surface hay on the side or sides of the bale that have been exposed to light for any considerable period will have turned (weathered) from green to a characteristic and distinct reddish shade of brown. While not quite as rich in protein, its total nutritive value is slightly greater than that of timothy. It is extensively used for feeding horses stabled in or near areas where this kind of hay is produced.

Johnson Grass Hay. Johnson grass hay is produced chiefly in the states bordering on the Gulf of Mexico. Johnson grass is a tall, perennial grass, native of southern Europe and Asia, which is grown for pasture and hay in the Southern and western parts of the United States. As it spreads rapidly by underground rootstalks and is difficult to eradicate in cultivated fields, it is considered a pest in certain sections. It is a member of the sorghum family and, like other members of this family, may at times produce hydrocyanic (prussic) acid poisoning when pastured or fed as uncured roughage. In general, the acid develops only when the normal growth of plants has been retarded or stopped by drought, frost, bruising, wilting, or other causes. There is little or no danger of the acid persisting in well-cured hay. Because the grass grows very rank, it must be cut while young in order to produce hay that is not too coarse. Good Johnson grass hay should contain few or no seed heads. Being cut while still succulent, it is at times rather difficult to cure properly and there is a greater likelihood of musty or moldy bales, or spots in bales, appearing in this kind of hay. For this reason purchases of this kind of hay should be limited to the U.S. No. 1 grade. Properly cured Johnson grass hay has a slightly higher feeding value than some of the other feeding hays, and is relished by horses. Johnson grass hay can usually be identified by the fact that the leaves always tend to fold along the midrib when cured, and by the frequent presence of a reddish or purplish spotting of the leaves caused by the so-called sorghum disease. Johnson grass is known in other countries by different names, such as Arabian millet, Aleppo grass, Syrian grass, Egyptian grass (dhourra), and maiden-cane.

Grain Hay. Grain hay is hay made from the cereal grasses (small grains), such as oats, wheat, and barley. This type of hay is produced in the Pacific states, particularly in California, where it is almost the sole feeding hay, and to a lesser extent in the Rocky Mountain states and in the so-called Southwestern states. The plant should be cut for hay while the grain is in the milk or early-dough stage, since at this stage most of the nutrients are still in the leaves and stems rather than concentrated in the grain. Grain hay seldom is as green as other types of hays, often being a greenish golden color, and for this reason has frequently been mistaken for straw by people not familiar with it. Much of the grain hay of California is a mixture of tame and wild oats. Some grain hay is produced that contains vetch or alfalfa. The Army does not buy barley hay, wheat hay made from bearded varieties, wild oat hay, mixed tame and wild oat hay, or any grain hay containing over ten percent of legumes. Grain hays have a total feeding value approximately equivalent to other feeding hays, but are somewhat richer in protein. They are much relished by horses and highly considered by horsemen in the areas in which they are produced. In the plains area of Western Canada and in various parts of the United States a considerable quantity of oats is cut with a binder while in the dough stage and fed as "sheaf oats" or "bundle oats." This type of roughage might be locally purchased and used by troops in the field, as was frequently the case in the Indian campaigns in the Great Plains area.

Grass Hay. Grass hay is hay made from any of the cultivated grasses or wild grasses, sedges, or rushes not previously mentioned and that have recognized feeding value. Some of the grasses in the United States that are cut for grass hay are redtop, orchard grass, Bermuda grass, Kentucky bluegrass, Canada bluegrass, bromegrass, ryegrass, paspalum, and quackgrass. While not from the grasses, the hay made from the wild sedges and rushes that grow in the high mountain "parks" or "meadows" of the Mountain States (particularly Colorado) is classed as grass hay. These plants provide excellent pasturage and produce a hay of high quality. Redtop is important as a hay grass in the New England States. Bermuda is much used for pastures and hay production in the cotton belt. Orchard grass, known in England as cocksfoot, is a fairly important hay grass in the southern part of the corn belt. Bluegrass, both

103

Kentucky and Canada, is highly prized in horse pastures, but is seldom cut for hay. Grass hay is generally the equivalent of other feeding hays. Purchases should usually be limited to the No. 1 grade.

LEGUME HAYS. Legumes are those plants which bear their seed in a pod or legume. Practically all the legume forage plants belong to the *pea* family and are richer in protein than the grasses or common roughages in the feeding hays. Legume roughages or hays are valuable as part of the hay component of the garrison ration because they provide, in a very effective manner, the proteins that are deficient in some of the cereal grains, such as corn; they are the highest in calcium among common feeds, although not rich in phosphorus; they are palatable and greatly relished by animals; and they are the richest source of vitamins A and D among the common feeds available for winter feeding. Legumes are not as easily made into hay as are the grasses, being more productive of waste on account of the loss of leaves in handling. Their succulence makes curing more difficult, and they are more readily affected by adverse weather conditions, resulting in brittleness and dustiness of the hay. Legumes must be fed judiciously because they have a laxative effect and cause excessive urination and sweating. This is especially true when feeding animals that are performing fast work during hot weather. The greater portion of the hay component for draft animals that are doing slow, hard work can be legumes. Regardless of the type of work being performed, any legume must be added gradually to the ration so that the change is not so abrupt as to cause the animals to become "washy." During the winter months when more carbohydrates are fed, the legume hays combine well with the other components in the ration and do not produce such a laxative effect.

Alfalfa. Alfalfa is a tall green plant having trifoliolate leaves and a bluish-purple, cloverlike flower in a loose head. It derives its name from the Spanish word *alfisfisah.* In other parts of the world it is known as *lucerne.* The name *purple medic* is commonly used in England. Alfalfa is said to be the oldest forage crop grown. Owing to its faculty of accommodating itself to wide differences in climatic conditions and different soils, it is now well distributed throughout the world. It is an important crop in central and western Asia, north and south Africa, Australia, the British Isles, Europe as far north as Sweden and Siberia, and in North and South America. It is grown in every state of the United States.

The excellence of alfalfa hay and other alfalfa forage is due to its high yield, its palatability, its richness in protein, its unusually high content of calcium, and its value as a source of vitamins A and D. It has a nutritive ratio (1:3.7) that more closely approximates that of grains than do the common roughages, and because of its high protein content combines well in a ration containing corn or other carbohydrate-rich feeds. Alfalfa has a stimulating effect on heat production and body metabolism and, therefore, is considered less desirable for feeding during hot weather. Alfalfa also causes increased sweating and urination because any protein-rich feed will require a greater intake of water, which, in turn, tends to increase excretions—sweat and urine. Alfalfa, especially if very leafy or early cut, is quite laxative in its effect, particularly on horses unaccustomed to it as a feed. For this reason, the change to alfalfa should be made gradually, beginning with two or three pounds daily. As a general rule, alfalfa should not comprise more than one half of the hay allowance. Five pounds fed once daily, usually at the noon feeding, is a convenient way of combining alfalfa with nonlegume hays for feeding horses. When feeding alfalfa care should be exercised in saving the leaves, which are the most nutritious part of the hay.

The foregoing statements concerning the use of alfalfa may lead one to believe that alfalfa must never be fed in greater amounts than five pounds per day. This is generally true; however, in some localities it may become necessary to use alfalfa as the only roughage in the ration in order to provide the bulk needed for proper digestion. Horses can build up a tolerance to large amounts of alfalfa without ill effects.

Alfalfa is the only legume hay authorized for purchase by the Army.

Clover. Red clover is the type of clover most generally used for the production of clover hay. It is a perennial found in the temperate regions of Europe, Africa, Western Asia, and Northern Africa. Its domestic distribution follows closely that of timothy, with which it is sown to a great extent. The greater bulk of timothy contains some clover in variable amounts. When fed alone it may make animals "washy." Because of its dustiness, clover hay is not recommended for use. Timothy mixed with not more than fifty percent of clover is purchased for use by the Army as a feeding hay. When feeding the timothy and clover mixture, alfalfa need not be added to the hay component of the ration. In many of our Eastern stations, timothy and clover mixture is the primary feeding hay.

Lespedeza. Lespedeza, sometimes called Japan clover, is a hot-weather annual, native to Eastern Asia. It is produced chiefly in the Southern and Southeastern parts of the United States. Its use has spread westward to eastern Kansas, Oklahoma, and Texas. Lespedeza grown on poor soil is used chiefly as a grazing crop, but that grown on rich soil can be cut and made into hay. Hay from the annual lespedezas is eaten readily by horses and is about equal to alfalfa in feeding value. In content of protein and total digestible nutrients, it averages slightly higher than clover hay. In the South, lespedeza is grown and combined with Bermuda grass, orchard grass, or redtop to make hay.

Lespedeza is not recommended for use ordinarily; however, it might be procured locally for use when the regular source of supply is disrupted or the prescribed hay component is not available.

OTHER LEGUMES. Under this heading are included those legumes which are not ordinarily authorized but which may be fed to horses in an emergency when other authorized hays are not available.

Soybean Hay. Soybeans are extensively grown in Northern China, Manchukuo, Japan, Russia, and the United States. The greatest area of production in the United States is, in general, the southern part of the corn belt and the northern part of the cotton belt. To secure the best quality of hay, the soybeans are cut when the seeds are about half developed. The portion of well-cured soybean hay that is eaten is about equal to alfalfa or clover hay in feeding value. However, there is more waste because of the coarseness of the stems. This kind of hay is frequently very dusty.

Cowpea Hay. The cowpea is a native of the tropics of Africa. It is extensively cultivated from the central part of the cotton belt southward and is the most important legume in the cotton belt. Cowpeas are cut for hay when the pods are fully matured. The hay is richer in proteins than alfalfa though slightly lower in total digestible nutrients. If well cured, it is equal in feeding value to clover or alfalfa hay and may be fed in the same amounts.

Peanut Hay. The peanut is a native of Brazil. It is cultivated throughout the southern part of the United States. Peanut hay is a by-product of the peanut crop. After the pods have been harvested the cured leaves and vines are used as hay or forage. Peanut hay, if well cured and not moldy, is a good substitute for other legume hay, although it contains less protein. If it carries much dust or dirt, which it frequently does, it is not suitable for feeding horses or mules.

GREEN ROUGHAGE. Fresh green feed for horses may be supplied by grazing in hand, pasturing, or by stall feeding of freshly harvested green feeds. Green feed, especially the grasses, is truly the natural diet of the horse. The domesticated horse, especially the military horse, probably receives too little of this kind of feed. It has been proved that green feed is not absolutely essential, but it is desirable when properly supplied.

Grazing. Grazing in hand should be practiced by both individual riders and organizations whenever it is feasible. It not only supplies a small amount of green feed, which is relished, but it also trains the soldier in the practice of grazing. Under field service conditions, grazing often becomes essential in order to supplement or replace the hay ration. When horses are first grazed, especially on the new grass in the spring, they should be grazed but a few minutes the first day, and the time gradually increased from day to day. Green feed is laxative and unless judiciously used will make the working horse too "washy." Special care must be exercised in grazing on legumes, especially if they are wet with dew, rain, or frost, since they are likely to cause bloating and are more laxative than the grasses. Except in an emergency, Johnson grass and the sorghums should not be grazed.

Pasturing. Many horses never have the opportunity of enjoying the benefits of being turned out in a good pasture. Pastures of any sort seldom are available, and when they are to be had they are usually so small and so overcrowded that they cannot supply more than a small part of the feed required. This results in overpasturing, and the pastures soon become little more than a corral. The carrying capacity of pastures varies a great deal depending upon the type of grass, soil fertility, and climatic conditions. From four to twelve acres of average grass pasture are required in the Great Plains area to supply a horse with necessary maintenance roughage during the pasture season. When pastures are overcrowded, horses will require nearly a full maintenance ration of grain and hay in order to keep them in flesh. Fall seedings of rye and winter wheat provide a good temporary pasture from about a month after seeding until winter stops the growth. Legume pastures will seldom be available, and they are somewhat less desirable than grass pastures because of the greater likelihood of digestive disturbances.

A complete rest, an improvement in the condition of the feet, and the good effects of a change of diet are some of the benefits that should be expected from a period in pasture. Too commonly the expected benefits fail to materialize because of improper management, and horses often come out of pasture in far worse shape than when they went in. Merely turning a horse in a field to shift for himself is not enough. He must have an adequate supply of grass; shelter so placed that he can take advantage of it, should he feel inclined to escape from wind, sun, cold, or rain; salt as he needs it; a good supply of water; and always the necessary amount of dry feed (oats, bran, and hay) to keep him properly nourished and in good flesh. Horses in pasture should be inspected frequently to determine their state of flesh and the condition of their feet.

Cut Green Forage. Stall feeding of limited amounts of freshly cut green roughage is sometimes practiced when horses cannot be grazed in hand or turned in a pasture. Grasses or other suitable green roughage can be fed in this way, but the same precautions must be taken as in the case of grazing. Freshly wilted forage is safe, but great care should be exercised to see that fermentation or spoilage has not commenced. It is always safest to feed it only on the day that it is cut. Remember that horses will gorge themselves on green feed, with possible disastrous results, if given the opportunity.

Silage, which might be classed as a preserved cut green roughage, is extensively used as a cattle feed in dairying countries and might be used as a locally procured roughage. It could be used in amounts of ten to fifteen pounds daily to supplement other roughage; however, it is not well relished by most horses.

Fruits and Roots. Fruits and roots are not a part of the natural diet of the horse, but certain of them are greatly relished and may be advantageously fed in small amounts to tempt the appetite of a shy feeder or a sick horse. They are high in moisture and low in nutrients and therefore add but little food value to the diet. They act more as appetizers and improve the digestion. Carrots seem to be greatly appreciated by all horses, and a pound or two a day often has a noticeably beneficial effect, especially during the winter when other green feeds are not available. They should be cleaned, sliced into small strips, and mixed with the grain. Carrots are particularly rich in vitamin A. Other roots such as potatoes, turnips, parsnips, and sugar beets can likewise safely be fed in small amounts, provided they are cut fine enough to prevent choking. Fruits, such as apples, are enjoyed by most horses.

COMMERCIALLY PREPARED FEEDS. *Ed. Note: Pelleted grains and pelleted complete diets were first extensively manufactured and distributed in the 1960s, two decades after the original cavalry treatise on feeds and feeding was written. Since commercially prepared feeds are now a significant and widely accepted diet for many horses—particularly for those not doing hard work—the information given below has been incorporated in this revised edition of cavalry doctrine even though the topic was not, for the obvious reasons, included in the original work. The information was prepared at the New York State College of Agriculture and Life Sciences by Doctors H. F. Schryver and H. F. Hintz, both leading researchers in equine nutrition.*

The use of commercial horse feeds has increased greatly in the last few years. Many manufacturers have different mixtures for the various classes of horses, the horse owner being given a wide selection.

There are two basic types of prepared horse feeds: "complete feeds" that contain some form of roughage and are designed to be fed without additional hay, and grain mixtures that do not contain roughage. Either type can be a loose mixture or compressed into pellets.

The complete, pelleted feed has several advantages over conventional hay-grain rations. Storage is decreased, there is less dust, and horses look better because they do not have hay bellies. Certain feeds and by-products that are nutritious but are not readily consumed by horses can be included in pelleted feeds. Total feed intake is usually increased when pellets are fed. Disadvantages include cost and an increase in bad habits such as wood chewing and tail biting when pellets are fed without any other roughage. There is also a slight decline in fiber digestion, but the decrease is not of great practical concern.

The feed selected should meet the needs of the horse but not provide costly excesses. A high-protein formula designed for weanlings would not be harmful to the mature horse, but he would waste it by excreting more nitrogen in the urine. Most companies clearly indicate the class of horse for which the feed is intended, but the feed tag should be scrutinized to be sure the feed is adequate. Feed tag requirements vary from state to state. Generally the minimum percentages of crude protein and crude fat, the maximum percentages of crude fiber, the maximum and minimum percentages of salt and calcium, and the minimum percentage of phosphorus must be guaranteed. *The higher the percentage of fiber, the lower the digestible energy.* A commercial mixture containing more than twelve percent fiber would probably contain less digestible energy per pound than oats (eleven to twelve percent fiber) and usually would not be considered as a high energy food. Complete feeds usually contain twenty to thirty percent fiber.

The feed should also be selected according to the type of forage that is being fed. Legumes such as alfalfa provide more protein and calcium than grasses such as timothy and orchard grass. The table given below can be used as a rough guide to determine the nutrients needed in commercial mixtures for various feeding situations. The table demonstrates an advantage of feeding a mixed or legume hay to weanlings because the grain mixture does not need as much protein. Protein is usually one of the most expensive ingredients in a commercial grain mixture. Grain mixtures for weanlings, yearlings, and producing mares should usually not contain more than ten to twelve percent fiber.

The feed tag also lists the ingredients. The wording is often ambiguous so that changes in formulation can be made to take advantage of price changes of the basic ingredients. Such adjustments result in a lower cost though the nutrient content still meets the guarantee. Other factors in addition to nutrient content determine the value of the feed. The palatability, or acceptance, by the horse must be satisfactory. The feed should not be moldy or dusty. Pelleted feeds should not contain a lot of fine or broken pellets.

APPROXIMATE NUTRIENT CONTENT NEEDED IN COMMERCIAL FEEDS TO MEET REQUIREMENTS FOR VARIOUS CLASSES OF HORSES

Class of Horse	Nutrient	Legume Hay	—Type of forage fed— Mixed Hay	Grass Hay	None*
		%	%	%	%
Weanlings	Crude protein**	14.0	16.0	18.0	14.0
	Calcium	0.2***	0.6	0.9	0.7
	Phosphorus	0.6	0.6	0.6	0.45
Yearlings. Mares	Crude protein	10.0	12.0	14.0	12.0
in late gestation	Calcium	0.1***	0.3	0.7	0.55
or lactation	Phosphorus	0.5	0.5	0.5	0.35
Mature horse	Crude protein	8.0	8.0	8.0	9.0
	Calcium	†	†	0.2	0.3
	Phosphorus	0.3	0.3	0.3	0.25

*Feeding small amounts of hay even when using complete feeds will help alleviate vices such as wood chewing.

**Protein should be good quality to supply the essential amino acids. Soybean meal, milk proteins, and meat meal are examples of reasonable protein sources.

***Many mixtures will contain calcium levels greater than 0.3 percent, but the extra calcium is not harmful when an adequate level of phosphorous is provided.

†The forage will normally provide all the calcium needed.

FOOD REQUIREMENT. The amount of food necessary to sustain an animal depends primarily on three factors; viz.,

The amount and character of the work being done.

The size of the animal.

The easy- or hard-keeping characteristics of the individual.

Bulk is essential in the diet of the horse. Concentrated feed, no matter how nourishing, cannot alone assure proper nutrition or take the place of roughage. The digestive apparatus does not well tolerate an unusually large grain ration, although a sufficient amount of bulk assists in caring for it. Horses, such as polo ponies, that are performing fast work require less bulk and more grain than those doing slow or ordinary work. In any group of horses there are always certain individuals that are hard-keepers. In order to keep in the same flesh as others these require more than the average amount of feed. This extra feed can be obtained from the savings made on the easy-keepers.

Underfeeding and Overfeeding. Underfeeding leads to loss of weight and strength, also to reduced power of resistance to disease. This occurs most commonly in campaign and is the underlying cause of a large amount of disability.

Overfeeding more often occurs in stable and is the most common cause of such diseases as colic, laminitis, azoturia, and lymphangitis. Most of the harm is caused by feeding too much grain regularly, or by failing to reduce the grain ration during a period of rest or reduced work. It is an infallible rule that normally regularly exercised horses should have their grain ration halved during periods of idleness.

PRINCIPLES OF FEEDING. The guiding principles in feeding are the result of long experience and are based on the anatomy and physiology of the digestive apparatus. These principles may be stated as follows:

Water Before Feeding. Watering before feeding is the established custom. Animals drink very rapidly, and the water passes quickly through both the stomach and small intestines into the cecum. Such a stream passing through an already full stomach washes a considerable portion of the contents into the bowels. If the meal has just been finished, the feed is only partially mixed with the gastric juices, and digestion is still incomplete. There is caused thereby a loss of nourishment, and indigestion or colic may result. Water may be given an hour after the meal. If possible, it is best to keep water in the stall at all times.

Feed in Small Quantities and Often. The digestive system of the horse and mule is so constituted as to permit leisurely feeding for many hours at a time. The stomach, being small, is unable to contain large quantities of feed, which does not stay long in the stomach. When the stomach is two-thirds full, and until feeding is finished, the feed passes through at the rate it is taken into the mouth. The stomach functions best when two-thirds full. If the periodic feeds are too large, there is danger of the stomach being overdistended, and the feed wasted by not being properly digested. A feed of three to four pounds of oats mixed with a half pound of bran and two handfuls of chop or chaff represents the approximate amount that the average animal should consume at a single meal. This may be followed by a long and slow consumption of hay. The gradual passage of food into the intestines then takes place under favorable conditions. If the total amount of grain is to be increased, it is better to increase the number of feeds rather than the size of the feeds. This plan of increasing the number of feeds is to be particularly recommended for conditioning horses or fattening thin horses.

Do Not Work Hard After a Full Feed. Immediately after a meal, the stomach and bowels are more distended than before; they contain more water and food, and perhaps contain gases resulting from the digestive processes. As a result, they require more space than just prior to feeding. This extra space is gained by a slight filling out of the abdomen and by the stomach bulging forward against the diaphragm. The size of the thoracic cavity is reduced thereby and the lungs are prevented from expanding to their fullest capacity. The animal, therefore, has difficulty in obtaining sufficient fresh air, and labored breathing is the result. This is an important point to keep in mind when feeding horses that are to be worked at very fast gaits. The chief danger in working an animal hard immediately after a full meal is the resultant interference with digestion. Digestion is accompanied by increased muscular activity of the bowels, increased blood supply to the digestive tract, and increased flow of secretions. Hard work diverts blood to other channels, tires the intestinal muscles, and reduces secretions. Obviously, digestion is retarded. This always results in loss of nourishment from the feed eaten, often in serious disorders of the digestive tract, and sometimes in death. Moderate exercise promotes digestion.

110

Do Not Feed an Exhausted Horse a Full Feed. The digestive organs of a very tired horse are just as fatigued as the rest of his body. The muscular layers of the stomach and intestines are tired, the nervous energy is depleted, and the glands of secretion are not ready to function normally because the bulk of the blood is still in the body muscles. Small amounts of water should be given at frequent intervals and the animal may be permitted to eat hay. If the fatigue is excessive, the first grain feed should be a bran mash or steamed oats fed after about thirty minutes of rest, or one-half to one-and-a-half pounds of oats after one to one-and-a-half hours of rest. The whole grain feed should be parceled out a little at a time. Failure to observe this principle very frequently results in the most serious colic, laminitis, or both.

Feed Hay Before Grain, or Feed Chop or Chaff with Grain. A small feed of hay before feeding grain stimulates an increased flow of saliva and gastric juices, takes the edge off the appetite, and quiets the nervous animal. In the morning, it is not necessary to feed hay first because the animal has generally been eating hay all night. An ideal way to feed hay is to keep it before the animal continuously by replenishing the supply frequently with a small quantity. Feeding chop or chaff with the grain adds bulk to the grain, forces the animal to eat more slowly, and consequently ensures more thorough mastication.

FEEDING MAXIMS. Water before feeding or wait until at least an hour after feeding.

Never feed grain to heated animals; hay will not harm them.

If expecting hard work immediately after feeding, give only a half feed.

Do not work the animal immediately after a full feed.

Use feed bags when mangers or feedboxes are not available.

When practicable, give a small feed of hay before each grain feed.

Whenever possible and practicable, feed from one-half to two pounds of dry bran per day mixed with the oats.

Bran mashes need not be routinely fed, but occasionally a bran mash is desirable when the condition of the animal or nature of the droppings seem to indicate.

Feed salt.

Never feed hay on the ground if it can be avoided.

When feeding in feed bags, remove them as each animal finishes.

Keep feeding utensils clean.

Supply clean feed.

Watch your horses feeding and know which are the slow and the shy feeders.

Watch their condition and fix the ration for each horse according to his needs.

Graze whenever possible.

Encourage men to bring handfuls of grass or other feed to their horses.

Be economical in feeding, waste nothing, let the horse get the full value of his ration.

Feed most of the ration, especially the hay, at night; the animal has plenty of time to eat and digest feed before working again.

Feed at regular hours each day.

111

Feed grain at least three times daily, and to thin horses four times.

Feed grain in small amounts and often.

Do not feed a very tired horse a full feed of grain.

FEEDING SPECIAL CASES.

Animals that Bolt Their Feed. In open stables animals learn to feed greedily. They consume their grain with the greatest rapidity, either to see what they can steal from their neighbors or from fear that they themselves will be robbed. To prevent the greedy habit as much as possible, chaff, chop, or bran should be mixed with the feed. Horses have difficulty in bolting crushed oats. Animals that bolt their grain in spite of this should have it spread out thinly over as large a surface as possible in order to prevent them from getting large mouthfuls. A feedbox with several bars across the top to divide it into compartments or a few large stones placed in the feed are other methods for preventing bolters from securing the huge mouthfuls or throwing grain out of feedboxes.

Windsuckers and Cribbers. Windsuckers and cribbers should, if possible, be fed apart from the other animals and in such a way as to prevent their practicing the habit. The best plan is to feed a cribber off the ground in a box stall with four blank walls. The habit may be acquired by adjacent animals; hence the desirability of segregating those which have acquired it.

Animals that "Stock." Animals that stock should have the amount of their feed very carefully regulated according to the work required of them. If they are rested, even for a short time, their rations must be proportionately decreased. After good condition has once been obtained, complete rest is not good for them. There must always be an amount of exercise sufficient to keep the circulation of the limbs active, and no more feed than suffices for their actual daily requirements.

Thin Animals. The horse and the mule are not by nature thin animals. Usually thin individuals are overworked, badly fed, or have something the matter with them. A thorough examination by an expert should be made to locate the specific cause or causes of the condition. In feeding a thin but otherwise healthy animal, take into account the fact the weakness of the muscles of his limbs is reflected in the muscles of his bowels and stomach. Until he gains strength, he is not capable of digesting large feeds without incurring the risk of indigestion or colic. In such cases, the rule of "little and often" must be strictly observed. As the bodily strength grows and the work is proportionately increased, the quantity of each feed may be also increased. An unlimited supply of water is also an important factor in the restoration of thin, weak animals.

FEEDING SCHEDULE. The times of feeding and watering should be definite and regular, and it is advisable to prepare a definite schedule for the guidance of those concerned. Assume that the following ration is being fed:

Oats . . . . 9 lbs.

Bran . . . . 1 lb.

Hay . . . . 14 lbs.

Salt . . . . As needed.

The dry bran is mixed with the oats in bulk. The following schedule is suggested for use where the animals are used for drill or exercised from about 7:30 to 10:30 in the morning and remain in the stables, or turned loose in the corral in the afternoon. The amounts shown are for the average animal in the stable. It must be borne in mind that the amount fed should be in accord with the need of each animal. The amounts of grain to be fed at each feed should be marked on a suitable card or blackboard on the heelpost in rear of each horse.

Feeding Grain Three Times Daily.

	A.M.					P.M.		
	5:30	7:30	11:00	11:15	11:45	1:30	4:30	4:35	5:00
Grain mixture (lbs)	3					3			4
Hay (lbs)				3				11	
Water			x	x			x	x	
Salt		Available in or near manger at all times.							

Water just before saddling and just before tying in stables after grooming, which follows the drill period.

If animals are to remain in stables in the afternoon, half of the hay ration may be fed at 11:15 A.M. Afternoon feeding of hay is in mangers before tying animals in stables.

If four or five pounds of alfalfa hay are included in the hay ration, it might well be fed at the 11:15 A.M. feeding, and the ordinary feeding hay fed at 4:35 P.M.

Feeding Grain Four Times Daily.

	A.M.					P.M.				
	5:30	7:30	11:10	11:15	11:45	1:30	4:30	4:35	5:00	6:45	7:00
Grain mixture (lbs)	2				3			2			3
Hay (lbs)				3			11				
Water		x	x			x	x			x	
Salt		Available in or near manger at all times.									

WEIGHTS OF GRAIN. The following table gives the approximate weights.

	Weight per bushel measure Lbs.	Weight per quart Lbs.	Weight per 12 qt. bucket level full Lbs.	Weight per mess kit spoonful;* heaping Oz.
Oats	32	1	12	
Oats, crushed	16-20	1/2	7	
Oats, ground	26	3/4	10	
Wheat bran	16	1/2	6	
Corn, shelled	56	1-3/4	21	
Corn, cracked	43	1-1/3	16	
Ear corn	40	Average 65 medium ears per bushel measure		
Barley	48	1-1/2	17	
Wheat	58	1-3/4	21	
Rye	54	1-3/4	20	
Kaffir	57	1-3/4	21	
Linseed meal	44	1-1/3	16	2/3
Salt, rock	85	2-1/2	32	1-1/4
Soda ash				3/4
Molasses		3		

*An approximate tablespoon. [Ed.]

GRADES OF GRAIN AND GRAIN INSPECTION. Most of the grain bought and sold in the grain markets is graded under federal standards that are promulgated by the Agricultural Marketing Service, United States Department of Agriculture. There are several grading factors used in determining the grade. The higher the grade, the higher the feeding value. The number of grades that are applicable varies with different grains. Oats are graded No. 1, No. 2, No. 3, No. 4, and Sample Grade, the last-named being the lowest grade. In addition there are several special qualifying grades that may modify any of the numerical grades or Sample Grade. Federal specifications specify that for Army use the No. 2 grade of oats will be procured, except that under certain circumstances a modified No. 3 grade may be purchased.

GRADES OF HAY AND HAY INSPECTION. The Official Hay Standards of the United States are promulgated by the Agricultural Marketing Service of the United States Department of Agriculture. All classes of hay under Federal standards are assigned grades as follows: No. 1, No. 2, No. 3, and Sample Grade, the last-named being of the lowest quality. There are in addition several special grades that may be given to modify any of the grades listed. The grading factors are factors that determine or influence the feeding quality of the hay. The important grading factors in all classes of hay are color, foreign material; and damage of various kinds. Leafiness and texture are important grading factors in certain kinds of hay. Federal specifications generally specify that the No. 2 grade of hay will be purchased for Army use.

Federal Inspection. The Federal inspection of hay is conducted in a manner very similar to that described for Federal grain inspection.

114

OTHER INSPECTIONS. The fact that all forage has been inspected does not relieve the stable manager from his responsibility for inspection of all forage at the time that it is fed. Forage may have been damaged while in storage. The inspection of carlots of grain and hay, as conducted by the civilian inspector or the veterinary inspector, is not an absolute and minute inspection of every sack or bale, but is sufficiently complete inspection to determine the grade of the lot as a whole. Such inspection cannot guarantee that there will not be small amounts that, when opened for feeding, may be unfit for use. It is the duty of the feeder to see that such damaged feed is not used. If there is any question as to the safeness of the feed, he should consult a veterinarian. The recognition of the various forms of damage to grains and hay is best learned by practical instruction.

7

Care of Horses in the Stable

Types. Various types of floors are used in stalls and aisles of stables. Permanent stables of good construction usually have floors of concrete or brick. Temporary stables are seldom provided with permanent flooring and the natural soil, clay, or crushed rock is used. For stables with tie stalls, rough-finished concrete provides the most satisfactory type of floor. It has many advantages and few disadvantages. It is sanitary, easily cleaned, and requires little repair. It is hard and cold, but these disadvantages are overcome if bedding is properly used. Brick floors are less desirable than concrete floors because they are slippery, less permanent, and more difficult to clean. Wooden floors, whether alone or laid over concrete, are not desirable, since they are slippery and unsanitary. Asphalt floors are not satisfactory. It is difficult to keep clay or crushed rock floors in a sanitary condition, and it takes an immense amount of labor to keep them properly repaired. A clay floor is very satisfactory in a box stall.

Cleanliness. The floors of stables and aisles should be thoroughly cleaned daily. During warm weather concrete and brick floors are best cleaned by scrubbing with water, using the hose and stable brooms. Earthen floors at all times, and hard-surfaced floors in cold weather, are cleaned by scraping with a shovel or hoe and sweeping with a stable broom.

Slippery Floors. If the floors wear smooth and become slippery, the surface should be roughened by chipping with a cold chisel. If slippery from ice, the surface should be sprinkled with sand or sifted ashes before the bedding is put down. Likewise, when necessary, the aisles should be covered temporarily with bedding and the approaches with sand and cinders to prevent the animals from slipping.

Maintenance of Earthen and Crushed Rock Floors. A great deal of work is required

116

to keep floors of this type clean and smooth. In tie stalls, horses tend to paw holes in the front part of the stall and a wet, urine-soaked depression appears in the back part of the stall. Repair of a stall floor by merely filling the hole or depression with new material is seldom satisfactory because of the difficulty of getting a proper bind between the old and new material. A stall is best repaired by removing all of the old material and replacing it with new; wetting it, tamping it, and allowing to dry out before use. To provide for stalls undergoing repair, the number of animals kept in a stable should be approximately five percent less than the rated stall capacity. The floor at the front of the stall, for a distance of about two feet from the rear edge of the manger, should be level in order that the animal's front feet may rest on a level surface. In back of this space the floor should slope gently to the rear to provide drainage. A drop of about two inches is sufficient.

MANGERS.

Construction of Mangers. It is quite generally agreed that the most satisfactory method of feeding horses in a stable is by means of a tight manger. Feeding hay on the floor of the stall will expose the horse to infestation by parasites. Feeding grain in the usual type feedbox results in waste from bolting the feed and throwing out the grain by greedy feeders. A tight manger will prevent all this. The feed will either be eaten or it will remain in the manger.

A satisfactory manger must be grain-tight, substantial, and so constructed that it can be readily and thoroughly cleaned.

The following manger has been found to meet the preceding requirements, and its dimensions are approximately correct for feeding horses. The details of construction are published herewith for the information of those who may be interested in building or improving a horse stable, since the feeding and watering facilities in a stable are of the greatest importance in animal management.

The manger is built of 2" clear pine and, in effect, is hung on two pieces of ¼", 2" x 2" angle iron bolted on the sides of the stall partition. It has a single board removable bottom.

Two V's are sawed out of one flange and the angle iron is bent as shown.

The top front board (2" x 6" manger bar) has a ring in it for tying the horse. The top and outside edge of this piece is covered with the same kind of angle iron to prevent damage from cribbing. Light-gauge sheet metal is not satisfactory as a protective covering because it soon becomes cracked and broken and is likely to injure the animal.

The wall of the stable makes the back of the manger; the partitions of the stall make the ends; the front is bolted or screwed to one flange of the angle iron; and the bottom board, by its own weight, rests on the angle iron and can be removed merely by tapping it up from below.

The completed manger is given two coats of linseed oil or creosote to preserve the wood. Paint is not recommended, since it will peel or chip, resulting in a pitted surface for the accumulation of dirt.

In a double stall it would probably be desirable to attach a piece of angle iron down the middle of the front boards to prevent warping and to make them more rigid.

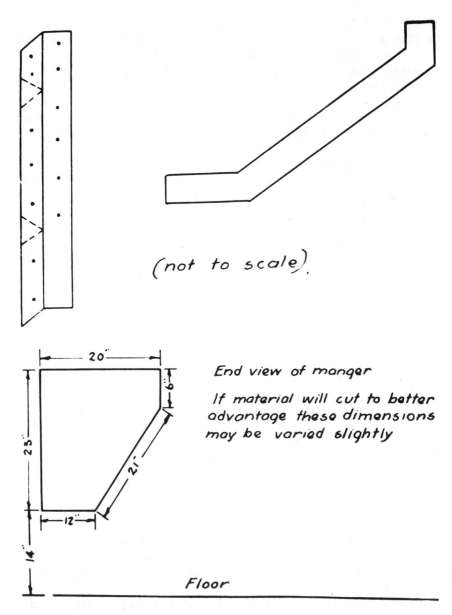

(not to scale)

20"

6"

End view of manger

If material will cut to better
advantage these dimensions
may be varied slightly

25"

21'

12"

14"

Floor

End of bottom board showing beveled edge

 Front edge

Manger Construction *The Cavalry School.*

118

Cleanliness. Feedboxes and mangers should be brushed out daily, care being taken that all particles of feed are removed and that the woodwork surrounding them is also kept free of particles of feed. This is especially important in warm weather when fermentation is most likely to occur. Advantage should be taken of exposure to sunlight and fresh air to keep feedboxes clean. In addition to the daily policing, which should be thorough, a monthly (or more often, if necessary) cleaning of feedboxes and the woodwork immediately surrounding them should be routine. This should be done by scraping and scrubbing with soda ash and hot water. Feedboxes should be washed immediately after each bran mash feeding.

Cleaning Solution. A five percent soda-ash solution (five pounds of soda ash to twelve gallons of water) should be used. To clean feedboxes this mixture should be placed in a kettle such as is used for cooking feeds, a galvanized can, or other suitable receptacle large enough for the purpose, and brought to the boiling point. The feedboxes should be freed of all loose dirt and then placed in the boiling solution for a period of from three to five minutes. They should be removed with a hook, and thoroughly rinsed. This is best done by the use of a hose when a water system is available. None of the soda-ash solution should be allowed to remain upon a feedbox, since it will irritate the mucous membranes of the mouth and lips of the animal. Care should be exercised by those handling the solution to prevent its coming into contact with the skin or mucous membranes (particularly of the eye), since the solution is irritating to such tissues.

WOODWORK. There should be no sharp or rough projections in the woodwork of the stables on which animals might injure themselves. All fittings should be flush with the surface to which they are attached. A well-appointed stable should contain sufficient box or single stalls for all animals. Kicking bars in double stalls offer some protection against injury from kicks, but unless properly constructed they may cause injury. When used, kicking bars should be adjusted to such height that they are level with a point midway between the hock and stifle. The rear end of the bar should be suspended in such a way that it will drop should an animal get a leg over the bar. The bar may be suspended with a section of light rope, a leather thong, or be equipped with a quick-release device. Use of such methods of suspension will result in the necessity for the rehanging of several dropped bars each day. Unless properly supervised, grooms, to avoid the labor of frequent replacement of the bars, are prone to refasten the bars in such a way as to prevent their proper release. A satisfactory quick-release device should not only permit the bar to come down if a horse gets over it, but should also be easy to reassemble.

Woodwork about the manger and front of the stall should be cleaned by scrubbing as frequently as may be necessary to maintain the wood free of stains or incrustations of dirt. Woodwork of that part of the stall which the animal cannot reach with his mouth may be left natural, treated with creosote, or painted, and should be washed frequently to remove dust and stain. Whitewash is not suitable for use in stables.

Three tablespoons of lye in a bucket of warm water make a good solution for cleaning the coating of dirt from the mangers and woodwork of the stalls, and improving the appearance of the stables. Care should be exercised when using this solution that none of it gets on forage or bedding.

WATER TROUGHS. Water troughs should be emptied and thoroughly cleaned each morning. A water trough placed in a corral should be kept plentifully supplied with water at all times when the animals are in the corral. The standing around the trough should have sufficient slope to provide for proper drainage. Under no circumstances should strange animals be permitted to drink at the water troughs or be fed in the stables. One animal with a communicable disease may infect all the animals. Animals suffering from a communicable disease should be watered from buckets. When a trough or bucket has heen used by an infected animal it should be thoroughly cleaned and then disinfected.

THE CORRAL.* The corral should be cleaned at least once a day. Thorough drainage should be provided and all depressions kept filled so that pools of water will not form after rains.

The corral fences should be of sufficient height and strength to restrain all animals turned into the corral. They should be able to withstand considerable shock and should be kept in a thorough state of repair at all times. They should be entirely free of all rough or sharp projections. When constructed of wooden posts and boards the posts should be on the outside.

The corral should be sprinkled when necessary to keep down the dust. Crude oil or used oil from crankcases of motors may be used to advantage. If there is no shade, shelter from the sun should be improvised from any available material. This is very important, since animals lose flesh rapidly if forced to stand in the hot sun for long periods of time.

The corral should never be crowded, since this is certain to result in animals being injured by kicking. Injury incurred by kicks while horses are in the corral is the most important cause of animal disability. Judicious use of the corral is necessary. Idle horses should not be turned loose in a corral with the expectation that the exercise they will voluntarily take will be a proper substitute for regular work or exercise. Horses that are known to kick should not be turned out with other horses. Horses with calked hind shoes should not be turned out.

TYING ANIMALS. For tying an animal in a stall, the proper length of rope is one that will permit him to reach all parts of his manger and to lie down with ease. The length of the permanently installed tie rope should usually be such that the snap hangs two or three inches above the floor. Permanently installed tie ropes of proper length will prevent many injuries caused by tying ropes too long, too short, or so insecurely that animals get loose. Ropes, not chains, should be used for this purpose. The rope is best fastened in the tie ring by splicing to ensure that it is not removed for other purposes. Any knot that is perfectly secure and capable of being untied rapidly may be used for securing animals.

---

*Particularly East of the Appalachians, the corral is normally referred to as a paddock. Either word describes a fenced-in area immediately adjacent to the stable, relatively small in size compared to a pasture, and utilized to turn horses out for rest and relaxation away from their stalls yet keeping them handy to catch up when wanted for feeding or work. [Ed.]

Nonslip Knot for a Rail, Pipe, or Picket Line *The Cavalry School.*

FIRE PREVENTION. All stables must be provided with the necessary fire equipment, which includes knives for cutting tie ropes. An extra tie rope for each horse, for use only in case of fire, should be available on the heelpost of the stall. Painting these ropes will aid in preventing the use of them for other purposes. Fire

121

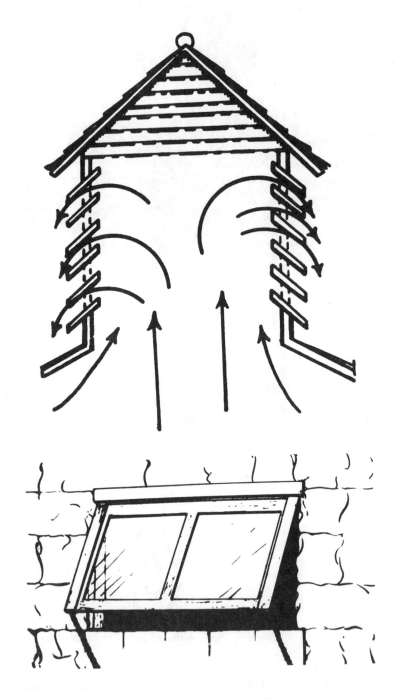

Ventilation of a Stable *The Cavalry School.*

drills should be held at irregular intervals and at times not previously announced. Smoking in stables must be strictly prohibited.

It must be borne in mind that animals will not leave a burning stable of their own volition. Merely cutting the tie ropes is not sufficient. Loose animals generally cannot be herded from a burning stable. Each horse must be led to safety. If turned loose outside of the stable, they are very likely to attempt to return to their stalls or to stampede. When led from the stable they should be put in some nearby stable or corral or tied on a picket line at a safe distance. The fire order should designate the place to which animals are to be moved in case of a fire in the stable.

VENTILATION. Ventilation must be thorough and continuous. In closed stables ventilation is effected by means of ventilators, louvre boards, windows, and doors. Animals rarely suffer from cold air, provided they are not in a direct draft. They do, however, suffer greatly from foul air; hence the importance of an abundant supply of fresh air. Ventilators and louvre boards are constructed in the stable roof to carry off the warm, tainted air. The principal supply of fresh air is obtained through windows and doors. Windows should be hinged at the bottom and open inward, thus forcing the incoming air up and over the animals, instead of directly on them. Doors are apt to cause drafts. They should be closed on the windward side in stormy weather. Any unpleasant odor on entering a stable is an indication of insufficient ventilation, which should be corrected immediately. The best time to inspect the ventilation of a stable is very late at night or early in the morning. Animals in cold stables are always healthier than those in close or warm stables.

BEDDING. A good bed in the stall contributes much to the comfort and efficiency of the animals. A clean and comfortable bed will induce the horse to lie down for considerable periods and thus get better rest. It provides a soft surface that will prevent bruising or abrasion of the elbows, hock, and other parts. It ensures warmth by insulating his body from the cold floor. It helps to keep his coat clean and thereby greatly lessens the labor of grooming. When the horse is standing, it provides a resilient surface that will do much toward the prevention of contracted heels, which is common among horses required to stand on unbedded floors. The bed should be level, dry, warm, and soft, and have a clean surface for the animal to lie upon. The allowance of bedding is five pounds per day for each animal.

Long, bright, clean straw from rye, wheat, rice, or oats is the best material for bedding. Numerous other materials, such as leaves, moss, shavings, sawdust, or even sand, may be used. Sand, however, is likely to be eaten and cause digestive disturbances.

Hay of the lower grades is frequently used as bedding.* Care must be exercised not to use it when moldy or very musty. Most forms of bedding hay absorb

*In allowing the use of hay for bedding, the cavalry had in mind horses in standing (as opposed to box) stalls where the horse was tied and therefore limited in the use of his head and neck. In those instances where a horse was stabled in a box stall the unit commander invariably forbade the use of hay as a bedding material. This prohibition was based on the need to prevent untethered animals from eating soiled hay. [Ed.]

moisture and become soggy more readily than good straw and for this reason are less satisfactory. Bedding hay is coming into more general use because much of the modern grain harvesting and threshing machinery breaks the straw into such short lengths that its value for bedding is greatly reduced.

In the morning the bedding should be removed from stalls and well shaken out, and only the dung and short or badly soaked refuse taken to the stable dump. Grooms require constant supervision in the sorting of bedding, otherwise bedding that should be saved will go out with the manure and the amount of bedding for stalls will be insufficient. That part of the bedding which can be used again should be spread out to air and dry. A good way to do this is to spread the bedding as thinly as possible over the floors of the aisleway in rear of the stalls and, with an occasional turning, leave it there until the stalls are bedded down in the afternoon. Bedding should not be stacked in the stalls. The floors of stalls should be thoroughly cleaned each morning and allowed to dry out during the day. Bedding racks, made of light material and with wire screen bottoms, are useful for drying bedding if they are procurable in sufficient numbers. They should be so constructed as to offer a maximum of drying surface, and the bedding should be turned several times. Ordinarily it is not practicable to construct these racks in sufficient numbers to make this system as efficient as spreading the bedding over the aisleway floors or the ground in rear of the stalls in open stables.

In the afternoon the dried bedding is mixed with such new bedding as may be necessary and the stalls are bedded. This should be done as late as possible in the afternoon to allow the maximum drying of bedding and stall floors. The bedding should be spread evenly over the bedded portion of the stall. Since a horse usually lies as far back in the stall as the length of the rope will permit, the bedding should not be right up to the front of the stall.

GROOMING. Good grooming is essential to the general health, condition, and appearance of animals that are stabled or that are exercised or worked. It cleans the hair and the pores of the skin so the skin can better perform its natural functions. This results in a cleaner and healthier skin that is less likely to become infested with skin parasites such as lice and mange mites. Good, vigorous grooming massages the underlying body muscles and thus improves their condition or fitness. In the field, the press of other demands or the discomfort of trying weather conditions is never a valid excuse for failing to groom thoroughly at least once a day. The value of grooming depends upon the thoroughness and speed with which it is done. Grooms should be encouraged to work hard and rapidly and to do a thorough job in a minimum time. Each man's grooming should be inspected as soon as practicable after completion and, if satisfactory, the man should be dismissed. Proper supervision of grooming is always essential, yet efficient grooming is possible only when the individual can be taught to take a personal pride in the appearance of his mount or team. Idle animals that are in a pasture do not need regular grooming; however, an occasional brushing of the coat is desirable.

Time of Grooming. Before the horse leaves the stable for work or exercise, the coat is brushed; mane, if any, neatly arranged; tail brushed; eyes cleaned; nostrils and dock wiped; and the feet cleaned.

On return from work or exercise grooming should be proceeding with immediately, except for necessary delay incident to wiping off and putting away equipment. Heated, wet, or sweating animals should be cooled out before being groomed. In the case of such horses the equipment should be removed and quickly put aside, then the horse given a brisk rubbing with a grooming or drying cloth to partially dry the coat. He should then be blanketed and walked till cool. Grain sacks cut into pieces of suitable size make good drying cloths. A couple of swallows of water every few minutes assists the cooling out and is beneficial to the animal.

GROOMING EQUIPMENT.

Standard Issue Equipment. Each groom should have the following grooming kit:

Currycomb. The currycomb is used to groom animals that have long, thick coats, to remove caked mud, to loosen matter scurf and dirt in the hair, and to clean the horse brush. The currycomb produces the best effect when applied gently in small circles rather than with pressure and in long strokes. It should never be used on the legs from the knees or hocks down, about the head, or over bonv prominences. The use of the currycomb should be prohibited in grooming animals recently clipped or that have a fine, thin coat of hair. In most cases the hair may be loosened and ruffled sufficiently with the grooming cloth or a compact handful of bedding or hay.

Horse Brush. The horse brush is the principal tool used for grooming. When properly used it reaches the skin, the bristles or fibers penetrating through the hair of the coat. It is also used for brushing the mane and tail.

Hoof Hook. The hoof hook is not a separate item but is attached to the back of the currycomb. It is used to clean out the feet.

Grooming Cloth. The grooming cloth is used to remove dust and dirt from the coat; to wipe out the ears, eyes, nostrils, lips, and dock; and to give the coat a final polish. In some cases it may be used to dry or ruffle the coat before brushing or to loosen dirt on the skin of recently slipped, light-coated, or thin-skinned horses where the use of the currycomb for this purpose might not be desirable. It is not an item of issue but is improvised from old toweling or condemned blankets. A convenient size is from eighteen to twenty-four inches square.

Miscellaneous Grooming Equipment. The following equipment is not standard but is sometimes purchased or improvised for use.

Dandy Brush. The dandy brush is a brush made of stiff whisk fiber. It has an elongated oval wooden back and the bristles are about two inches in length. Its use is strongly recommended whenever it can be procured. It can be used in place of the currycomb for removing light dirt from the skin and is more effective than the horse brush for brushing the coat. It is very useful for brushing the mane and tail.

Improvised Hoof Hook. This article is used to clean out the feet. It can be easily made by the horseshoer. A 3/8-inch rod or a horseshoe drawn out to that dimension is excellent for this purpose. The rod should be eight inches long to begin with. The end is sharpened slightly and given a rounded point, then bent at right angles about one and a quarter inches from the point. The other end can be turned into a small ring for a handle. This is a more useful hoof hook than the one that is attached to the currycomb.

Drying Cloth. A cloth suitable for drying horses or massaging the skin can be made from the material in an ordinary burlap sack.

Wisp. A compact handful of bedding or hay, or a twisted or braided pad of such material is called a wisp. It is useful in ruffling and drying the coat of sweating horses or working loose hair out of the coat.

"Rubber." A piece of grooming equipment useful during the shedding seasons is made as· follows: Prepare a piece of wood about two inches by four inches by six or eight inches and slightly round the long edges. Cut out a rectangular piece of automobile inner tube large enough to cover one face, except the ends. Stretch the rubber, with the roughened or mold side to the outside, around the block and tack in position with carpet tacks. This article is used by slapping or stroking the coat in the direction of the lie of the coat, with the block somewhat canted. It is very effective in removing loose hair and stimulating shedding. Its use is more effective when the working face of the rubber is slightly dampened by passing over a damp sponge between strokes.

WASHING AND DISINFECTING GROOMING EQUIPMENT. Grooming tools should be washed occasionally to clean them, and disinfected when necessary as a precaution against the spread of skin diseases. The currycomb and horse brush should be cleaned in soda-ash solution (a pint of soda-ash to a bucketful of water) and rinsed in clean water. Grooming cloths should be washed with soap and water once a week. To stiffen the bristles of brushes after washing or disinfecting, soak in strong salt solution (add salt to water until no more salt can be dissolved) for several minutes and stand with bristles down to dry. The horse brush and currycomb may be disinfected by immersing for thirty minutes in a three-percent cresolis solution (two quarts of cresolis to a bucket of water). The currycomb may also be boiled.*

METHOD OF GROOMING. Clean out the feet. Work from the heels toward the toe. Most important is a thorough cleaning of the bottom of the commissures or depressions between the frog and the bars. The deepest part of each depression is near the heels. It is the part most often cleaned improperly, and is the usual seat of thrush. The cleft or depression at the back of the frog must be thoroughly cleaned, but care must be exercised that this depression is not deepened by cutting the horn. At this time the feet should be inspected for thrush and loose shoes. Loose pieces of the horny frog or small underrun sections of the frog that may harbor filth should be removed by the horseshoer. Cases of thrush should be reported to the veterinarian. A thorough washing of the under surface of the foot once a week is advisable. A hoof that is well cleaned once daily and given proper shoeing attention cannot develop thrush.

Many commercial disinfectants, including Lysol, are available in convenient form for application to grooming equipment. [Ed.]

126

Take the currycomb in the right hand, fingers over the back of the comb, and the brush in the left hand. First use the currycomb on the left side of the animal, beginning on the neck, then breast, withers, shoulders, and foreleg down to the knee; then back, side, belly, croup. and hind leg down to the hock. Strike the edge of the currycomb against the heel frequently to free it from dirt. The currycomb should never be used about the head nor on the legs from the knees and hocks downward. When it is necessary to loosen mud or matted hair on the fleshy parts of the body, apply the currycomb gently. Take the brush in the left hand and currycomb in the right; brush entire left side of the animal in the same order as when the currycomb was used, except that in brushing the legs brush down to the hoof. After every few strokes clean the dust and hair from the brush with the currycomb. In using the brush the man should stand well away from the animal, keep his arm stiff, and throw the weight of the body against the brush. In grooming the belly apply the brush the way of the hair, the brush in the left hand on the left side and in the right hand on the right side. The skin under the flanks and between the fore and hind legs must be soft and clean. Special care must be exercised to keep the skin at the points of the elbows and back surfaces of the pastern free from scurf and crusts. The skin in these regions must be kept soft and pliable.

Pass to the right side of the animal, change the brush to the right hand and the currycomb to the left, and groom the right side in the same order as prescribed in the preceding paragraph.

Brush the head, mane, and tail. When cleaning mane and tail, begin brushing at the ends of the hair and gradually work up to the roots, separating the locks with the fingers so as to get out scurf and dirt. Tails require occasional washing with warm water and soap.

Finally, with grooming cloth wipe about the ears, face, eyes, nostrils, lips, sheath, and dock, and give a final polish to the coat.

Special Method of Grooming (For Fine-Coated and Clipped Animals). Use the normal method, omitting the use of the currycomb, except occasionally to remove caked mud. In place of the currycomb the dandy brush should be used.

Inspection of Grooming. Examine the feet to see that they have been thoroughly cleaned, especially in the depths of the commissures. Pass the fingertips against the lie of the hair to get a view of the skin. If the coat and skin is not clean, gray lines on the coat will mark the passage of the fingers and the tips of the fingers will be covered with scurf. Between the branches of the lower jaw, under the crownpiece of the halter or bridle, the bends of the knee and hock, the folds of skin between the forelegs, the belly, the inner surface of the thighs, and the dock are the places most frequently neglected when the work has not been thorough. These regions should be checked when inspecting grooming.

Hand-rubbing (Massage). Hand-rubbing (massage) is restful to tired muscles, stimulates the circulation, removes loose hair, and helps to produce a glossy coat. Hand-rubbing of backs and legs is particularly beneficial after a long ride, or at the end of a day's march. The back should be massaged after the reversed blanket has been removed. The back is best massaged by using the palms and heels of the open hand. Place the hands firmly against the skin and massage deeply with a circular

127

motion. Most of the movement is between the skin and underlying muscles rather than between the hand and the skin. The legs are massaged below the knees and hocks with special attention to the tendons. Brisk but gentle rubbing with the fingers and palms in the direction of the hair is an excellent stimulant to the circulation of the legs after hard work. The back and legs should be examined for injuries before being massaged.

METHODS OF CARE OF A HORSE AFTER WORK. The exact procedure to follow in the case of a horse after work must in all instances be varied to suit the condition of the horse, the equipment available, weather, and other factors. The methods outlined below are proven methods, but it must be borne in mind that each should be modified as necessary to meet the existing conditions.

Care of Horse After Moderate Normal Work when Horse Is Returned to Stables Well Cooled Out.

Example: After a one hour trail ride:

Remove equipment in spot out of draft.

Cover back and loins with cooler or blanket.

Fold blanket back on loin and with gunny sack or wisp, dry and rub back and loins. Massage back with hands. Do not slap. Replace blanket on back.

Examine feet, legs, and back for injuries.

Sponge nostrils, eyes, face, and dock.

Groom. If horse is damp with sweat, dry with gunnysack or wisp before grooming. Do not wash legs. Groom as outlined on page   . Remember that *vigorous* grooming with a good brush is what massages the skin and improves the coat. A mere removal of dirt is not sufficient. A thorough cleaning of the feet is a very essential part of proper grooming. If weather is cool and horse covers are used, they should be put on as soon as grooming is completed.

Thirty to forty-five minutes have now elapsed and the horse may be watered. Do not allow to drink excessively.

Place in stall with plenty of good hay.

Grain may be fed thirty minutes after putting in stall.

Care of a Horse Cooled Out but Fatigued After Hard Work.

Example: After a long cross-country ride, or after a long hunt:

Remove equipment in spot out of draft.

Cover back and loins with blanket or cooler.

Fold blanket back on loin and with gunnysack or wisp, dry and rub back and loins. Massage and replace cover.

Examine back, legs, and feet for injury.

Sponge nostrils, eyes, face, and dock.

Groom. If hair is damp, dry with gunnysack before grooming. Replace blanket.

Give one-half pail of water, not too cold.

Walk for five to ten minutes. If second sweat breaks out rub dry and go over horse with brush and grooming cloth.

If it is desirable to use cold packs on legs, they are put on at this time. Do not leave on longer than two or three hours.

Put horse in stall with plenty of hay but no water.

In thirty minutes, put bucket of water in stall and keep filled thereafter.

Do not feed grain until horse has been in stall for *one hour,* then give a small feed of grain.

At end of two hours, remove the wet bandages and dry legs well. Massage legs. Dry rest bandages may be put on at this time.

Horse Brought in Hot and Tired After Fast, Hard Work.

Example: After a polo game:

Remove all equipment in a spot out of a draft.

Cover with blanket or cooler.

Sponge head and dock with water which has had the chill taken off.

Walk slowly two or three minutes.

Sponge off body with lukewarm water. Swipe down thoroughly and replace cover at once. Omit sponging the body if the weather is cold or there is danger of the horse chilling.*

Examine back, legs, and feet for injury.

Give a few swallows of water and walk slowly until thoroughly cooled out. A little water, three or four swallows, may be given every few minutes while cooling. Do not let the total exceed three-fourths to one bucketfull.

Put in stall with plenty of good hay. If animal is not dry, remove the cover and rub with a grain sack until dry. Replace cover and leave animal alone for twenty minutes to eat hay.

Give the horse a half bucketful of water. Groom thoroughly.

Put wet derby bandages on front legs. Leave on two or three hours.

Water. Keep water in stall.

Grain should not be fed in less than one hour after putting horse in stall. The grain feed should be light.

The army discouraged the washing down of horses as a grooming aid for a number of reasons, one very cogent objection being that an inept groom can cause laminitis by dousing a hot horse with excessive cold water. It should be noted, however, that many knowledgeable trainers of racehorses, polo stable managers, and other horsemen concerned with the care of expensive horseflesh do use water judiciously with beneficial results. The advantages of water include: the efficacious removal of dirt and sweat, a considerable saving in grooming time as compared with brushing and rag-rubbing, and the elimination of "elbow grease." The basic principles are: (1) Only clipped horses, or those with summer hair, are washed. Thick coats, or those not yet molted, must not have water applied. (2) Tepid water, not colder than the prevailing temperature, must be used. (3) A disinfectant and fungicide composed of approximately 5.25% sodium hypochloride in solution with inert matter is added to the tepid water in a ratio of two to four ounces in an eight- to ten-quart pail of water (several commercial brands of household bleach, including Clorox, are satisfactory for this purpose). (4) The reinforced tepid water is then applied to the horse's coat with a large sponge, rubbing briskly against the grain and thoroughly soaking the hair. Excess water is then immediately removed with a scraper applied in the direction of hair growth. (5) On cold or windy days the horse is then blanketed, or covered with a cooler if conditions are not too intemperate. If the horse is to be vanned or trailered care must be taken to avoid direct drafts until he has dried out; it is best to wait until he is dry before loading. [Ed.]

Remove wet bandages and dry and massage legs thoroughly. Rest bandages may be used if desirable.

CLEANING THE SHEATH. The sheaths of all geldings should be examined occasionally and those cleaned which show a considerable accumulation of dirt and secretion. Some horses require it more often then others, especially those which urinate without protruding the penis. This habit is frequently induced by the accumulation of dirt. The sheath should be cleaned with warm water, a sponge, and a mild soap. Form a lather in the sponge and carefully remove the secretions, including the "bean" or ball of waxy secretion that sometimes develops in a depression in the head of the penis and that may interfere with urination. In certain warm or tropical areas the possibility of the infestation of the sheath with maggots (screwworms) from fly attacks renders close attention to this detail very necessary. Stable personnel should be trained in the proper method of cleaning the sheath.

PLUCKING MANES AND TAILS. If the manes and forelocks are not clipped, they should be kept properly plucked (not trimmed) so as to present a neat and uniform appearance.

Docking and banging of tails is prohibited. The hair of the tail may be trimmed immediately below the hock, but will otherwise only be plucked to prevent shagginess of appearance. Plucking is done by grasping a few hairs at a time, sliding the hand up close to the roots, and pulling the hairs out by the roots with a quick jerk. Always work on the longest hairs and mostly on the under side of the tail.

TRIMMING MANES AND FETLOCKS. The fetlocks should be kept neatly trimmed by shearing. The back of the fetlock and pastern should not be clipped or trimmed too closely, since this practice is likely to cause skin irritation (scratches), especially during cold weather. A moderate length of hair offers proper protection to the part, permits proper grooming, and presents a neat appearance.

Clipping of manes is strongly recommended, especially for field service. Clipping ("hogging") of manes is almost universally practiced in the Army. Both the mane and forelock are clipped and should be reclipped as frequently as may be necessary to present a neat appearance.

BRAIDING THE TAIL. When the hair of the tail is done up for wet weather the braid should look well and be uniform in appearance with that of the other animals. It should not hurt the tail bone and irritate the animal, and yet should be secure enough to stay in place.

In plaiting the tail, gather in all the short hairs and get them well in hand by grasping the tail with both hands and sliding them down three or four times to the end of the tail bone. At this point divide the hair into three sections, the center section slightly thicker than the other two, and begin plaiting the three sections into a braid. Exercise care to plait the braid smooth and snug, though not too tight. When about twelve or fourteen inches from the end of the tail, change the three sections into two equal ones, fold the braid up, and wrap the two ends of the unplaited sections in opposite directions around the tail until they pass each other underneath. With the thumb and forefinger work two holes through the hair close to and on each side of the tail bone just above the point where the two ends of the braid lie, then pass the two ends from underneath outward through the holes thus made and draw them snug but not too tight. Divide the two sections into three again and plait down to the end. Secure the end by taking a half hitch over it with a few hairs. Weave the small braid back and forth between the strands of the large braid and finish by hiding the end. With a little practice a soldier easily learns to braid the tail of his animal in a few minutes.

CLIPPING. As a rule, clipping of working animals with heavy coats is recommended. Clipping has many advantages and some disadvantages. Whether clipping is advisable depends upon the nature of the coat, the climatic conditions, the amount and character of the work to be performed by the animal, the character of the stables, the amount of clothing, the availability of personnel, and the time for grooming. A decision can be reached only after careful consideration of the

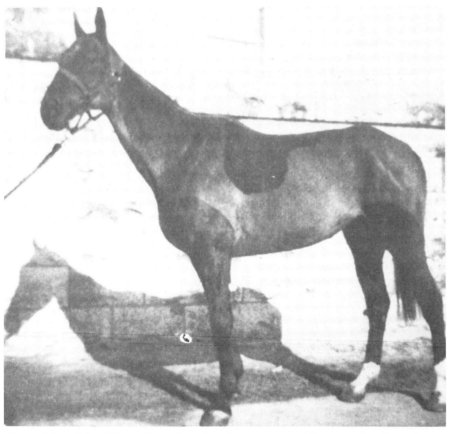

Horse Clipped for Winter *Not clipped on breast to provide protection from thorns or brush. In more open country it is customary to clip to the leg line. [Ed.] The Cavalry School.*

131

influencing factors in each instance. Clipping is not recommended under field conditions during moderately cool or cold weather, or when field service under such conditions is expected. During the severe weather in colder climates it is not advisable in most cases to clip the legs. Where animals are to receive considerable work under the saddle. it is advisable to leave a saddle patch the size of the folded blanket. This will afford protection from abrasions or from wearing away the hair of the back and is very helpful in preventing the infections of the back under the saddle that are often prevalent just before or during the spring shedding.

If clipping is practiced, it should begin in the fall before the winter coat becomes heavy. Animals should be reclipped during the winter as often as the length of the coat warrants it. Clipping under most conditions should cease as soon as spring shedding begins. Clipped animals should be warmly clothed and not exposed to low temperatures in corrals or stables. To turn clipped animals in corrals for considerable periods with protection defeats every object of clipping. As a rule, during cold weather, when not actually at work, clipped animals should be stabled and warmly blanketed. When animals are reclipped during cold weather it is advisable to exercise the animals immediately after clipping until a light sweat appears and then dry, groom thoroughly, hand-rub the body, and blanket them. Clipping must not be used as a substitute for proper grooming. Clipping lessens the labor of grooming, but the clipped animal needs the same thorough and vigorous grooming as an animal in full coat.

Power clippers are best for clipping animals, though hand clippers will serve the purpose. Clipper heads and blades must be used with care, since they are easily dulled and broken. They can and should be resharpened as often as may be necessary. Clipping should follow grooming, since many blades are broken by sand and dirt in an animal's dirty coat. While using power clippers a small pan of kerosene oil should be at hand and the clipper head immersed frequently with the machine running.

WASHING OF ANIMALS. Washing of animals as a general practice is to be strongly condemned. Routine cleaning of mud from the lower legs by washing should be prohibited. At times it may be necessary to wash the lower leg or other parts of the body to remove stain from the hair that cannot be removed by other means. Thorough drying of the wetted hair and skin is very necessary to prevent scratches or chilling. *(See footnote, page 126. Ed.)*

BLANKETING. Blankets are used for the following purposes:
    As a protection against cold and storm.
    To cool out wet or heated animals.
    To conserve the ration by conservation of heat energy during severe weather.
    To improve the coat.
    To protect thin-skinned and clipped animals from flies.
    As a protection against chill in the case of sick animals.
    Both lined and unlined blankets are issued. A serviceable fly sheet can be made from grain sacks. Horse blankets should be worn while at rest only.
    Blankets must be properly adjusted and secured; otherwise, they are apt to slip

off and become torn. All straps and fastenings must be kept in good repair. Blankets must be kept clean. Those used on animals suffering from communicable diseases must be thoroughly disinfected before being used on other animals. To assist in preventing the possible spread of skin diseases or parasites, it is advisable to stencil on the blanket the name of the horse and confine its use to that animal only.

WATERING. Under average conditions animals require about eight gallons of water per day. Excessive heat and heavy work will double ordinary requirements.

Animals suffering from communicable diseases should always have a separate watering place. When practicable, such animals should be watered from individual buckets. Neglect of these precautions may cause a disease to spread throughout the stable.

During watering there must be no shouting or confusion of any kind.

Restless and kicking animals should be watered separately.

Never allow an exhausted animal to drink his fill at once, especially if he has not been watered for some time. Give him a little at a time at five or ten-minute intervals until he is satisfied.

WATERING IN CAMP. In camp animals should be watered three times daily under average conditions. At work, especially when the weather is warm, four times daily should be the rule. Water should be given before feeding.

Amimals should not be watered for at least an hour after feeding, but they may be allowed to drink freely while at work, even though sweating. If brought in hot, they may be given a few swallows at intervals, but should be kept moving until they have cooled down.

Care should be taken not to allow too many animals to water at one time. Only such number as can be watered without crowding should be taken to the trough. They should be allowed ample time to drink their fill and not be led away the first time they raise their heads from the water. This must be carefully explained to the untrained man. Animals should be led to and from water at a walk. One man should not lead more than two animals.

EXERCISE AND CONDITIONING. These subjects are very closely related, since conditioning is largely dependent upon the exercise and feed given. Animals are considered to be in fit condition when the body and muscular organs are in condition to perform the work required without injury. Fit condition is attained by systematic exercise and feeding, which must be continued even after the condition has been attained. The work required of military animals of any type is usually done at relatively slow rates of speed, but may be continued for long hours, and possibly day after day on short rations. Endurance, stamina, a good state of flesh, and resistance to disease are necessary. These qualities can be attained only by intelligent feeding and long periods of conditioning work at the slower gaits—largely the walk. It must always be borne in mind that the riding animal for field use must carry the weight of full field equipment, and that this weight must be carried during the latter part of the conditioning period. Continued exercise with stripped saddles will never condition the animal for field service. This perfectly obvious fact has been too frequently overlooked.

The exercise must be regular and graduated, and always within the limits of the animal's strength. Working tired animals when unfit is very likely to cause accidents or disease. This is the time when they are most likely to suffer bad falls and sprains. Once animals are put in fit condition any work within reason not only is performed without great effort but adds to the quality of the condition already attained.

If animals are not worked for any considerable time the process of conditioning has to be repeated. The minimum amount of systematic exercise necessary to maintain animals in condition is two hours daily. The character of the work given animals under routine is seldom such as to maintain the animals at all times in condition to perform strenuous marching or field service. It is not desirable to maintain animals at all times at the peak of condition for field duty, but rather to have them in such condition that a relatively short period of carefully scheduled work will put them in fit condition for the anticipated duty. Ordinarily, animals regularly exercised six days a week do not suffer from being given a full day's rest on Sunday. In fact all working animals should have at least one day of rest each week, but it is important that the grain allowance be cut in half if the animals are given two or more consecutive days of complete rest.

The kind and amount of exercise given to animals depends upon the work they are to perform, the condition of the animals, and the number of men available to give the exercise. When there is one man available to exercise one or two animals, as in a troop of cavalry, the most satisfactory exercise can be had by organization under the supervision of the troop officers. But when there are many animals and few men, special means must be adopted.

Length of Time Necessary. The amount of time necessary to condition a horse properly depends upon the age, the amount and kind of previous work, the state of flesh, and the health of the animal. The mature horse that has been ridden a year or more requires at least two or three months; a five- or six-year-old that has been ridden or worked a little requires about six months; and a green, immature four-year-old requires from nine months to a year.

Any form of exercise should begin with a period of ten or fifteen minutes at a walk so that good circulation may be established. It should end at a walk in order that animals may be returned to the stables dry and breathing normally. Dirt roads should be used habitually for exercise, with only enough work on hard roads to accustom the animals to traveling on them. When one man is exercising two horses he should ordinarily ride one out and the other in, and he should lead each horse alternately on his right and left. Playful or vicious animals should be led with a very short rein to prevent accidents.

The walk is the prime conditioning gait, and is the only one not likely to be overused. As a rule, the troop horse gets more than enough galloping during the necessary training of men and maneuvering, and most of his exercise should be at the walk and trot. The length of the trot periods must be suited to the condition of the animal, but in no case should they exceed seven minutes. Walking develops muscle, and trotting and galloping develop wind. If either the trot or the gallop is used to excess, the animal will lose rather than gain condition. When horses have attained fit condition for field service, the proportion of time used at the various gaits during a daily two-hour exercise period might be: walk seven minutes, trot two minutes, gallop one minute.

The routes selected for exercise should be varied from day to day to avoid monotony. It is best to return by a different route from the one taken going out so that animals do not fret when they are headed toward the stables.

Draft and pack animals should do a considerable part of their exercise drawing loads and carrying packs so that their muscles may be hardened to the work.

Fitness of condition can be conclusively demonstrated only by a satisfactory performance of actual duty of the type for which the animal was conditioned. Test marches near the end of the conditioning period and at its termination may be made for the purpose of testing conditioning progress and determining the final degree of attained condition. The fitness of condition can, however, be less accurately judged by observation of the animal's appearance and actions. An animal in fit condition presents the general aspect of good health. He will have alert eyes and ears; a fine, glossy coat; soft, elastic skin; supple and well-developed muscles; well-let-down flanks; a good covering of flesh; a watery sweat that does not lather easily; a lack of undue thirst after hard work; a quick return to normal breathing after fast work; a good appetite; and a free, springy gait. The tendons and joints should be smooth and clean. The lower legs should not be swollen or feverish the morning following a day of hard work.

Conditioning Schedule. When it is desired to condition horses for a particular use it is necessary that a well-conceived plan and schedule of work be prepared. The nature of the plan and schedule will be determined by many influencing factors that must be carefully considered. Granting that the objective in training be the same for both, it is hardly probable that two different groups of horses will begin this conditioning period on an entirely equal basis. Each will present a separate problem. For this reason it is not feasible to outline in detail a standard schedule of conditioning work that can be indiscriminately applied. Even the plan and schedule prepared at the beginning of a conditioning period for a specific group of horses must be elastic so that it may be modified to suit the actual progress of conditioning. More, less, or different work may be desirable—the needs cannot always be foreseen.

The following is a suggested nine-week schedule aimed at fitting the horses of an average troop of cavalry for march, maneuver, or other forms of field service. It is assumed that the horses are mature, seasoned, and doing average garrison duty, which is approximately the equivalent of the work prescribed in the first week of the schedule. The animals are at what might be called the garrison level of condition. The amount and kind of feed and the methods of feeding will be varied as necessary to best meet the requirements of the individual horse and the group as a whole.

1st Week: Two hours' work daily, all at the walk except one five-minute trot period each hour; stripped saddles.

2nd Week: Two hours' work daily, all at the walk except one seven-minute trot period each hour; stripped saddles.

3rd Week: Two and one-half hours' work daily, all at the walk except one seven-minute trot period each hour; up and down gentle slopes; stripped saddles.

4th Week: Two and one-half hours' work daily, all at the walk except two seven-minute trot periods each hour; rolling country; saddles packed to carry one-half normal weight.

5th Week: Three hours' work daily, all at the walk except two seven-minute trot periods each hour; rolling country; saddles packed to carry one-half normal load.

6th Week: Same as 5th week, except carry full pack. Include a slow gallop of one mile every other day to improve wind.

7th Week: Three hours' work daily, all at the walk except three seven-minute trot periods each hour and a slow gallop of one mile every other day for wind; full pack; use one day to march eighteen miles in three hours.

8th Week: Same as 7th week, except use on day to march twenty-five miles in about five hours; and include two gallops (12 mph) of one mile each, with a ten-minute walk between, on every other day.

9th Week: Two and one-half hours' work daily, all at the walk except two or three seven-minute trot periods each hour; full pack; gallop same as 8th week.

Throughout this schedule reduce the work to about half of the usual amount on Saturdays. The horses should be turned loose in the corral for a part of the day, grazed for a half hour or more, or exercised in hand for about twenty minutes on Sundays. Do not forget that it is important that the regulation gaits be maintained at all times while marching or exercising. A five- or ten-minute halt should be made each hour to rest the animals and readjust equipment.

The following schedule of conditioning is one that was successfully used for conditioning selected Army horses for the Eastern Endurance Rides. These rides were three hundred miles in length, sixty miles per day for five days, and each day's ride to be completed within ten hours.

1st and 2nd Weeks: A.M. Monday, Wednesday, Friday: Eight miles at 6 mph. Tuesday, Thursday, Saturday: Twelve miles at 6 mph, 175 pounds up. Sunday: 1 hour walk, 15 minutes grazing.

P.M. One hour walk, 15 minutes grazing.

3rd Week: A.M. Monday, Wednesday, Friday: Walk one mile; trot and canter 3 miles (1-3 canter, 2-3 trot); then 6 miles at 6 mph, 175 pounds up. Tuesday, Thursday, Saturday: Twelve miles at 6 mph. Sunday: One hour walk, 15 minutes grazing.

P.M. One hour walk; no extra weight.

4th and 5th Weeks: A.M. Monday, Wednesday, Friday: One mile walk, 3 miles trot and canter (1-3 canter, 2-3 trot), then 6 miles at 6 mph, 175 pounds up. Tuesday, Thursday, Saturday: Fifteen miles at 6 mph, 190 pounds and up. Sunday: One hour walk; no grazing.

P.M. One hour walk; no extra weight.

136

6th Week:	A.M.	Monday, Wednesday, Friday: Walk 1 mile, trot and canter 3 miles (1-3 canter, 2-3 trot), then 6 miles at 6 mph, 175 pounds up. Tuesday, Thursday, Saturday: Fifteen miles at 6 mph, 200 pounds up.
	P.M.	One hour walk; no extra weight.
7th Week:	A.M.	Sunday, Tuesday, Thursday: Walk 1 mile, trot and canter 3 miles (½ canter, ½ trot), then 8 miles at 6½ mph, 175 pounds up. Monday, Wednesday: Eighteen miles at 6½ mph with 205 pounds up. Friday: Forty miles in 6 hours with 225 pounds up. Weigh horses before starting and after finishing, give veterinary examination after completing ride. Saturday: Inspect, weigh, and give 2 hours walk.
	P.M.	One hour walk except Friday. Further training should be same as 6th week, except full weight should be carried on days when no cantering is done.

The horses were fed in accordance with each animal's individual need up to fourteen pounds of oats and fourteen pounds of hay. Oats were fed four times daily—at 6:00 A.M., 11:30 A.M., 4:30 P.M., and 8:30 P.M. Hay was fed two pounds at 11:00 A.M., and twelve pounds at 4:00 P.M. A small quantity of bran was also fed during the first two weeks of training. Prior to the ride all horses were clipped, except a small patch on the back corresponding to the size of the saddle blanket, which gave additional padding for the saddle. Service-issue lightweight shoes were used. The shoes on the hind feet were prepared with a clip, while on the forefeet the rocker-toe shoe was used.

The following is a schedule of conditioning for point-to-point races and steeplechases.

1st Week:	Monday: School—work slowly—1 to 1½ hours.
	Tuesday: Jump course or school 1 hour.
	Wednesday: Gallop 1 mile, 15 mph—walk or lead 1 hour.
	Thursday: Work slowly 2 hours.
	Friday: Jump course or school 1 hour.
	Saturday: Gallop 1 mile, 15 mph—walk 1 hour.
	Sunday: Rest, graze 15 or 20 minutes, ½ hour lead in hand.
2nd Week:	Same as 1st week, except as noted below.
	Saturday: Gallop 1 mile, followed by 1/8 mile breeze (full speed).
3rd Week:	Same as 2nd week.
	Wednesday: Gallop cross country 3 miles.
4th Week:	Same as 1st week, except as noted below.
	Wednesday: Gallop cross country 4 miles or more.
	Saturday: Gallop 1 mile, followed by ¼ mile breeze.

5th Week: Monday: Gallop 1 mile at 20 mph—breeze ¼ mile.

                Tuesday: Work slowly—school at slow gaits—1 to 1½ hours.

                Wednesday: Jump course or school.

                Thursday: Two canters of 1 mile each at 20 mph. (Breeze ¼ mile if wind is not yet good.)

                Friday: Work very slowly—school or have led.

                Saturday: Jump course or gallop 2 miles at 12 mph.

                Sunday: Rest, graze.

6th Week: Same as 5th week.

                Saturday: Take a long cross country ride. Gallop at least 4 miles at about 20 mph.

7th Week: Same as 5th week.

                Thursday: Increase breeze to ½ mile if horse needs more wind.

8th Week: Plan on having your horse's wind and muscle at a maximum by the end of this week or just about one week before the test. Any strenuous work done the last 5 or 6 days before the test will take something out of the horse that will not come back before the test. If the horse has not enough wind a week before the test he never will have it.

                Work—Approximately the same as the 5th week.

                A week before the test the horse should get a long, cross-country gallop to really open his lungs. After that the galloping should be only short breezes of about ¼ mile, with the last breeze 2 days before the test.

RESTRAINT AND CONTROL OF ANIMALS. In the management of animals special restraint is sometimes necessary. The methods are varied, and the one to be used depends largely upon the individual animal and the object of the restraint. Always select the mildest and least dangerous method that will accomplish the end sought. It must always be remembered that kindness, perserverance, and tact will often accomplish the desired purpose with resort to special means of restraint.

Twitch. The twitch is the simplest, handiest, and most common method of the special restraint. It is, however, too often resorted to in many stables in lieu of gentler methods of persuasion. It is effective as a simple measure in the majority of cases. It should always be used with caution and only when necessary. Since it shuts off the circulation in the lip, it should never be used continuously for an extended period of time, and never with greater force than is necessary.

    A twitch is made by running a small piece of rope or rawhide through a hole in the end of a rounded piece of wood two or three feet long, such as an ax handle, and tying it into a short loop.

    A loop of the twitch is passed over the upper lip, which is seized by the hand and drawn forward, care being taken to turn the edges of the lips in so as to prevent injury to the mucous membranes. The cord is then twisted by turning the stick until sufficient pressure is obtained. As soon as the twitch is removed from the lip, the latter should be rubbed with the palm of the hand to assist in restoring the circulation. The twitch should never be applied to the ear or tongue.

Side Stick. This method of restraint is used for vicious animals to prevent them from biting while being groomed or to prevent an animal from doing injury to a wound. The side stick is a stout wooden rod from three to four feet in length, with a small cord or strap at each end, one for attaching to the noseband of the halter, the other to the surcingle.

Muzzle. This means of restraint is useful to prevent an animal from eating bedding, or chewing or tearing the dressing from a wound. Muzzles are best made of leather. They should be provided with attachments for fastening to the halter rings, or with straps that are sewed to the muzzle and fastened over the poll.

Crosstie. This consists of tying the head in an elevated position with two tie ropes. The ropes extend from the tie ring in the halter to opposite sides of the stall. The crosstie is useful in preventing an animal from chewing a wound or dressing and from lying down when it is desired to keep him standing.

Blind. Blinds are used as a means of restraint for nervous or vicious animals. The desired docility is attained by depriving the animal of sight. A blind may be made in the form of a hood or of a piece of leather broad enough to cover the eyes and provided with strings for fastening to the halter. Blindfolding is most effective when the animal is not to be moved.

Knee Strap. In shoeing an animal, or when operating on him, it may be necessary to fix a foreleg. A strap or rope is used to fasten the pastern to the forearm. The leg is first well bent at the knee. A rope or strap is then attached to the pastern by means of a loop and the free end passed over the forearm and back to the pastern, drawn tight, and tied or buckled.

Side Line. The side line is used for securing a hind leg. It is made with about twenty feet of five-eighths-inch rope and a leather hobble provided with a ring. The hobble is buckled snugly around the pastern of the leg to be raised. One end of the rope is secured around the animal's neck with a nonslip knot, and the free end of the rope is passed through the hobble ring and brought back through the neck loop. The leg is then brought forward by pulling on the free end of the rope, which is held in the desired position by an attendant, or tied to the neck loop with a single bowknot, which may be quickly released. If desired, the leg may be drawn backward by tying a rope to the hobble and having an attendant draw the leg to the rear.

Casting Rope. The casting rope is made of five-eighths- or three-fourths-inch rope and is about thirty feet long. This is doubled and then from three to four feet of the doubled end tied in a nonslip loop, which is passed over the animal's head and adjusted about the neck. The free ends are passed backward between the forelegs and around the rear pastern or through hobbles, if used, thence upward and back through the loop at the neck. A strong man should hold the animal by the head, standing on the side on which it is desired to throw the animal. When standing on the left side, the left hand should grasp the halter firmly, and when standing on the right, the right hand is used. The halter shank should be brought over the top of the neck and held in the opposite hand. Two or more assistants grasp the free end of the rope and by a quick pull to the rear, take the animal off his feet. The man at the head, acting in conjunction with them, pulls the head and neck to the ground.

139

When the animal is down the man at the head should hold the head firmly against the ground. At the same time the attendant handling the ropes on the side not against the ground should quickly draw the legs up against the side and secure them by a double half hitch made of the free ends of the rope. When one side is thus secured the animal may be rolled over and the other legs tied in a similar manner. Keeping the animal down is facilitated by the man at the head placing one knee on the neck and raising the animal's muzzle from the ground.

The animal can be cast more easily if one foreleg is secured with a knee strap. If it is desired to cast the animal on his left side, place the knee strap on the left foreleg, turn the head toward the right, and pull the left hind leg forward slightly before pulling on the right hobble rope. Should it become necessary to cast an animal without the use of hobbles, the pasterns should be bandaged to prevent rope burning.

Assistance to Cast Animals. In going to the assistance of a horse or mule that is down and unable to rise without aid the following procedure is suggested:

See that the animal has plenty of room. If it is in a single stall, pull it out into the aisle.

Turn it over, by attaching ropes to the lower hind and forefeet. Then see that the feet are on the same level with or lower than the back.

Assist the animal to roll up on its breast, and allow it to remain quiet for a few minutes.

Pull the front feet out in the position naturally assumed by a horse when it is about to rise.

Stand close against the buttocks and grasp the tail. Be prepared to exert a pull upward and forward. Leave the head alone.

Now speak sharply to the animal or slap it lightly with a strap and lift on the tail as directed above.

In case it is impossible to raise the animal by the method just described, it may be necessary to use a sling. The articles required are a block and tackle of sufficient strength and forty feet or more of rope. The block may be fastened above the animal in the stable, or in the field a tripod may be improvised from strong poles. The rope is placed around the animal as follows:

Double it, put the head through the loop, and carry the loop back to the collar seat. Pass the free ends of the rope between the front legs, crossing the ropes just before they go between the legs. Pass the lower rope under the body so that it emerges just in back of the withers.

Lay the upper rope over the chest so that it crosses the lower rope at this point.

Pass the upper rope under the body in a position corresponding to the other rope, crossing the two ropes as they emerge from between the hind legs.

Bring both ropes up over the buttocks, one on each side of the tail, and pass them forward along the back, under the crossed ropes, and tie to the loop that lies at the top of the neck. Draw the ropes as tight as possible before the knot is tied. Now attach the hook of the block under all the ropes at the point on the back where they intersect, namely, the single strands crossing to go between the hind legs and the double strand coming forward from the tail, and you are ready to raise the animal.

140

RECORDS. *Ed Note: In the cavalry it was mandatory for the stable sergeant to maintain the following records: List of public animals by brand number, record of stable property, forage record, shoeing record, morning report (showing number of horses and mules available for duty, in hospital, sick in stable, or being shod), and sick report. Of these, only the shoeing record is reproduced below.*

SHOEING RECORD

NAME	JAN	FEB	MAR	APR	MAY	JUN	JUL	AUG	SEP	OCT	NOV	DEC	REMARKS
Ranger	(3)	(9)	(11)	(10)	(15)	— —	—	— —	(26)	(18)	(20)	(19)	(23)	Hind shoes removed and not replaced March 11. All shoes removed May 15. Sick in stable May 15 to August 25
	(15)	— —	— —	(22)	— —	— —	—	— —	(30)	—	— —	— — —	

Explanation: The circle appearing in the rectangle for any month represents the body of the horse. The lines outward from the circumference represent the legs. The number in the circle is the day of the month. Thus in the case of Ranger, this horse lost the shoe from his right fore on January 3 and the record shows it was replaced that date. On January 15 the other three feet were shod. On February 9 he was shod all around. On March 11 he was shod in front and the Remarks show that his hind shoes were pulled and left off. On April 10 he was shod in front. On April 22 he was shod behind. On May 15 all shoes were removed and not replaced. On August 26 he was again shod all around.

8

Care of Horses in the Field

Ed Note: In the original Cavalry Manual *this chapter dealt extensively with the care of animals on campaign, where the exigencies of wartime conditions were stressed. Adapted below are those sections which would pertain particularly to endurance trail rides and, to a limited extent, to fox hunting, three day eventing (combined training), or mounted camping trips. The term* field *service as used herein is intended, therefore, to cover strenuous mounted activities away from the normal stable facilities to which the horse is accustomed.*

The general principles of caring for horses in the field are the same as those governing their care in stable, as discussed in other chapters of this text. The methods of care in the field are but modifications of those employed in stable. They are modified only to the extent ddemanded by the changed and changing conditions encountered. The feed bag replaces the feedbox, the ground replaces the niceties of well-bedded stall and serves as a manger, while a few trees or the lee of a hill afford the horse's only protection from the elements. The horse works harder in the field, has less protection, and often has to eat less than in stable. For these reasons, the care given him must be the best possible under every circumstance or condition.

PREPARATION FOR FIELD SERVICE. The foundation of successful work in the field is laid in the stable. In addition to the routine training of horses and riders, the following subjects must be given careful attention in the final stages of preparation.

Selection and Elimination of Horses. Active competition away from normal stabling facilities is far more rigorous than that conducted under normal routine. Many horses suitable for routine riding are wholly unsuitable for extended work. Among

142

these are horses that are too young or too old, those with partially disabling unsoundness, those with defects of conformation, which will result in injuries when they are worked hard, and those which by their past performances have proved themselves to be lacking in stamina. These animals should be eliminated before the final stages of training, and care must be exercised that such animals are not selected for use by newly activated units. Horses under five years of age are too young, and often six years is a better minimum age. Those over fifteen years of age are approaching the age of senility, but some individuals beyond this age will render excellent service.

Conditioning. If great losses are to be avoided, horses must be properly conditioned before going to field service. The importance of fit condition cannot be over-emphasized. Conditioning is continuous because every minute of properly conducted routine work or exercise contributes to the animal's physical fitness. However, during a period of about two months just prior to entering upon field service, special attention should be given, concurrently with other training, to a systematic program aimed at attaining the high level of condition so necessary for field service. The details of conditioning are discussed on page

Shoeing. The normal sequence of shoeing should not be disrupted by a frenzied attempt to reshoe all horses within the last few days before going into the field. If it is, most of the animals will require their next reshoeing in the field within a limited space of time and the horseshoers will be overworked. Horses should be conditioned while wearing the type and weight of shoe to be worn in the field. Light or medium weight shoes are most suitable; or medium weight in size three and larger. The rougher footing usually encountered during field service makes bruises and penetrations of the sole more probable, and for this reason more sole must be left on the foot than is usually the case in garrison shoeing. The extra fitted shoes, one fore and one hind, required for each horse should be of recent make and properly identified. When horses are used on average routes with fifty to seventy-five percent of the distance hard-surfaced, the average life of the service issue shoe will probably be about 250-275 miles. Certain types of concrete roads will wear shoes out in half of this distance.

Equipment. Saddle and harness equipment should be fitted to the individual horse prior to the conditioning period so that it may shape to the animal and be well broken in. Thereafter it should not be shifted from animal to animal, except when a change may be made necessary by a marked gain or loss of flesh. Last-minute issue of stiff, new saddle and harness equipment is certain to result in many equipment-caused injuries.

Clipping. As a general rule, horses should not be clipped for field service, except during hot weather or in warm or tropical climates.

CARE ON THE MARCH. The factors discussed in the following pages directly or indirectly affect the animal's efficiency while marching and must be given proper consideration in march planning and in the conduct of the march.

Rate and Length of March. Horse cavalry on good roads in daylight under favorable conditions, well-seasoned and properly conditioned, is able to march thirty-five miles per day at the rate of five to five and one-half miles per hour for six days a week as long as the situation requires. However, this rate and length of march will probably result in a considerable loss in flesh after a week or ten days of marching. When the mission and tactical situation demand, cavalry can, for short periods, materially increase its length of march. Ordinarily, forced marches are made by increasing the number of marching hours rather than by increasing the hourly rate of march. For short forced marches the rate may be increased. Marches over thirty-five miles per day are classed as forced marches. Marches up to one hundred miles in length can be made within twenty-four hours. If horses are to be marched many days and not lose flesh during the march, it is probable that the weekly march cannot exceed about one hundred and fifty miles. Long marches at more rapid rates and long forced marches should be followed by a period of rest or lighter work for recuperation and regaining of lost flesh. Horse artillery can travel at the same rate as cavalry on roads and under favorable conditions cross-country. Light wagons can travel at the same rate as mounted units except under difficult cross-country conditions. Assuming the horses are in fit condition, there are many factors concerning the well-being of the animals that will influence the march. These factors will be discussed in the following pages. From the horse's point of view, the length of a march is not only to be estimated in miles, but also with regard to the number of hours the load is to be carried. This latter consideration may be the more important of the two. If the load is carried all of the time, a march of five miles in four hours may be more productive of fatigue and injury than a march of fifteen or twenty miles in the same time. A march of twenty-five to thirty miles in four hours might be even more conducive to bad effects. A proper balance of time and rate must be struck. The maintenance of a good average rate throughout the march is to be desired, and provided it is not unduly hurried at any point, the quicker a march is completed the less fatiguing it is to both horse and rider.

Route. Other things being equal, the shortest route should be selected. Level or slightly rolling terrain is least tiring. If watering en route might be advisable or necessary, the availabilty of watering points must be considered. Where roads are used, the type of road surface must be considered with reference to its effect on the marching rate and the production of fatigue or injuries. From the viewpoint of ease of travel and minimum likelihood of injury to the animal, a road of fine, closely packed, pebble gravel is quite ideal under practically all conditions of weather. Improved dirt roads, except when muddy or rather dusty, are equally good. Because of their slippery or boggy condition, muddy roads are very fatiguing, cause sprains and strains, sometimes loosen the shoes, and always increase the number of interfering wounds. Dust is not particularly bothersome to individual horsemen or small groups, but in larger commands dust may be very harmful to the animal's efficiency. A horse probably can travel on a concrete road with the least fatigue, but at the expense of rapid wear on the shoes and greater likelihood of injury to the feet caused by concussion, especially at the more rapid rates of march. Much marching on concrete, or other types of equally hard roads, is certain to result in an appreciable increase in the incidence of lameness due to corns and other foot injuries caused by concussion. Sprains of joints and strains of tendons will be less common than when traveling on soft but uneven roads. Gravel or rock roads bound with road oil or asphalt are quite satisfactory when the temperature is moderate. During hot weather the surface frequently softens and becomes sticky. In addition to causing loosened or cast shoes, it makes traveling more difficult and the feet may become hot from the heat transmitted from the road surface. During very cool or cold weather, such a road surface becomes very firm and often extremely slippery. Loose, coarse, crushed rock, sometimes found on new roads of this type and frequently along the shoulders of hard-surfaced roads, offers very poor footing and often causes severe injuries to the soles of the feet. Travel in dry sand is very fatiguing, but wet sand furnishes ideal footing. When moving cross-country, firm turf, the perfect footing, should be sought.

Weather. Weather conditions have a marked effect on the marching efficiency of horses. Temperature is the most important single factor. Horses suffer far less from extremes of cold than from even moderate heat. Low temperatures alone have little or no effect on the marching ability of the horse. However, he must be prevented from chilling during halts, particularly if sweaty. Wet snow packs firmly in the feet, causes slipping, and makes travel very difficult. Dry snow, unless it is very deep, is not a considerable hinderance to marching. Sleet- or ice-covered roads or ground are very hazardous and may make movement difficult or well nigh impossible. Changing to calked shoes in the field to meet this hazard, which is usually temporary, is seldom practicable. High temperature has a more adverse affect on the rate of march more than it has on the length of the day's march. Dry heat is far less damaging than moist heat. The former greatly increases the horse's need for water. Heat associated with a high degree of humidity is ever more enervating for horses than for men. It will greatly reduce the marching rate, since it causes thumps, overheating (heat prostration), and exhaustion—the most common forms of disability occurring during the day's march. The temperature for the horse's most efficient marching performance is probably below sixty degrees Fahrenheit, and his efficiency begins to drop quite markedly when the temperature rises above seventy-five to eighty degrees. Moderate or intermittent rains are refreshing, but long-continued wet weather is productive of troubles other than those caused by its bad effect on the footing. The equipment becomes waterlogged and the load carried by the horse is thereby considerably increased; the sodden and mud-splattered blanket softens, abrades, or scalds the skin of the back; the disease known as scratches may appear; and the overly softened hoofs hold the shoes less securely. Sudden and violent hail storms frighten horses and have caused marching units to stampede. Wind is desirable, except when weather is cold or when it creates dust storms.

Time of Departure. It is seldom advisable to start the day march before daylight, even with the object of avoiding heat. In the dark, feeding arrangements are not satisfactory, saddles and equipment are often not properly adjusted, and articles may be unseen and left behind. However, day marches in the combat area will be the exception rather than the rule. If the hour of departure is long after dark, saddling in the dark will be necessary, but the equipment may be packed ready for saddling before darkness falls. Night marches are always more fatiguing than day marches, mainly because of the slower rate necessary. Injuries to the heels of the hind feet (treads) caused by jamming up in the column, and other accidental injuries, are more common during night marches.

Gaits. The normal marching gaits are the lead and walk at four miles per hour and the trot at eight miles per hour. The gallop, normally twelve to fourteen miles per hour, is used only under exceptional circumstances. Moderately frequent changes of the gait used are desirable for the well-being of the horse.

The lead is used chiefly for the purpose of resting both the horse and his rider. It should be used for a few minutes at the beginning of the day's march as a means of limbering the horse and establishing good circulation in his feet before he is mounted. A short lead of about three minutes into each hourly halt is desirable. There are more benefits derived from leading into a halt than from leading out of a halt. Horses should always be led to and from water and up and down long steep hills. Longer periods at the lead may become desirable or even necessary when the horse becomes excessively fatigued or exhausted on a long march. Under such circumstances and when leading up long hills, the maintenance of regulation rate is often impracticable. Horses should be led the last half mile into the bivouac site.* Most benefit is derived by leading with loosened cinches, except when to do so will cause a marked displacement of the saddle.

Since the walking rate of four miles per hour is somewhat faster than the average horse will attain if given his own choice in the matter, it is necessary that he be trained to maintain this rate. Walking is the gait that can be performed with least expenditure of energy, but if maintained uninterruptedly for long periods it becomes very tiring to the horse because of the weight he is carrying and the continued use of particular muscles.

The trot at eight miles per hour is quite easily attained by even the horses that are the slowest in their execution of this gait. Unlike at the walk, the usual fault at the trot lies in exceeding the prescribed gait, especially during the early stages of the day's march when the horses are fresh and spirited. There can be no doubt that the trot requires a greater expenditure of energy than the walk. It has been estimated that it takes approximately twice as much energy to trot a given distance as it takes to walk the same distance. Since the rate of the trot is twice that of the walk, it is obvious that any given period of time at the trot uses up four times as much energy as would be used during the same period at the walk. For this reason trot periods should be relatively short to avoid the fatigue caused by undue taxing of the body muscles, heart, and wind. Short periods at the trot, not to exceed seven minutes, alternated with short walks, are probably the most economical way of utilizing the horse's power in marching. Trotting should be confined as far as possible to level ground or up and down gentle grades. It is better to trot down a hill than to trot up a hill, and trotting up or down long or steep slopes should be avoided. Trotting on hard-surfaced roads is to be avoided if more suitable footing can be selected.

*Bivouac *is the military term for a temporary campsite.* [*Ed.*]

Formation. The type of formation affects the animal efficiency of a marching command in several ways. Marching in a column of twos keeps the animals cooler during hot weather and causes fewer tread wounds than marching in a column of fours. A column of twos, with a column of riders on each shoulder or edge of the road surface, is excellent for the horses, provided the road is not dusty and swept by a cross wind or is not carrying heavy motor traffic. In the case of dusty roads or heavy traffic it is better to travel in a column of twos on one road shoulder or side of the road surface proper, and on the leeward side in the case of dust. Distances between units should, if possible, be increased when marching on dusty roads. Few modern motorists realize that a horse cannot always be steered with the same precision as a car. This has led to many serious accidents. Placing an outrider at the head of the column and one at the tail of the column for the purpose of warning motor traffic is frequently a worthwhile procedure. Proper distance between horses, four feet from head to croup, must be maintained. The tendency is always toward a lesser distance, resulting in injury to the heels of the horse in front and possibly kick injuries to the horse that is closing the distance. When marching cross-country, dispersed formations with a wide front add to the horses' comfort.

Halts. Halts are made during a day's march for the purpose of resting the animals and men and preparing for the next period of marching. It is well to think of a day's march as being composed of a series of short marches, each of less than an hour's duration, usually fifty to fifty-five minutes, and each followed by a five- to ten-minute period of rest and preparation for the next short march.

The first halt of the day is of ten to fifteen minutes duration and is best made after about thirty to forty-five minutes of marching. This is often referred to appropriately as the "shakedown" halt. It follows a short period of relatively slow marching during which the horses are slowly warmed up by leading and walking for ten to fifteen minutes and then given one or two short trots, which will suffice to shake down the equipment so as to expose errors in the packing or saddling. The "shakedown" march is usually two or three miles in length. This early morning exercise usually stimulates the bowels and kidneys to the extent that the horses have a desire to relieve themselves. The riders are likewise frequently so affected. After attending to these matters, the feet are examined, the errors of packing and saddling are corrected, the cinches tightened, and the command is ready to get on with the serious business of the day's march.

After the shakedown halt, halts of five to ten minutes duration are made after each fifty to fifty-five minutes of marching. These are called hourly halts. It is best that they be preceded immediately by a short lead of about three minutes, preferably with the cinches loosened. At each halt the rider examines his horse's feet and shoes, checks the general condition of his horse, and makes such adjustments of his riding equipment as may be necessary. The cinch is not tightened until just before resuming the march. When marching on roads, the road should be cleared at the halt. More injuries are caused by vehicles passing during halts than while marching. The few mouthfuls of grass that the horse may be offered or may snatch at each halt can do him no harm, but on the contrary help to augment his never-too-plentiful field ration, and the few swallows of water that he may be so fortunate as to find in some roadside depression should not be denied him. To prevent dis-

147

comfort or chilling during cold weather, the halt need be only long enough to complete the usual necessary tasks. During very hot weather, the hourly halt may of necessity be extended beyond the usual maximum of ten minutes in order to give the fatigued or exhausted horses adequate rest. The necessary length of halts can seldom be foreseen and fully provided for in a march schedule prepared before the march. A halt for watering during the day's march should, whenever possible, be made to coincide with the hourly halt.

A long halt of one to four hours is sometimes made near the middle of a long day's march to escape the midday heat, to give the horses a chance to rest and be fed, or possibly to take advantage of a good opportunity to graze. Except to avoid excessive midday heat, long halts are not ordinarily considered necessary unless the total day's marching time is in excess of six or eight hours. The wisdom of using long halts was repeatedly proven by cavalry and wagon train commanders in the days of our American Indian campaigns. During a long halt the horses are unsaddled, bridles are removed, the horses watered as soon as cool enough, a feed of grain is given, and the men eat their carried lunch. The horses are often grazed before resaddling and resuming the march.

Watering. Under favorable weather conditions (cool or cold) horses can complete a normal day's march without being watered en route and suffer no ill effects. On the other hand, when weather is hot and dry and the marching rate is fast, the horses may be rather seriously in need of water as frequently as every two or three hours. The horse's need for water is in direct proportion to the amount of water lost by sweating. It must be borne in mind that a comparatively dry coat is not always an indication that the horse is not losing a great deal of water by sweating. When the day is hot and the humidity low, the sweat evaporates rapidly and the horse may appear to be sweating very little yet may be sweating excessively and losing great quantities of water. When the humidity is high the same amount of work may cause the horse to be dripping with sweat, yet the water loss is no higher than in the former instance. In the latter case the cooling effect of sweating is very slight, and it is under these conditions that horses suffer most and may become overheated.

Were it always possible and feasible to water horses whenever they are thirsty, they would unquestionably hold up under field service much better than is ordinarily the case. Frequently the scarcity of water or the exigencies of service make it necessary that horses go without water longer than is good for them. Nothing contributes more to a rapid loss of flesh and condition than a shortage of water. When a horse is receiving insufficient water or is deprived of water, he loses much of his appetite for feed and is unable to digest and assimilate properly what he does eat. Horses that receive an adequate amount of salt will suffer less from sweating and shortage of water. Horses can carry on without water for many hours. The horses of several of the divisions in Allenby's force during the Palestine and Egyptian campaigns (1917) were unavoidably forced to go without water for periods of thirty-six to eighty-four hours. They, of course, suffered much and lost a great deal of flesh, which was hard to replace, but the military mission was accomplished.

Horses should be watered just before leaving the bivouac site at the beginning of the day's march. Whether the horses will need watering one or more times during the day's march must be determined by the factors previously discussed above. Unless excessively thirsty, horses on the march, even though they be warm and sweaty, may be given their fill of water with safety, provided they are immediately continued on the march at the walk for a period of at least ten to fifteen minutes before they are halted or trotted. Horses should be led to and away from the watering points, not more than two horses per man. The bridle should be removed and the horse held by the tie rope after passing the neck loop over the head. Halting at the watering point after watering may cause the animals to chill. In estimating the number of animals that can be watered at one time along a given water frontage, it has been customary to assume that each animal requires about six feet of space; however, horses may be quite satisfactorily watered on a frontage of three feet for each horse. Clear, clean water is desirable, but seemingly horses can drink almost any kind of water with safety, except that which is contaminated with specific disease-producing organisms or chemical poisons. Anthrax is the only serious disease of horses that is likely to be water-borne in running streams. Horses can safely drink water that would be wholly unfit for human consumption. Sewage contamination, which is so dangerous to humans, does not in itself render water unsafe for horses. Water in swamps, stagnant ponds, or roadside pools, even though covered with a scum of water fungi, should not be considered unusable in an emergency, or rejected as a source, except when better water is available. Water in water troughs or tanks used by civilian animals is the most dangerous and should be avoided, especially in territory recently held by the enemy. Practical determination in the field as to the freedom of water in streams from disease-producing or chemical contamination may of necessity be limited to an upstream reconnaissance for the presence of animal carcasses or other evidence of gross contamination. Horses seem to exercise little aesthetic sense in their selection of water, but at times even the rather thirsty horse will refuse water with certain off flavors or odors. However, this can seldom be taken as an indication of its unfitness for use. Long-continued consumption of water roiled with rather coarse sand from the bottom of a stream or pond may result in the intake of enough sand to cause sand colic or a general unthriftiness. Canvas buckets are used when watering from wells or when the nature of the banks of a stream or pond makes it impossible to lead the horse to water. When the amount of water is limited, watering from a bucket will often prevent wastage. Even a very few swallows of water will do much to revive a fatigued horse. Wiping the eyes, nostrils, and lips with a wet grooming cloth will help to refresh the horse, especially when marching on dusty roads.

Feeding. Horses are not fed during a day's march other than has been discussed on page 148.

Shoeing. In a group of any size some shoes are certain to loosen and others to be lost in the course of a day's march. Loose shoes are tightened on the march by the horseshoer. In the case of a lost shoe, the foot is temporarily reshod by the horseshoer with one of the fitted shoes carried by the rider for that purpose, or, if the remaining distance and road surface will permit completing the march without severe damage to the hoof, the foot may be left unshod until the bivouac site is reached. In case the lost shoe cannot be replaced, a grooming cloth or sack wrapped over the bottom of the foot will help to prevent damage to the hoof. The rider should be trained to watch for loosening shoes on horses near him, particularly on the horse in front of him in column whose feet he can readily observe.

Swimming. Horses are often forced to cross streams by fording or swimming. Both of these methods may effect the well-being of the horse. Accidents occur frequently when horses become bogged in the deep mud of stream banks. Should a bogged horse be unable to extricate himself after being freed of his equipment and urged to exert himself, it will be necessary to use force to pull him out. Although this method is not without hazard the best way to apply force is by pulling on a rope that has been run through the halter ring and then tied rather loosely around the horse's neck with a nonslip knot. The traction applied should be steady and, if possible, straightforward in prolongation of the long axis of the body. When horses are wet after fording or swimming a stream, they should not be halted and permitted to chill, but should be kept moving. The horse is a natural and very powerful swimmer, being able to breast successfully a current that would sweep a man away. He is not naturally a water-loving animal and will rarely enter the water and swim unless urged to do so or in order to follow another animal. Horses frequently drown or suffer from water-inhalation pneumonia following immersion as a result of failure to appreciate the fact that a swimming horse must not be pulled through the water by a rope attached to the halter. He can be guided readily with the halter rope, but when a strong pulling traction is applied, the horse's head will go under, he will become frantic, and may give up and quickly drown. Horses can swim while carrying a saddle and rider, and even while carrying a loaded pack saddle. However, pack saddle loads should be removed whenever possible. Top-heavy loads are particularly dangerous, since they are likely to turn the horse over on his back in the water and cause certain drowning.

Diseases and Injuries. All personnel should be constantly alert for the detection of sick or injured animals during the day's march. Every horse should be examined for evidence of injury at each halt. While the symptoms of almost any disease may first become apparent during the day's march, the diseases or conditions caused by overwork or fatigue—thumps. overheating, and exhaustion—are several times more likely to appear than all of the other diseases combined. They are all caused by overwork, and the means of prevention are self-evident. Thumps is usually the first of these diseases to occur, and it should be taken as a warning that unless the rate of march is reduced, dangerous overheating or exhaustion is certain to follow. Equipment-caused injuries are the type of injury most frequently incurred during the day's march. They seldom are of such immediate severity that they affect the animal's ability to complete the days' march, but they will, unless properly relieved, lead to the loss of use of the animal. Many equipment-caused injuries can best be prevented by exercising proper preventive measures during the day's march. (See page 188 for a complete discussion of the causes, prevention, and first-aid treatment of injuries of this type.) Wounds caused by interfering are of rather frequent occurrence. They may be prevented by the use of leather interfering boots. Each group should be equipped with a few of these boots. They are not an item of issue but can be made by any saddler. The prevention and first-aid treatment of the various other diseases and injuries that may affect animals during the day's march are fully outlined in chapter 9.

Last Hour of March. The last period of marching before arrival at the bivouac should be almost an exact reversal of the marching procedure followed in the initial or "shakedown" period of marching at the beginning of the day's march. As the horses were gradually warmed up at the beginning of the march, so should they be cooled out as the march is ending. About the last fifteen minutes should be at the walk, including a lead with cinches loosened for about the last half mile into the bivouac (five to eight minutes). This not only rests the horse and cools him out, but rests the rider and takes the kinks out of his muscles so that he is better able to care for his horse as soon as the bivouac is reached.

BIVOUAC SITE. The factors that influence the comfort and safety of the horses must be considered in the selection of a bivouac site. Water for animals, as well as for men, must be available at or close to the bivouac of a mounted command. Streams of ponds, preferably the former, are the usual sources of water for animals. A very small stream may have to be dammed in order to provide sufficient water. Frequently the most level and inviting area for a bivouac along a stream will be within a bend of the stream and but slightly above sea level. Such a site should be avoided if there is the slightest danger of a sudden rain causing a flooding of the stream. The high-water level of a stream is usually marked by the presence of driftwood and debris in bushes and trees, and a site above its level should be selected. Many bivouacs have been washed out and valuable equipment and lives lost by failure to observe this simple rule. Next to water, natural cover or protection from the elements and enemy observation or fire is the most important consideration. Trees, bushes, or even the leeward side of a hill will supply needed cover. The best possible standings for the horses should be selected. They should be as level as possible and free from large rocks so that the tired horse may lie down and get his much-needed rest. The area provided for the animals should be sufficiently large that animals can be reasonably dispersed so as to minimize injury to each other and reduce casualties should the area be bombed or shelled. The area used should have sufficient exits so that the animals may be quickly and widely dispersed or the command moved out promptly in case of an attack.

CARE OF ANIMALS IN BIVOUAC OR CAMP. Like the hourly halt, the halt for the night is for the purpose of resting the animals.

Care of Animals Upon Arrival in Bivouac. Upon arrival in the assigned area, the horses are tied to trees or on picket lines if use of the latter is necessary or desirable, and unbridled. To facilitate unsaddling, the cantle roll is removed and the loads are removed from the pack saddles. The saddles are removed at once so as to relieve the horse of his load at the earliest possible moment. The folded saddle blanket is turned over and immediately placed on the horse's back with the dry side next to the back, being secured in position with the surcingle. This protects the hot and sweaty back from chilling or sunburning and allows the back to dry and cool out slowly. If hay is available, about a fourth of the day's ration is now placed in front of the horse and the tie rope adjusted to the proper length for feeding. The horse is not bothered for about twenty minutes while he eats hay. Like a very tired person under similar circumstances, the fatigued horse seems to appreciate and be considerably benefitted by this period of undisturbed rest and relaxation. The blanket is then removed, unfolded, and spread out to sun and dry. The back is examined for swellings or other evidences of injury. Any swelling on the back should be given prompt first-aid treatment by the rider. Apply a cold wet pack made from a folded grooming cloth or sponge soaked in cold water and held in place with the surcingle. Should the back not be entirely dry when the blanket is removed, the hair should be ruffled and dried with the grooming cloth or a wisp of grass or hay. The back and legs are then massaged and the horse groomed. Forty-five minutes or more having elapsed since arrival in bivouac, the horse is watered, being allowed to drink his fill. As soon as he returns from watering he will be fed about a third of the daily ration of grain, which has been placed in the feed bag. The feed bag must be properly adjusted. The poll strap should be adjusted so that the horse can reach the grain and yet not be so tight as to force the muzzle against the bottom of the bag. The neck strap, placed well forward on the neck, should be adjusted short enough so that the grain will slide forward toward the horse's mouth when his head is lowered. The muzzle opening adjusting strap should be adjusted tight enough that grain will not be thrown out if the head is tossed and yet not so tight as to interfere with the animal's breathing. A wad of hay placed between the sides of the opening will help prevent grain from being tossed out of the bag and yet will not interfere with breathing. A very tired or exhausted horse will often refuse his grain at this time. Should the horse not eat, remove the feed bag and allow him to eat hay for an hour or more before again offering grain. The horse will usually eat after this further period of rest. The feed bag should be removed as soon as the horse has finished eating and its inner surfaces wiped with grass or hay and exposed to the sun to dry.

Restraint. Whether horses are tied to trees or to picket lines, the tie should be of the proper length and the knot secure. Many horses are injured in bivouac or camp because of improper tying. Tie ropes that are tied too long are certain to result in leg injuries (rope burns). Insecure tying results in loose horses, which are subjected to kicks or which may gain access to and gorge themselves on grain. All personnel in a group should be trained to tie with the same kind of knot. The knots shown on pages   and   are excellent knots for tying to a picket line, and the modified clove hitch shown on page 153 is the best type of knot for use on a tree or post. The modified clove hitch is very secure, can be easily untied, and the tie will not slip down the tree. The length of tie shown is correct. When picket lines are used, they should be at a height of about four to five feet, securely anchored, and taut. In wooded terrain they may be stretched between trees, but in open areas they must be elevated by the use of improvised supports and ends of the lines securely anchored to pins, stakes, or a deadman. Tying horses to dead limbs or trees may lead to serious accidents.

Feeding. The methods of feeding shortly after arrival in bivouac have been explained above.

Hay should always be fed in bivouac and never at march halts, although grazing

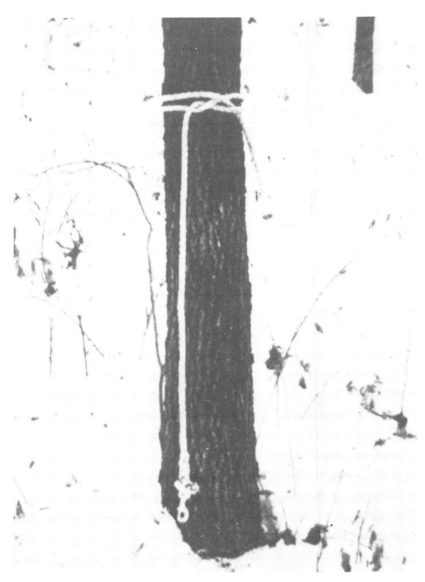

Modified Clove Hitch *The Cavalry School.*

at halts should be encouraged. After feeding about one-fourth of the daily allowance soon after arrival in bivouac, the balance of the hay should be fed in small amounts several times during the day, the last feeding being just at nightfall. Feeding in small amounts prevents wastage caused by hay being blown away or trampled into the ground. The picket-line guard should keep the hay raked into the center of the line or within reach of the horses if they are tied to trees. The bales of hay should be opened on the line or wherever they are to be fed so as to avoid the wastage certain to result should they be opened elsewhere and the loose hay carried

153

to the horses. Protection of baled hay from ground moisture or rain is of no importance in an overnight bivouac, but if a camp is to be occupied for a longer period the hay should be placed on some type of dunnage and covered with canvas. Hay that has become wet is safe for feeding, provided it is not fermenting or has not become moldy. While the feeding of moldy hay is not considered a good practice, there may well be times in the field when shortage of forage and the pressing need for feed will warrant its use. Moldy bales should be opened, aired, sunned, and shaken out before use.

Grain should be fed at least three times daily if possible. The first grain feed is given shortly after arrival in bivouac. The next feed is given after the late afternoon or evening watering, and the last feed is given early the following morning. If a long halt for feeding has been made during the day's march, only an evening and morning feed is given in bivouac. Grain should be measured into the feed bags directly from the sacks. To assure accurate feeding and to save work the following morning, the grain for the morning feed should be put in the feed bags after the evening feeding of grain and the grain that is to be carried on the next day's march put in the grain bags. If it can be definitely foreseen that feeding during the day's march will not be necessary and that grain will be available at the next bivouac, grain should not be carried in the grain bag. The eight pounds of oats, two feeds, in a full grain bag adds materially to the horse's tiring load. The comments made with reference to the protection of hay and feeding of wet or damaged hay are equally applicable to grain. In addition, it is important that grain be protected from loose horses. A loose horse that eats his fill of grain is almost certain to develop colic or laminitis. Should grain be spilled on the ground in front of a horse, especially if the ground is sandy, it should be swept up, for in retrieving the spilled grain the horse may eat harmful amounts of sand.

Salt is a very essential part of a horse's diet in the field, and it should be fed as described on page 101.

Watering. Horses are watered shortly after arrival in bivouac. They are watered one or more times before nightfall, depending upon the hour of going into bivouac and their need for water. The evening watering should be shortly before the evening feed of grain. Should the horse's pasterns get wet and muddy they should be wiped dry after returning from water so as to prevent scratches, especially during cold weather. Horses are not watered in the morning before feeding grain, since they usually will not drink well at that time. They should be watered as late as possible before beginning the day's march, usually just prior to saddling or after saddling and before moving out. This is an hour or more after their morning grain is fed, and they may be watered with safety and should be encouraged to drink their fill. Methods of watering and sources and quality of water have been discussed on page 148.

Grooming. One complete and thorough grooming, which is given within the first hour after arrival, is normally the only complete grooming during an overnight bivouac. However, just before saddling in the morning the feet should be cleaned, and the coat quickly brushed to remove adherent dirt, paying particular attention to see that the back is clean.

Protection from Weather. While the horse can endure extremes of temperature and changes of weather better than man can, such conditions do affect his state of flesh and condition, and he should be afforded every practical protection in the field. Extremes of heat and the usually associated bothersome insects are very conducive to weight loss. When a saddle blanket is used as a cover for the horse in bivouac, it usually finds its way to where most blankets get—under the hind feet. This results in dirty and torn blankets that will cause back injuries when they are put to their normal use under the saddle. Carrying stable horse covers in the field is unthinkable. Trees, brushes, and terrain features must be utilized to their fullest advantage. Horses should not be clipped during field service, except as necessary in some cases in a semitropical or tropical climate or when horses are moved from a cool to a hot climate.

Standings. A good place for the horse to stand and lie down while he is in bivouac is essential if he is to get the maximum amount of rest and proper protection from injuries. A good, firm turf is unexcelled as a standing. In any event the standing should be as firm, smooth, and well drained as possible. The standing should be free of rocks and stubs that may cause injury. In swamps and jungles the ground should be freed of trailing or creeping vines in which the horse's feet may become entangled. When an area is to be occupied for several days, clearing the weeds and underbrush from the vicinity of the horse lines will greatly abate the insect nuisance. Grading or leveling of picket-line standings or frequent changes of their location will be necessary during wet weather if the camping area is occupied more than a day or so.

Care of Equipment. Proper attention to the care and necessary readjustment of riding equipment while in bivouac will do much to prevent equipment-caused injuries during the march. The cause of any saddle sore inflicted during the march should be determined, the cause removed, and steps taken to protect the injured area during the subsequent marches. As soon as the saddle blanket has been dried in the sun, it should be cleaned by alternately working the caked or sweat-marked areas between the two hands and brushing with the horse brush until it is clean and soft. It should be refolded by employing the same folds previously used. Just before saddling, the side to be placed next to the back should be given a final inspection. Blankets should be washed, stretched, and dried whenever their condition requires and the situation permits. Fold lines should be changed after washing to avoid excessive wear along the folds. Bits should be kept free of caked dirt, but the exposed portions of the bit should not be polished. Leather should be clean and pliable so that those parts which contact the horse will be less likely to cause injury. Excessive oiling or soaping of such parts will irritate the skin, especially during hot weather.

Shoeing. All well-finished jobs of shoeing must of necessity be done while the horses are in bivouac. At the end of the day's march each horse's feet should be inspected and the animals with lost or loose shoes given first attention. When a lost shoe has been hurriedly replaced with a fitted shoe during the day's march, it will frequently be found desirable to smooth up the job or reset the shoe in bivouac. Because of the increased amount of shoeing that must be done with limited equipment, it is not to be expected that the shoeing job will have the niceties of finish expected in stable. Utility rather than smoothness of finish should be sought. Clinches should be strong, even though rough, so long as they do not cause injury. They should not be weakened by rasping to improve their appearance. Weak clinches are the most common cause of loosened and lost shoes. Horses are almost always reshod in stable because the hoof has grown too long. Worn-out shoes will likely be the reason for reshoeing in the field in at least half of the instances. Shoes should be used to the limit of their wearing life—until broken or ready to break or worn so thin that they do not offer adequate protection. Shoes are often replaced in stable before they are much more than half worn out When a command is marching 150 miles or more each week over an extended period, it will probably be necessary to reshoe the equivalent of at least six or seven percent of the horses each day. Under some conditions the number will be much greater. Horseshoers almost always have to work on march rest days in order to keep the horses shod. On protracted marches, rest days may have to be ordered for no other reason than to provide time for shoeing.

Stampedes. Animals are liable to panic and may stampede for what appear to be very trivial causes. Sudden storms; noise of an unexpected nature, such as thunder or hail; the presence of loose animals; wild animals passing through the camp; swarms of bees or flies; and grass fires in the vicinity are all known causes, but on some occasions the reason has not been apparent. Should a large body of animals suddenly dash in one direction, probably nothing can stop them. A strict supervision over the picket lines and the presence of men at the heads of the animals, when the occasion can be foreseen, are the best means of averting disaster. Turning animals loose on the way to and from the watering place should be prohibited. Stray animals of every sort should be prevented from entering camp.

Sanitation. Animal sanitation in a overnight bivouac does not present much of a problem. The sanitary considerations in connection with water have largely been discussed on page 149. The point selected on a stream for watering horses should be downstream from the point for water for cooking and drinking and upstream from the points designated for bathing or washing clothing, vehicles, or equipment. When vacating an overnight bivouac, the manure should be thinly scattered on the ground in the vicinity of the lines so that it will dry out quickly and not serve as a breeding place for flies that will molest future occupants of the area.

When an area is occupied for more than a day, the manure should be removed daily from the horse standings and disposed of at some distance from the camp by burning, spreading thinly over large areas, or composting. The site for disposal of wastes should be downstream from the camp. The standings must be kept level and free from dung or moist depressions in which flies may breed. It is often necessary to fill or grade the standings in order to prevent mud and provide for adequate drainage. Whenever the size of the area will permit, rather frequent changing of the location of the horse lines will be a sanitary advantage. The cutting of tall weeds, grass, or underbrush in the vicinity of the standings will greatly reduce the incidence of mosquitoes and flies, which in addition to being annoying to horses, may be carriers of disease. It is far safer to avoid the use of barns or stables that may have been occupied by civilian animals, since such places may harbor infection or parasites. Should a horse die or be destroyed, the carcass should be burned or deeply buried.

9

Diseases, Injuries, and First-Aid Treatment

The purpose of the proper care of animals is to keep them at their highest degree of efficiency by the prevention of disease and injury. Most diseases and injuries are preventable if all concerned are vigilant, intelligent, and untiring in the application of simple preventive measures. Frequently the development of serious diseases or injuries can be prevented by prompt first-aid measures and early treatment. In succeeding paragraphs, the causes, prevention, symptoms, and first-aid treatment of the more common diseases and injuries are discussed. Medical treatment, as outlined, is limited to the drugs that the veterinarian might issue for emergency use.* All sick and injured horses should be reported promptly to the veterinarian.

THE HORSE IN HEALTH. Health is the condition of the body in which all the functions thereof are performed in a normal manner. It is particularly essential that the normal functions of the body of the animal be thoroughly understood, else one cannot hope to recognize any departure therefrom. Even the most elementary study of diseased conditions must be founded upon a very thorough knowledge of the normal body.

Posture. The standing posture is the most common posture of the horse. Normally, the front feet will both be on the same transverse line and bear weight equally. Any

The science of veterinary medicine is constantly improving as new methods and drugs are developed. While the symptoms and descriptions of diseases and injuries discussed herein are accurate, the treatments given—while in all cases effective—are not necessarily the most modern therapy in all instances. [Ed.]

158

other posture of a forefoot is spoken of as *pointing* and is an indication of trouble. The hind legs are rested alternately; rarely does the horse stand with both hind feet squarely together on the ground; in fact, it is difficult to make him take or maintain this position. Due to certain peculiarities of structure, the horse can maintain the standing position without tiring and can sleep standing. Some few horses never lie down, but they probably would rest better and their legs would last longer if they did. The horse lies down either obliquely on the chest with the legs somewhat folded under the body and head extended with the chin or teeth on the floor, or flat on his side with the legs and head extended. The horse is a very light sleeper, sleeping with his eyes partly open. He gets his deepest sleep and greatest rest when lying down.

Skin. The skin is loose, supple, and easily moved about over the structures underneath. One should be able to grasp a handful of skin with ease. The coat is smooth, sleek, and glossy. The hair may stand up, and the coat becomes coarse and heavy during cold weather. The old coat should be shed quickly and easily in the spring.

Pulse. The normal pulse rate varies from thirty-six to forty per minute depending upon the age, sex, temperament, and breeding of the horse. The pulse rate increases with exercise or excitement. The rate after a five-minute gallop will be sixty or seventy per minute. After very strenuous work, the rate may be as high as eighty to ninety. In a horse that is well conditioned, the rate should return to approximately normal in a few minutes after exercise. The pulse rate will not return to the normal at rest as rapidly as the respiratory rate will subside. The pulse should feel strong, full, and regular. Its rate is determined by placing the tips of the fingers over an artery and counting the pulsations for fifteen to thirty seconds at least twice, averaging the counts, and multiplying the average by four or two. The count is commonly made from the artery that rounds the jawbone in front of the large cheek muscle.

Respiration. The breathing should be free, soft, and noiseless. After fast work, the breathing is heard as a rushing sound of air; but there should be no harsh, fluttering, whistling, or roaring sound. The breathing rate per minute is approximately as follows:

```
At rest ............................... 9-12
After walking 200 yards .................... 28
After trotting 5 minutes ................... 52
After galloping 5 minutes ............... 52-70
```

The preceding rates are for horses in good condition. After cessation of exercise, the breathing rate should subside quickly to normal. The quickness with which the breathing rate subsides is an excellent indication of the fitness or condition of the horse. The breathing rate increases with exercise more rapidly than the pulse rate, and after work subsides more quickly than the pulse rate. The breathing rate is counted by watching the rise and fall of the flanks, the movements of the nostrils, or, on a cold day, the steamy expiration of breath.

Temperature. The normal body temperature of the horse at rest is about 100°F. but may vary one degree in either direction; however, a temperature of 101°F. is uncommon. The temperature varies with exercise, excitement, and air temperature. One hour's work at the walk and trot may raise the temperature one or two degrees. Hard, fast, or prolonged work, especially under a hot sun, may build the body heat up to 104° to 107° F. When the temperature reaches this reading, the horse is approaching "overheating." (See page 166.) The temperature is taken with a clinical thermometer in the rectum. The thermometer is moistened or oiled, the mercury is shaken down to 96° or below, the bulb of the thermometer is inserted in the anus and allowed to remain three minutes, and then it is withdrawn and the temperature noted.

Urine. Urine is passed several times daily in quantities of a quart or more. During the act of urination, the horse straddles, grunts, and assumes a very awkward position that might be mistaken for an indication of pain. Lack of water and profuse sweating decreases the amount of urine voided. Some horses hesitate to urinate on a hard floor, but habitually wait until placed on bedding. The urine of the horse is a thick, yellowish fluid and is at times cloudy.

Defecation. Defecation occurs eight to ten times in twenty-four hours. Normal droppings should be fairly well formed but soft enough to flatten when dropped; free from offensive odor or mucous slime; vary in color from yellow to green, according to the nature of the feed; and not be filled with grains that are either wholly or partially unmasticated. The amount of droppings passed in twenty-four hours varies from thirty-six to forty pounds, depending upon the size of the animal and the amount of feed consumed.

Because the droppings are a good indication of the condition of the teeth and the digestive tract, an examination of the fresh droppings should be made frequently. An examination may reveal the following irregularities:

Hard droppings may indicate a lack of water, a lack of exercise, too dry and indigestible feed, or a combination of all of these. This can be corrected by giving a few bran mashes, by watching the watering, by grazing, and by an hour of exercise daily.

Very soft or watery droppings may indicate too hard work, fatigue, too much grazing, excessive use of bran, or a slight irritation of the intestines. Reduce the work; omit bran and grazing. If condition persists, withhold all feed for twenty-four hours.

Slimy or mucous-covered droppings, or those having an offensive odor, indicate too highly concentrated feed or an irritation of the intestines. Reduce the feed; give bran mashes and plenty of water.

Unmasticated grains indicate that the teeth are sharp or diseased, or that the animal eats too rapidly. Have the teeth examined, feed chop and dry bran with the grain.

INDICATIONS OF DISEASE. Every disease has different indications, and the symptoms vary so greatly that only exhaustive study can acquaint one with all of them. In order that sick animals may be detected in the early stages of the disease and brought to the attention of a veterinarian, the cavalry officer must be prepared to recognize the more common early deviations from normal.

The most common preliminary indications of disease are partial or complete loss of appetite, elevation of temperature (101°F. or more), accelerated breathing, increased pulse rate, listlessness, dejected countenance, profuse sweating, stiffness, nasal discharge, cough, diarrhea, constipation, pawing, rolling, lameness, inflamed mucous membranes, unhealthy coat of hair, loss of hair, itching, or unnatural heat or swelling in any part of the body.

Inspection for Sick Animals. The best times to inspect animals for evidence of sickness and injury are just after they have been fed and at the time of grooming. One of the first and most important symptoms of sickness is impairment of the appetite. A sick horse will often nibble at his hay but refuse his grain. Sick animals in a corral are inclined to stand by themselves. Move each animal around, look for nasal discharge, and listen for coughing.

NURSING. Good nursing is indispensable in the treatment of sick and injured animals. The chief points to consider in nursing are discussed on the following pages.

Ventilation. Allow plenty of fresh air, but protect from drafts. Avoid extremes of temperature, and in the field, provide shelter from wind and rain.

Clothing. The amount of clothing should be regulated according to the weather. Woolen leg bandages and extra body cover may be necessary during cold weather. A fly sheet is often desirable in summer. The latter can be improvised from grain sacks.

Bedding. A good, clean bed encourages the sick animal to lie down and thus get needed rest. It should be shaken up several times daily and the droppings and urine-soaked bedding removed.

Stalls. A roomy, well-bedded box stall should be used whenever possible. Keep a bucket of water in the stall and change the water frequently.

Exercise. Convalescent patients should receive as much exercise as their condition warrants. The sick animal should in most cases have complete rest.

Grooming. Animals that are weak and depressed should not be worried with unnecessary grooming. Such animals should be carefully hand-rubbed at least once a day; and their eyes, nostrils, and docks should be wiped out with a sponge or soft cloth. The feet should also be cleaned. Animals that are only slightly indisposed should be groomed in the usual way. Animals with tetanus should not be cleaned at all.

Feed. Some sick animals retain a good appetite. The principal things to observe in such patients are that they are not overfed, that droppings are kept soft, and that they have plenty of water. Sick animals with impaired appetites require special attention. They often relish a change of diet, such as a bran mash, steamed oats, chopped alfalfa, grass, roots, and apples. Feed small amounts often, do not allow uneaten portions to remain in front of them, keep mangers and feedboxes clean,

161

induce eating by hand feeding, and sprinkle a little sweetened water over the hay and grain. The forced feeding of liquid foods by means of drenches or enema may be used as a last resort.

USES OF BANDAGES. Bandages are one of the oldest forms of surgical apparatus and are employed under varying conditions for many purposes. The chief uses for bandages are to:

Keep the legs warm and the circulation active.
Give support to the blood vessels and synovial capsules.
Compress specific parts.
Hold dressings or medicated packs in position.
Afford a vehicle for applying hot or cold lotions.
Immobilize a part.
Protect the legs from injury.

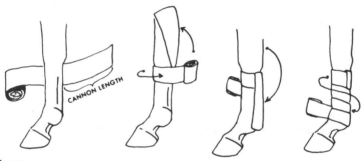

Types of Bandages

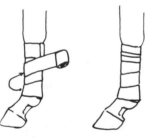

BANDAGING LEGS

Start just below knee. Hold cannon length of bandage up; make a snug wrap around below knee. Smooth loose end down back of leg. Continue wrapping snugly to fetlock. Make one wrap around fetlock. Bandage should cover most of fetlock but not interfere with action. Continue back up to knee. Fastener should be on outside of cannon. Adhesive tape or special elastic straps may be used as extra precaution. Hind legs are done in same manner; longer cannon requires compensation in wrap thickness and overlap.

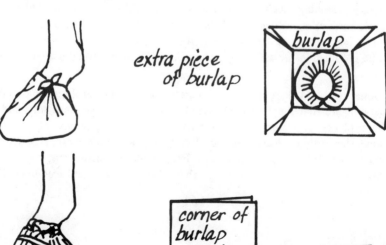

extra piece of burlap

burlap

corner of burlap sack

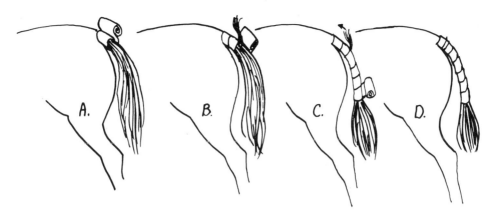

A. Make one or two snug wraps around top of the tail as close to the body as possible. Use a special tail bandage or a track or derby bandage.

B. Start wrapping down the tail, overlapping each wrap. After every two or three turns pull a small swatch of hair out and up to anchor the wrap.

C. At the end of the dock reverse and start wrapping up the tail. With the loose hair pointed up toward the top of the tail, wrap up and over it to the top.

D. A finished tail wrap. If there is extra bandage length, continue down part way and then fasten. Fasten bandage with its own ribbons, over which a strip of adhesive or masking tape may be applied to make sure bow knot will not untie. *Do not wrap the tail too tightly,* since this will restrict or cut off circulation. A wet brush will straighten the pulled-up anchor hairs.

CLASSIFICATION AND APPLICATION OF BANDAGES.

Roller bandages consist of long strips of various lengths and widths, and can be obtained in an assortment of materials. For convenience of application, they are wound into snug rolls. Roller bandages are used particularly on the legs from the knee and hock down to and including the foot. The greatest danger in applying a roller bandage to the leg above the foot lies in getting it so tight throughout, or at one or more points, that the underlying blood vessels are compressed and circulation of the blood is interfered with. This is particularly true when horses are worked in bandages, or the inelastic type of material is used. The following general rules are applicable for all roller bandages:

Use one hand to hold and direct the roll, the other to keep each lap smooth and to hold the turn while changing direction or taking up slack.

Wrap snugly enough to exert the desired amount of pressure and prevent slipping, but be careful not to shut off circulation by too much pressure.

Secure the end with the same pressure used in wrapping.

Always fasten the bandage on the outside of the leg.

Bandages may be secured as follows:

Pass the tapes on the end around the last wrap in opposite directions and tie in a bowknot.

Slit the last twelve or fourteen inches of the gauze or muslin with scissors.

Tie the two slits with a straight knot and proceed as with the tapes.

Double back the last twenty inches of the gauze or muslin bandage around the last wrap and tie that end with the folded end.

Secure the bandage with safety pins by pinning the end to the wrap underneath.

Leave a bight protruding at the start and tie the end to this bight.

Roller bandages are made of gauze, muslin, Canton flannel, wool, and knitted elastic material. Aside from gauze, bias-cut muslin, and Canton flannel bandages, the most commonly used bandage is the derby bandage. The latter is not an article of issue but is often purchased for polo and horseshow use. The exact operation of the application and uses of the various roller bandages is difficult to describe.

Foot Bandage. The five-inch, bias-cut muslin bandage is most suitable for bandaging the foot. Hold the foot in the same manner that a horseshoer holds it when shoeing. Hold out a bight twelve inches long, make one complete turn around the foot one-half inch below the coronet, and take a half turn around the bight by holding the end of the bight in the left hand and the roll in the right. After drawing up snugly, take another turn around the foot in the opposite direction to the first. Complete by another half turn and pull around the bight. Make these half turns around the bight come over the quarter. Continue the turns around the foot by working down toward the toe and back so as to cover the whole foot. Take a half turn around the bight each time and draw the bandage tight before starting a new wrap. Secure by tying the end to the bight.

Eye Bandage. In certain injuries to the eyes, it is necessary to apply wet, antiseptic compresses. This form of treatment also produces very good results by virtue of excluding light. This bandage may be made from a grain sack. Hold the material up to the head and mark the place to cut openings for the ears and the sound eye. Lay it on a flat surface and cut out elliptical holes large enough for the base of each ear. Cut a circular hole for the sound eye about four inches in diameter. Then cut four strips, each about eight inches long, on each lower border. Sew a gauze and cotton compress on the inside so it comes over the injured eye. Apply the bandage by laying it on the face and forehead, placing the ears in their proper holes, and adjusting it so the sound eye is in the center of the hole cut for that purpose. Tie the four pairs of strips underneath the jaw.

Many-Tailed. The many-tailed type of bandage is used principally on the knee and hock. It acts only as a protection and support for a compress held in place by a loosely applied roller bandage.

Maltese Cross. The Maltese cross bandage is an accessory foot bandage and is used as a protection for a compress that has first been secured by a roller bandage.

Foot Pouch. The foot pouch is an accessory bandage cut from the corner of a burlap sack and has the same function as the Maltese cross.

Lay a burlap grain sack on the floor with the open end toward the operator. Starting at the open end and two inches inside the left-hand seam, cut straight down toward the bottom and parallel to the seam until about eight or ten inches from the bottom of the sack. Repeat this cut two inches inside the right-hand seam. Join these two cuts by cutting across the sack, parallel to and eight to ten inches above the bottom edge. This leaves the bottom eight to ten inches of the sack intact with long strips, one on each side. Grasp the bottom left-hand corner with the left hand, and the bottom right-hand corner with the right hand, and invert the sack by pushing the right corner into the left corner. This leaves the sack shaped similar to a bonnet with both strings together on the left side. Cut a hole one inch in diameter in the corner diagonally opposite the corner to which the strips are attached. Tie the strips together with a simple knot and pass in opposite directions through the hole just cut. This serves as a puckering string for the pouch.

Place on the foot by inserting the toe in the corner opposite the one in which a hole was cut for the strips to pass through. Pull up snugly around the foot, and wrap the loose ends around the coronet and pastern. Secure by passing the strips in opposite directions around the coronet and tying over the wall below the coronet.

NONCOMMUNICABLE DISEASES. Noncommunicable diseases are those diseases which are not "catching" or transmissible from animal to animal either through direct or indirect contact. Likewise, they are not transmissible to man, as are some of the communicable diseases. In stable, noncommunicable diseases are the cause of a little more than one-third of all times lost (disability) due to disease and injury combined, while communicable diseases are responsible for about one-tenth and injuries more than one-half. Due to the great increase in the incidence of injuries when in the field, and the fact that horses in field service are better seasoned and conditioned, noncommunicable diseases usually cause less than one-fifth of the total animal disability, and communicable diseases are often of small consequence. There are many more noncommunicable diseases than there are communicable diseases. No noncommunicable disease causes as much time lost as does any one of the communicable respiratory diseases. However, as a group, the noncommunicable diseases cause more deaths than do communicable diseases.

The various causes of noncommunicable diseases can be united under one general cause—poor animal management. This includes improper feeds, feeding, watering, general care, and work or exercise. The three most important noncommunicable diseases, from the standpoint of days lost, are caused by improper methods of feeding and watering.

There are certain measures of "weapons" that can be employed to prevent many of the noncommunicable diseases. The weapon "good general care" is certainly effective, since this implies good feeding, good grooming, and the avoidance of overwork or other things that lower the horse's natural resistance and vitality. Daily inspection is effective for the early detection of the sick and, likewise, for detecting those conditions which might affect the health of the animals. Cleanliness is important in both a direct and indirect way. A dirty, ill-kept stable is a direct indication that stable practices which affect the health of the animals are equally negligent.

The group consisting of thumps, overheating, and exhaustion is relatively unimportant in the stable, but in the field it is often responsible for one half of the time loss due to disease.

THUMPS (*Spasms of Diaphragm*).

Causes. Overwork or fast work during hot weather, especially among animals not properly conditioned.

Prevention. Have animals in good condition and avoid overwork in hot weather. Regulate the rate of march to suit the condition of animals. This condition frequently is an early symptom of overheating.

Symptoms. General symptoms of fatigue with spasmodic, jerking contraction of the muscles of the diaphragm that is noticeable in the belly and flanks.

Nursing and First-Aid Treatment. If marching, halt the animal and, if the temperature is elevated, reduce it by sponging the body with cold water. Have the animal ridden or led into camp at the walk. The condition will usually disappear in less than two or three hours if the animal is given complete rest.

HEAT EXHAUSTION (*Overheating–Sunstroke*). A noncommunicable disease with disturbances of the nervous system due to a marked rise in the body temperature.

Causes. Caused by long-continued hard or fast work during hot or very humid weather, especially among animals not in good condition or having heavy coats.

Prevention. Keep animals in good condition to perform work required. Do not overtax the strength of the animal. Fit the marching rate and frequency of halts to the condition of the animals. Watch animals for early symptoms. Clip animals that have heavy coats. Water frequently on hot days.

Symptoms. Thumps, a condition described above, often precedes overheating. The animal that has been sweating freely will cease to sweat, or sweating will diminish, and the animal will be dull and require urging. The gait is staggering or wobbly, especially in the hindquarters. If halted, the animal stands with the legs spraddled, breathing very rapid and shallow, nostrils dilated, expression drawn and anxious, nasal membranes bluish-red in color, and trembling of body muscles. The body feels hot to the hand and the temperature will be from 103° to 109° F. If in this stage the animal is forced to continue on the march, he will soon fail and probably die later.

Nursing and First-Aid Treatment. Prompt first-aid treatment is of utmost importance. Stop the animal at once in the shade, if any is nearby. Remove the equipment and apply large quantities of cold water to all parts of the body but especially to the head, sides of the neck, groins, and flanks. Wash out the mouth and nostrils with cold water. Give the animal three or four swallows of water every few minutes. Under this treatment the temperature will drop quite rapidly, and as improvement is noted move the animal about very slowly and rub the body to prevent chilling. As soon as the temperature is near normal, the animal may be moved slowly into camp. If possible, he should be excused from work the following day but may continue the march as a leg animal.

EXHAUSTION.

Causes. Overexertion, excessive or prolonged heavy work, or lack of condition.

166

Prevention. Prevent the causes.

Symptoms. After the animal arrives in camp or stable he may lie down and refuse his feed, especially his grain, yet drink considerable quantities of water. The temperature may be slightly elevated and the pulse may be weak and thready. Sweating may be quite noticeable and possibly patchy, yet the body may feel cold and clammy.

Nursing and First-Aid Treatment. Make a comfortable place for the animal to lie. Cover the body with a blanket to prevent chilling. Hand-rub the legs. Give small amounts of water frequently. Do not annoy the animal by too much attention. A period of rest is all that is needed to recuperate from his excessive fatigue. When rested, he will resume eating. Refusal of animals to eat for some little time after the termination of a hard day's march is not uncommon.

COLIC. A general term applied to abdominal pain caused by some form of digestive disturbance. For practical purposes, it is often classified as spasmodic or flatulent (gas colic).

Causes. The causes of both forms of colic are very similar, but flatulent colic is more frequently caused by feeds likely to ferment in the digestive tract, such as green clover or alfalfa, especially when wet or after being frosted. General causes are indigestible or spoiled feeds, sudden changes in feed, overeating, eating while fatigued, working too soon after feeding, watering while exhausted or hot, bolting the feed, overeating or green feed, and watering too soon after feeding. Wind sucking is frequently a cause of flatulent colic. Parasites, tumors, and abnormalities of any of the digestive organs may be a cause. Collections of sand in the bowel, resulting from an animal eating on a sandy picket line, may cause repeated attacks of colic.

Prevention. Feeding suitable feed of good quality, and attention to the principles of feeding and watering will prevent most cases of colic not due to internal causes.

Symptoms. Pain is indicated by restlessness, pawing, stamping of the feet, looking around at the flanks, kicking at the abdomen, lying down, rolling, sweating, and frequent attempts to defecate usually resulting in the passage of but a few pellets of dung or a discharge of gas. In the so-called spasmodic form, the attacks of pain are often intermittent with short periods of a few minutes of apparent freedom from pain. In the flatulent (gas) type of colic, the digestive tract is filled with gas and the belly is often greatly distended. Breathing is often difficult because of pressure on the lungs caused by the bloat. The temperature is normal or but slightly elevated in the beginning of all forms of colic. If the sickness continues for a day or so, the temperature may rise considerably.

Nursing and First-Aid Treatment. Rational treatment includes relief of pain and elimination of the irritating bowel contents. Place the animal in a well-bedded box stall, or if in camp, bed down a section of the picket line and have an attendant hold the animal's tie rope. Do not force an animal with colic to move about at a trot, since it will not do the animal any good and often will cause great harm, or may cause death if the animal is bloated. Get a veterinarian at once. Do not attempt to keep the animal from rolling unless he is throwing himself to the ground so violently that it is evident he may rupture some organ. Give frequent rectal injections of two or three gallons of warm soapy water. Wring blankets out of hot water and wrap around the belly and flanks as hot as can be borne without burning the hands or animal. Do not allow any feed, but water may be given in small amounts. Do not attempt to drench the animal with the various concoctions that may be suggested. Improper or excessive medication has resulted in the death of many animals that otherwise would have recovered. Withhold all feed for at least twelve hours after all pain has disappeared and feed sparingly for two or three days.

DIARRHEA.

Causes. Spoiled feed; overfeeding of "washy" feeds such as alfalfa, clover, and bran; nervousness; sudden changes of diet; and errors of feeding.

Prevention. Careful attention to kind, quality, and quantity of feed and methods of feeding. Exclude "washy" feeds from diet of animals that tend to scour.

Symptoms. The droppings are frequent and of semifluid nature. They may be of a normal color and odor or of a gray color and fetid odor. If the condition persists, the animal loses flesh and the appetite is lost.

Nursing and First-Aid Treatment. In mild cases, correction of diet will be sufficient. Give the animal absolute rest for twenty-four to forty-eight hours while withholding all feed and limiting the amount of water. After this period, feed lightly and do not allow excessive amounts of water. Rest the animal until the droppings have returned to their normal consistency.

AZOTURIA *(Monday Morning Disease).*

Causes. Caused by more or less strenuous exercise following two or more days of rest during which the grain ration has not been appropriately reduced. It occurs most frequently in horses that are in good, fit condition. It is most likely to occur during cool or cold weather.

Prevention. When conditioned animals accustomed to regular work are given a period of complete rest for longer than a day, reduce the grain ration by at least one-half or one-fourth of the usual allowance and give more hay. When animals are first exercised after a period of rest, they should be first walked for a period of at least twenty minutes after leaving the stables and not called upon to do more than *a very small amount of fast work the first day.*

Symptoms. The disease usually appears within the first twenty minutes after leaving the stable if the animal is restive or in high spirits and exerts himself accordingly, but it may not appear until much later. Increased excitability, profuse sweating, and rapid breathing are the first symptoms. Very soon the animal begins to stiffen in his hindquarters, drag the hind legs, and knuckle over in thè hind fetlocks. The muscles over the croup and loins become swollen and firm, but not sensitive to pressure. There is no marked increase in temperature, but because of exercise and excitement the temperature may be as high as 102° F. If continued in work, the animal will become completely incapable of supporting weight on the hind legs and fall to the ground; in such cases the chances of recovery are remote. The urine is scanty and red or coffee-colored.

Nursing and First-Aid Treatment. Stop the animal immediately when the first symptoms are observed. Remove the saddle or harness at once and cover with one or more blankets. Keep the animal standing, if possible; if not, provide a good bed. If hot water can be made available, a hot blanket pack placed over the back and loins and covered with dry blankets is very beneficial. They should be changed frequently. After a few hours, the average case can be moved slowly to the stable, provided the distance is not too great. At this time, he should be given a laxative and fed on bran mashes, grass, and hay for a few days.

LAMINITIS (*Grain and road founder*).

Causes. Overeating of grain, eating improper or spoiled feed, colic, exhaustion, sudden chilling, overexertion, long-continued work on hard-surfaced roads, and drinking more than small amounts of cold water while overheated.

Prevention. Avoid the causes of the disease.

Symptoms. In the acute form of the disease, an intense lameness appears quickly. Usually only the forefeet are affected, although occasionally all four are involved. The forefeet are placed well forward and the horse rocks back on his hind feet so as to take as much weight as possible off the forefeet. The posture assumed by the horse shown is very characteristic. The affected feet are hot. The pulse and respiration are considerably accelerated and the temperature may reach 105° F. The animal can be turned or moved only with difficulty. In a mild case, such as is often caused by continuous marching on hard roads, the animal moves stiffly, taking short, quick, shuffling steps with the forefeet while planting the hind feet well forward under the body.

Nursing and First-Aid Treatment. Remove the shoes from the affected feet and place the animal in a well-bedded box stall. Cover the affected feet and legs as high as the knees and hocks with several layers of burlap sacking and keep the packs saturated with cold water. If a stream is available, the horse may stand in it. In this case, the shoes need not be removed. Laxative diet is indicated. Feed bran mashes and a little hay. Cases that are not cured in four or five days are liable to develop the disease in a chronic form. Chronic laminitis is practically incurable. Early treatment is an important factor. As soon as the acute pain has diminished, moderate walking exercise each day is beneficial. Following the attack, shoe with a bar shoe over a leather pad covering a tar and oakum pack.

SCRATCHES. An inflammation of the back of the pastern.

Causes. Wet, muddy, and filthy standings; failure to dry legs that have been wetted from slush, rain, or washing; pasterns not thoroughly cleaned while grooming; and short clipping of the hair on the back of the pasterns. Most prevalent during wet, cold weather.

169

Prevention. Proper attention to standings for animals, and good grooming, especially when in the field.

Symptoms. Redness, heat, pain and swelling of the skin on the back of the pastern. Later, the surface of the skin becomes moist and raw. Dust and dirt dries with the secretions to form a scabby mass that sticks to the skin and hair, and the skin may crack. Usually there is lameness.

Nursing and First-Aid Treatment. With soap and warm water, thoroughly clean the region and carefully soak off all accumulated dirt and dried secretions. Rinse with clean, warm water and dry. Apply a white lotion pack under a bandage twice daily. Rest the animal on clean, dry standings and feed laxative feeds. After the moistness of the skin has decreased, apply dry dressings or leave unbandaged. Avoid the use of water after the first cleansing.

ACUTE LYMPHANGITIS (*Big leg*).

Causes. Failure to reduce the grain ration of a heavily fed, well-conditioned animal during a period of idleness.

Prevention. Reduce the grain ration by at least one-half whenever an animal is idle for two days or more.

Symptoms. The acute form of the disease is characterized by marked swelling, heat, tenderness, and lameness in one or both hind legs. Usually but one hind leg is affected. The tenderness is most pronounced on the inside of the leg between the hock and body. There is a loss of appetite, rapid pulse and respiration, and a temperature of 102° to 106° F. The leg may swell to twice its normal size. The skin may become moist with exuding serum. In milder cases, the swelling may be confined to the lower leg and the general systemic symptoms will be less severe. Recovery is seldom complete and there is a tendency for the condition to become chronic, resulting in a permanently enlarged or "filled" leg.

Nursing and First-Aid Treatment. Feed hay only. Allow plenty of water. Shower leg with cold water for twenty minutes several times daily. After each showering or bathing of the leg, apply white lotion solution. After pain has diminished give slow walking exercise, followed immediately by warm bathing and hand-rubbing of the leg.

THRUSH.

Causes. Lack of proper grooming of the feet, particularly failure to clean out thoroughly the depths of the commissures and cleft of the frog. Lack of frog pressure, insufficient exercise, filthy standings, dryness of the feet, and cuts or tears in the horny frog are all contributing causes.

Prevention. A hoof that is properly cleaned once each day will not develop thrush. A thorough washing of the under surface of the hoof once a week will materially assist in the prevention of this disease. (See grooming, page 126.)

Symptoms. Cracks, depressions, or fissures in the horn of the frog in which is found a thick, dark-colored discharge with a very offensive odor. The cleft of the frog and the sides of the frog at the depths of the commissures are the parts usually diseased. The destruction of horn is progressive, and the horn may be underrun and loosened some distance back from the edges of the external opening. Lameness is usually absent, except in advanced cases where the destruction of horn was extended to the sensitive tissues.

Nursing and First-Aid Treatment. Clean and wash the hoof. With a sharp hoof knife, trim away all diseased and underrun horn and all ragged pieces. This is very important. With cresolis solution (one and one-half mess-kit spoonfuls to a mess cup full of water) and a stiff brush, thoroughly scrub the horn. After it has dried, paint the area with tincture of iodine. Repeat the washing and iodine treatment daily until the horn begins to appear dry, and then apply pine tar. If the hoof is contracted, shoe to correct. Ordinary cases of thrush can be cured readily. Cases in which the horn in the cleft has been completely destroyed and a deep fissure extends up between the bulbs of the heels are more difficult to cure, and if not carefully watched will recur.

DRY FEET.

Causes. Lack of frog pressure, lack of exercise, dry weather, allowing the shoes to remain on the feet too long, and loss of the waxlike horny covering (periople) of the horny wall.

Prevention. Make provision for frog pressure and exercise the animal regularly. Pack the bottom of the hoof with wet clay during dry weather.

Symptoms. A hard, dry, and inelastic condition of the horn. The first symptom of lack of moisture in the hoof is the hardness and dryness of the horny frog. While dryness in itself may not cause lameness, it is an indirect cause of such conditions as contracted heels, corns, and thrush.

Nursing and First-Aid Treatment. The first step should be to correct errors in shoeing, and the second to restore and maintain the normal moisture content of the horn. Moisture may be restored to the horn by packing the feet daily with wet clay, by standing the animal in a shallow clay mud bath, by wet packs on the feet, or by standing in a foot bath. After the use of wet packs or foot baths is discontinued, the application of some vegetable or animal oil to the wall of the hoof will assist in preventing the loss of moisture by evaporation. A light dressing with pine tar is also useful for this purpose.

CONTRACTED FEET.

Causes. Dry feet, insufficient exercise, thrush, cutting of the bars, opening up the heels, cutting away the horny frog, continued use of heel calks on open shoes, and allowing the shoes to remain on the feet too long.

Symptoms. The contracted foot is easily recognized from its appearance. The quarters, and especially the heels, are narrower and higher than normal, and there is little or no frog pressure. The foot may resemble the foot of a mule more than that of a horse. The frog is reduced in size and is often affected with thrush.

Treatment. Soften the feet as prescribed for dry feet.

If the contraction is not pronounced and the horny frog is in a healthy condition and of sufficient size to come in contact with a bar shoe, shoe with a bar shoe with a well-rolled toe after packing the foot with tar and oakum covered with a leather pad. Pack the feet at one shoeing and omit at the next.

If the contraction is pronounced, the following method may be used. Thin the wall of the affected quarter or quarters from a point near the bend or widest part of the hoof back to and including the buttress, and from the coronary band to the lower border of the hoof. The wall should be well thinned with the rasp and knife, care being taken not to draw blood. Shoe with a bar shoe after packing the foot with pine tar and oakum. Dress the cut surface of the wall with pine tar.

COMMUNICABLE DISEASES. Communicable diseases are caused by specific living causative agents that are transmitted from animal to animal either by direct contact between sick and well animals or indirectly through the medium of the water troughs, feed pans, corrals, stockcars, or equipment. Specific infective agents are *bacteria (germs), viruses, fungi,* and *parasites.* The diseased animal passes off infective material in the discharges from its nose, mouth, digestive system, urinary system, or skin, and the infection is spread by direct or indirect means. Some of the communicable diseases are incurable, some are transmissible to man, and all may cause great losses during campaign.

In the stable, communicable diseases cause but eleven percent of the total time lost. The percentage seems relatively low when compared to the time lost due to noncommunicable diseases and injuries. However, their true importance is much greater than figures indicate. The low incidence of communicable diseases is the result of continual application of preventative measures being relaxed, at which point communicable diseases will become rampant and cause a great amount of damage.

CAUSES.

Predisposing. Certain causes or conditions that lower the vitality and natural resistance of animals to disease, thereby rendering them more susceptible to infection, are termed predisposing causes. These predisposing causes are more important than is generally realized. While they cannot in themselves produce communicable disease, it is certain that if they can be avoided the incidence of disease will be very greatly reduced. They seem to be very important to the development of the communicable respiratory diseases. The following are some of the important predisposing causes:

Exposure.
Working animals hard before they are in good condition.
Overwork.
Lack of sufficient feed.
Improper grooming.
Change of environment.
Long shipment by rail or sea.
Other diseases.
General debility.

Exciting. The exciting or specific causes of disease are those living causative agents known as *bacteria* ("germs") that produce strangles and anthrax; *virus* that produces influenza, rabies, and sleeping sickness; *fungus* that produces ringworm; and *parasites* that produce mange and pediculosis (lousiness). All of these causative agents are spread from animal to animal by direct or indirect means. When any of these specific agents enter the body of the horse, there is an elapse of time, usually less than twenty-one days, before the first symptom (sign) or symptoms appear. This period of time is known as the incubation period. In some horses, there is a protective force known as immunity that destroys the disease-producing powers of the infection. Immunity may be natural or acquired. Natural immunity implies that protective forces are normally present in the body. Acquired immunity is that immunity produced by the injection of some immunizing agent (vaccine, bacterin, antitoxin).

PREVENTION. There are several general preventive measures that are applicable in the prevention and control of all communicable diseases. In other words, there are several "weapons" that can always be effectively employed in the battle against any communicable disease. In addition to the general "weapons," the special weapon, vaccination, can be used in attacking certain diseases that have been proved to be vulnerable to the weapon.

Preventive Measures. The preventive measures that can be used to combat and control communicable diseases are *daily inspection, cleanliness, disinfection, isolation, quarantine, good general care,* and *vaccination.*

Daily inspection must be performed. The daily inspection of animals is not confined to the suspected animals, but also includes all other animals in the stable. The purpose of the daily inspection is to detect sick animals at the earliest possible moment so that they may be promptly isolated and treated or destroyed, as the case may warrant. Constant vigilance is necessary to prevent the spread of disease throughout a stable. The daily inspection should include an inspection of the methods of animal and stable management that directly affect the well-being of the animals.

Cleanliness, like daily inspections, must be maintained at all times whether or not there is a disease among the animals. The woodwork, mangers, water troughs, floors, feed pans, and other things that will harbor dirt and filth must be kept clean. Dirty and unsanitary conditions about a stable tend to lower the animal's vitality and natural resistance to disease. (See chapter 7 for methods of cleaning equipment and fixtures in a stable.)

Disinfection is the destruction of the infective agent, or inhibition of its growth, by the use of chemical agents known as disinfectants. No disease has been made wholly extinct by this method; however, many diseases can be controlled by it. To destroy the infection within an animal would be ideal, but the more general method is the cleaning and disinfection of places that harbor infection. A thorough cleaning with soda-ash or lye and water should always precede disinfection. Spraying a disinfectant on a dirt-encrusted object is not effective. Liquor cresolis compositus is a commonly used chemical disinfectant. Heat and sunlight are also used in disinfection.

173

Isolation is the separation or segregation of a diseased animal so as to prevent the spread of infection from that animal to other animals that are susceptible to the disease. The diseased animal is usually placed in the isolation ward of a veterinary hospital if one is available. Any place is suitable provided the diseased animal cannot come in direct or indirect contact with susceptible animals.

Quarantine is the segregation of a group of animals that have been exposed to or are suspected of having been exposed to infection. The purpose of the quarantine is to prevent the spread of infection. It is a physical control over the animals in which a disease may be in the incubative stage. Daily inspection must be made in order to detect sick animals. If a quarantined animal is found to be infected, it should be immediately placed in isolation. (The quarantine period is extended for twenty-one days more following the detection of a new case.) The Army adopted the twenty-one-day quarantine on the basis that nearly all communicable diseases have an incubation period of less than twenty-one days. Animals are placed in quarantine whenever they are *known* to have been in contact with an animal affected with a communicable disease, or whenever they are received in a station or camp from any source.

In case of newly purchased animals and of animals known or suspected to have been exposed to communicable disease, the quarantine should be absolute. In the case of the shipment of seasoned animals, where there has been little or no opportunity for exposure en route, the quarantine may be a working quarantine provided the animals do not come in contact with other animals in the stable. The veterinary officer will make such modifications as may be indicated from time to time, and he will recommend when the animals are to be released.

Good general care includes the application of proper methods of feeding, watering, grooming, work or exercise, and stable management. While communicable diseases are caused by living infective agents, the predisposing causes are equally as important. If a high, natural vitality and resistance can be maintained through proper care, the animal may remain healthy even though the "germs" are present. It will lessen the severity of the attack should the animal become affected.

Vaccination is an effective preventive in certain diseases. All Army animals are immunized against tetanus by the use of tetanus toxoid; and each spring, all animals are routinely vaccinated against sleeping sickness. Anthrax vaccination is not a routine procedure, but it is given to all animals if they are to go into a known anthrax area. Up to the present time, there is no successful means of immunizing animals against the most important communicable diseases, the acute respiratory group.

COUGHS AND COLDS. Animals suffer from coughs and colds quite similarly to man but to a lesser degree. They are mildly infectious inflammations of the membranes of the nose and throat. A simple cough or cold is of minor importance; however, these conditions may lower the resistance of the animal so that he may develop a more serious respiratory disease.

Causes. Exposure to wet or cold, particularly when tired and heated; damp or poorly ventilated stables; and sudden changes in weather.

Prevention. Means of prevention are suggested by the nature of the causes.

Symptoms. Dryness and redness of the nasal membranes followed by a watery discharge that in a day or so becomes grayish and thickened, later yellow in color. If the throat is affected, the cough is at first dry and later moist. The nasal discharge is odorless. In the early stages, the animal is somewhat listless and may run a slight temperature, 101° to 102° F.

Nursing and First-Aid Treatment. From early symptoms it is difficult to tell whether the condition is a simple cold or the beginning of influenza, or possibly strangles, and for this reason the animal should be handled as if he had the more serious disease. (See below.) Simple colds will usually respond to rest and a mild laxative diet. The animal must be protected from cold, drafts, and overheating.

STRANGLES (*Distemper*). Strangles is a communicable disease, more often seen in young animals, affecting chiefly the glands in the region of the throat. It is spread by both direct and indirect contact.

Causes. The disease is caused by the infection (nasal, abscess, or other body discharges of a diseased animal) coming in contact with the nasal membranes, or by entering the digestive tract through the mouth.

Prevention. The remarks under prevention of influenza, on page 176, apply to this disease. The greatest danger of spread is by infected watering and feeding utensils. One attack usually renders the animal immune for several years, if not for life. Since newly purchased horses usually develop this disease while in the remount depot, the disease is not common among animals with riders.

Symptoms. Early symptoms are loss of appetite, increased temperature, pronounced moist cough, profuse watery nasal discharge that later becomes thick and yellow, head and neck extended stiffly, and a hot and painful swelling between the jaws. Early depression and weakness are not as pronounced as in influenza. The swelling usually develops, after about a week, into an abscess containing very thick, yellow pus. In more serious cases, abscesses may develop in other parts of the body. This disease often occurs with influenza following shipment.

Nursing and First-Aid Treatment. Segregate sick animals. Absolute rest. Clothe the body according to the weather, and prevent drafts but provide plenty of fresh air. Paint the swelling between the jaws with tincture of iodine once daily. Tempt the appetite and provide feed that is easily chewed. Clean the discharge from the nostrils two or three times daily with cresolis solution of the strength for washing wounds, and after the abscess opens, clean two or three times daily with the same solution. Do not open the abscess with a knife until it is well "pointed" and nearly ready to burst as indicated by loosening of hair, and softening and moistening of skin at the most prominent point. After recovery, the animal may be reconditioned more rapidly than after influenza.

INFLUENZA. This is a very communicable disease affecting chiefly the respiratory system. It is also known as shipping fever. It is spread by both direct and indirect contact.

Causes. Influenza is caused by the animal eating or breathing some of the body

175

discharges of a diseased animal, particularly the nasal and bowel discharges.

Prevention. Cleaniness of surroundings and good condition of animals. Prevention of undue fatigue or exposure, especially incident to shipping. Young, unseasoned animals are particularly susceptible. There is no means of preventive innoculation. Animals that recover are partly immune to subsequent attacks. Quarantine newly acquired animals for twenty-one days. Segregate diseased animals. Disinfect stalls and equipment.

Symptoms. The symptoms are very similar to those of influenza in man. The first symptoms noticed are depression, great weakness, and loss of appetite. Often the first symptoms noticed will be lack of usual vigor; more rapid breathing, a slight, dry, hacking cough; and possibly a slight, watery nasal discharge. At this stage, the temperature is elevated (101.5° to 106° F.) and the mucous membrane of the eyelids will have a sort of brick-red color tinged with yellow. Later, the nasal discharge often becomes more profuse and usually thick and yellow. The acute symptoms usually last about a week. Complications may bring about other symptoms such as swelling of the legs or belly, and diarrhea. Pneumonia is often a complication. Young animals frequently develop strangles at the same time they have influenza.

Nursing and First-Aid Treatment. Isolate the diseased animal. Ordinary drugs are of little use in this disease. Procure the services of a veterinarian. Absolute rest and good nursing are very important. Keep the animal warm with blankets and leg bandages if the weather is at all cold. Allow plenty of sunshine and fresh air but protect the body from drafts. Do everything possible to induce the animal to eat, since the disease is very wasting and it is important to maintain strength. Give plenty of water. Do not give cathartics. After recovery, the animal should be given a week or more of rest and then slowly reconditioned.

PNEUMONIA. Pneumonia is an inflammation of the lung tissue. It may occur in a simple form but is usually a complication of influenza. It should be considered and handled as a communicable disease.

Causes. A complication of other communicable diseases of the respiratory system, especially of influenza; overexposure to cold, especially when heated; overexertion; or irritating fluids or gases entering the lungs.

Prevention. The nature of preventive measures is obvious after considering the causes. Good veterinary attention is essential to prevent the disease occurring as a complication of influenza.

Symptoms. A severe chill, with a temperature varying from 103° to 107° F.; redness of the visible mucous membranes; rapid, difficult breathing; and a full rapid pulse (from fifty to eighty per minute). The nostrils are dilated and the expired air is quite warm. The animal is usually constipated at first, and the urine is scanty and highly colored. The legs and ears are cold, and there is great weakness. The patient may remain constantly standing with the elbows turned out and the head drooping, or it may lie down for short periods. There is frequently a reddish discharge from the nostrils and there may or may not be a cough.

Nursing and First-Aid Treatment. Isolate the animal in a clean, dry place free from drafts, but abundantly supplied with fresh air. Clothe the body according to the season, rub the legs well and bandage warmly. Remove the bandages twice daily, rub the legs well and reapply. Feed easily digested feeds (bran mashes, grass, good hay, and steamed oats), and keep a supply of fresh water within reach at all times. Convalescence from this disease is always slow, and great care must be taken that the amount of exercise or work is suitable to the strength of the animal.

SLEEPING SICKNESS (*Equine Encephalomyelitis*). Equine encephalomyelitis is an acute infectious disease of horses and mules affecting the central nervous system. It is a disease transmissible to man.

Cause. The disease is caused by a filtrable virus. The infective virus is carried from the sick to well animals only through the medium of infected mosquitoes. A few days after biting a diseased animal, the mosquito becomes infective and by its bite may transmit the disease to well animals or to man.

Prevention. Avoid areas of infection. Use all possible means to protect animals from mosquitoes. All Army animals are vaccinated against this disease each spring. This vaccination is very effective, since it produces a strong immunity.

Symptoms. The animal usually shows symptoms of drowsiness. Excitement is sometimes shown in the early stages. The gait is staggering and the animal frequently walks aimlessly in circles or may stand quietly with the head pressed against a stall or fence. Often the animal can swallow only with difficulty or not at all, and saliva mixed with partially chewed feed may drool from the mouth and nose. Later, the animal may fall to the ground and be unable to rise.

Nursing and First-Aid Treatment. Immediate isolation of suspected and diseased animals with complete protection from mosquitoes. Encourage eating and supply plenty of clean drinking water. Endeavor to keep the animal standing. Cold packs applied to the poll and changed frequently are of value. Procure the services of a veterinarian.

GLANDERS. Glanders is a chronic, incurable, and very communicable disease affecting horses and mules. Man also is susceptible.

Causes. The organism that causes the disease is found in the nasal discharges, bowel discharges, and secretions from ulcers on the skin. It may enter the body through the respiratory system, digestive system, or surface wounds. The animal, which by all ordinary signs appears healthy, may be diseased and spreading the disease to other animals. Direct contact between diseased animals is not necessary to spread the disease.

Prevention. The most effective weapon in preventing the disease is the diagnostic *mallein test.* This test detects the infected animals in the early stages of the disease before they have become spreaders of infection or before they have shown any external signs of disease. The infected animals are at once destroyed. By this method, veterinary science has very nearly eradicated the dread disease from the United States.

Symptoms. There is no need for a description of the symptoms in this manual, for it is doubtful that the reader will ever see a diseased animal that will show any visible symptoms.

Nursing and First-Aid Treatment. The disease is incurable and diseased animals must be destroyed as soon as detected by the mallein test.

TETANUS (*Lockjaw*). Tetanus is a disease that affects the nervous system. The disease affects man, but is not considered directly transmissible from horse to man.

Causes. A germ that gains entrance to the body through deep, penetrating wounds or those which do not drain properly. The germ that causes the disease is found in the ground, and in much greater quantities in some localities than others. Soil fertilized with manure is most likely to harbor the germ. Nail punctures of the hoof or deep wounds of the legs are mostly likely to be infected. A minor nail puncture of the hoof, which because of its mild nature may not receive proper treatment, often results in tetanus in an unvaccinated animal.

Prevention. All animals should be permanently immunized against tetanus by vaccination with tetanus toxoid. The vaccination is the same as that for man, except the dose is larger and the stimulating dose is given every two years. The use of tetanus antitoxin as a preventive has been discontinued. Antitoxin is still used in the treatment of the disease. While immunization with tetanus toxoid is highly effective, it is possible that an occasional animal will fail to develop a full protective immunity and may come infected.

Symptoms. Stiffness and spasms of some or all of the voluntary muscles are constant symptoms that usually develop within less than five days after infection. Spasms of the jaw muscles, which fix the jaw so that the mouth can be but partially opened, are usually an early symptom. The first symptom is general muscular stiffness interfering with movement, mastication, swallowing, and drinking. If the head is raised by elevating the muzzle, the haw or third eyelid is drawn partly across the surface of the eyeball. As the disease progresses the gait becomes stilted, with little bending of the joints, and the head is carried stiffly extended. The animal is easily excited and thrown into a spasm of muscular rigidity by any sudden noise. There is little or no increase in temperature in the early stages.

Nursing and First-Aid Treatment. Isolate the animal in a quiet, darkened stall where he will be free from anything that may excite him. Any wounds that can be found should be thoroughly disinfected with tincture of iodine. The diseased animal is not a menace to other animals, since the disease cannot be transmitted directly, except by wound infection with discharges from an infected wound. Feed gruels or thin mashes and keep water in front of the animal at all times. Do not annoy the animal by frequent observation; absolute quiet is the best treatment. Diseased animals that live as long as ten days usually recover.

ANTHRAX (*Charbon*). Anthrax is a very communicable disease most frequently observed in cattle, but also attacking horses and mules. Man is sometimes infected through wounds.

Causes. A germ found in soil, on forage, or in the water of stagnant pools where it may remain alive for long periods. It gains entrance to the body through the digestive system, respiratory system, or through wounds. The disease usually occurs only in certain localities, especially in low-lying land, and usually in summer.

Prevention. Since the disease is quite frequently caused by infected hay, care should be exercised to prevent the use of hay produced on infected land or in an area in which the disease is prevalent. Grazing in such areas should be avoided. Diseased animals should be destroyed and the unopened carcasses burned, together with all discharges, bedding, and feed with which they may have been in contact. All other animals should be vaccinated.

Symptoms. The general symptoms are the same in all animals: high fever, want of appetite, rapidly increased swellings in various parts of the body, spotting and purple coloring of the mucous membranes of the eye and nose, bloody discharges from the nostrils and sometimes the bowels, and rapid death. In the horse or mule, the patient may be found in many cases with rapidly increasing swelling of the throat. This swelling is rather soft and doughy to the feel. The finger pressed into it will leave a dent. It may occur on the chest or belly. Later, a rusty or bloody nasal discharge may be observed. Death usually occurs in about twenty-four to forty-eight hours.

Treatment. Curative measures are usually of no avail. Upon discovery of the first case in a stable, veterinary service should be obtained at once and the rest of the animals should be immunized.

MANGE. Mange is a communicable parasitic skin disease spread by both direct and indirect contact. It is rare in horses and mules in North America, but occurs in other parts of the world, having been very prevalent and having caused a great deal of disability among Army horses in Europe during World War I. In rare instances man may become infected with the horse mange mite.

Causes. A very small parasite (mange mite) that lives on or in the skin. It may be spread by immediate contact with diseased animals or by infected equipment, stables, and cars. Animals in run-down condition are most susceptible, especially if poorly groomed.

Prevention. Maintain animals in good condition and groom well. Avoid the use of civilian stables that may be infected. Segregate diseased animals and disinfect all stables and equipment that may have become contaminated. Properly treat the diseased. Inspect to detect diseased animals. Avoid interchanging equipment among animals. Use individual grooming equipment.

Symptoms. Patchy loss of hair associated with intense itching. The surface of the affected areas is likely to be moist and raw or scabby due to the activity of the parasite and scratching or rubbing by the animal. Later the skin becomes much thickened and tends to lie in ridges.

Nursing and First-Aid Treatment. Segregate diseased animals. Clip and burn hair. For small areas, scrubbing the skin with cresolis of strength recommended for washing wounds may be of some benefit. Routine hand treatment or dipping with lime and sulphur or arsenical dip is the usual method of treatment employed.

179

RINGWORM. Ringworm is a communicable skin disease spread by direct and indirect contact. The type infecting horses is sometimes mildly infective to man.

Causes. Caused by a low form of vegetable life (fungus) quite similar to ordinary mold. The causative fungus will remain infective in stables and corrals and on equipment for long periods.

Prevention. Good grooming. Use only clean equipment. Avoid interchange of grooming tools and other equipment that come in contact with animals. Segregate infected animals. Disinfect all infected horse equipment and stables. Clipped animals are less frequently infected. Young and unseasoned animals are most susceptible, and the disease frequently follows the shipment of this class of animals.

Symptoms. It may be seen in horses of all ages and affects the body, head, and neck particularly. The hair becomes erect and dull on the affected area. After a few days, this hair, with a dry scab, falls off and leaves a bare, circular patch varying in size from a penny to a dollar. The bare surface is slate gray in color and appears scaly. Another variety is mainfested by grayish-white crusts on the bare patches. There is no itching. The hair that covers healed areas is usually of a somewhat darker shade than the surrounding coat.

Nursing and First-Aid Treatment. Segregate diseased animals and disinfect equipment. Scrub the affected area and outside the affected area for several inches with cresolis solution of the strength of one tablespoonful to a pint of water. Loosen and remove scabs. Thereafter, apply tincture of iodine about every second day after rubbing off the loose scabs or scales.

LICE. Lice are small parasites that live on the skin surface.

Causes. Animals with long coats that are not groomed are most frequently infested. Occurs most frequently in late winter or just before spring shedding. Usually contracted from stables that may remain infested from year to year if not disinfected. Spread by direct contact between animals and by infested stables or equipment.

Prevention. Good grooming, clipping, isolation of infested animals, and disinfection of stables and equipment.

Symptoms. Scratching, loss of hair due to rubbing, presence of lice, and the presence of small white eggs (nits) stuck to shafts of some of the hairs. Neck, mane, and back are the regions most frequently infested.

Nursing and First-Aid Treatment. Segregate infested animals. Clip the animal and burn the hair. Wet the entire body with cresolis of the strength solution of one mess-kit spoonful of cresolis to a mess-kit cup brimful of water. Bathe the body again in this solution at the end of five days. Disinfect stables and equipment. Man dose not become infested with horse lice.

INJURIES. An injury, in general, is any break in the continuity of any body tissue or tissues caused by violence, usually external violence. The common types of injuries are *wounds,* of any kind or cause, *bruises, strains, sprains,* and *fractures.* In the stable, injuries are responsible for over half of the total time lost, but in the field they cause over four-fifths of the total noneffectiveness.

Injuries can be prevented very largely by the application of proper methods of animal management. From the standpoint of prevention, the size, type, location, or severity of an injury is of little importance, but a knowledge of the cause of the wound is essential. Injuries can be prevented if the causes can be found and eliminated. Kicks cause nearly half of all animal noneffectiveness in the stable, and equipment injuries are usually the cause of two-thirds or more of the disability in the field.

TENDINITIS. Tendinitis is an inflammation of the large tendons on back of the leg in the cannon region, usually caused by injury rather than disease.

Causes. A strain of these tendons; long toes and low heels; violent efforts and sudden checks, as in jumping or galloping over rocky, uneven ground; long-continued exertion in which the muscles tire and are more easily strained; lack of fit condition; and tight bandaging. A form of tendinitis is sometimes a complication of influenza and strangles.

Prevention. Proper balance and shoeing of the feet. Have the animal in good, fit condition. Avoid other causes of the injury.

Symptoms. Lameness, heat and swelling in the tendon, and sensitiveness of the tendon to pressure. The tendons of the forelegs are far more frequently affected than are those of the hind legs. The entire length of the tendons in the cannon region may be affected or only a part of their length. The lameness and swelling may not be noticeable until the day following the actual injury.

Nursing and First-Aid Treatment. Absolute rest is most essential. As soon as the injury is discovered, shower the leg with cold water from a hose throughout the day or apply cold or ice water packs, and for the night apply a white lotion pack over the injured tendon. After two or three days of this treatment the swelling, heat, and tenderness will have subsided or disappeared in many cases. After the acute swelling and tenderness have disappeared, it is often beneficial to bathe with hot water followed by massage. Tincture of iodine rubbed briskly on the skin over the tendon once daily after the acute soreness has disappeared is often beneficial.

ROPE BURN. Rope burn is an injury usually occurring on the back of the pastern.

Causes. Often caused by the animal getting his foot, usually a hind foot, over his own or an adjacent horse's tie rope, or entangled in a loose picket-line guy rope. An improperly made or improperly used side line or casting rope often results in rope burns. Tying with the tie rope too long is the most frequent cause.

Prevention. Correct methods of restraint. (See page 138.)

Symptoms. The injury may be a simple chafe or abrasion of the skin or it may, if deep, involve the underlying tendon. Lameness is always a symptom.

Nursing and First-Aid Treatment. General method of treatment the same as for scratches (page 169), except that white lotion packs should not be used if the injury is more than a surface one.

SPRAINS. A sprain is a joint injury, usually without any break or injury of the overlying skin.

Causes. Caused by twisting or pulling of the joint or bending the joint beyond its normal range of action. This results in stretching or tearing of the ligaments, which hold the ends of the bones in their proper position to form the joint.

Symptoms. Marked lameness, heat and swelling over the joint, and tenderness on pressure or manipulation. In severe sprains, the animal may refuse to bear any weight on the affected leg.

Nursing and First-Aid Treatment. The treatment should be the same as that outlined for tendinitis on page 181. However, it will be found that recovery from sprains is likely to be much slower.

FRACTURES. A fracture is a broken bone.

Causes. Most fractures result from kicks inflicted by other animals. Fractures of the bones of the legs are sometimes caused by sudden turns or stepping in holes. The tibia, the long bone just under the skin on the inside of the hind leg between the hock and stifle joints, is the most frequently fractured bone in the body. This is accounted for by the fact that it has no muscular protection on the inside of the leg. A kick delivered from one side of the animal may pass under the belly and strike the inside of the opposite hind leg. The bone forming the point of the hip may be fractured by falling or striking it against the side of a doorway.

Symptoms. When any long supporting bone of the leg is completely fractured, the leg dangles helplessly and will bear no weight. The skin over the fractured bone may or may not be broken. When the bone forming the point of the hip is fractured, the animal may show but few symptoms other than lameness, difficulty in advancing the hind leg on that side, tenderness, swelling over the seat of injury, and a noticeable lowering of the point of the hip of that side.

Nursing and First-Aid Treatment. Complete fractures of any of the supporting bones of the legs of horses or mules are considered incurable, and the destruction of the animal is authorized without delay. An incomplete fracture (no separation of the bony fragments) will often heal without impairment of function. A fracture of the bone forming the point of the hip will heal provided the animal is given complete rest for a month or six weeks. After local soreness has disappeared, the animal may receive slow exercise gradually increased. A form of nonpainful, mechanical lameness will disappear in a matter of months.

WOUNDS. Wounds are breaks in the continuity of any soft tissue. They are usually caused by external violence and most frequently involve the skin and underlying tissues. Depending upon their character, they are described as incised (sharp cut), lacerated (torn), penetrating (small opening), and perforating.

Causes. There are many possible causes of wounds. In the stable, kicks are the cause of nearly half of all wounds. In the field most of the wounds are caused by the equipment carried by the horse, especially by the saddle.

182

Treatment of Wounds. The great principle in the successful treatment of wounds may be summed up in the word *cleanliness.* Cleanliness of the wound itself, of the dressing, and of the dresser are of the greatest importance.

Bleeding. If bleeding is profuse, the hemorrhage should be controlled before any attempt is made to clean or close the wound. The easiest means of stopping bleeding is by pressure. Pressure may be applied by tight bandaging above and below the wound, or by placing a pad on the wound and bandaging over it. For ordinary wounds, a simple pad and bandage are usually sufficient to control the flow. If a large vessel happens to be cut and the end exposed, it should be tied with clean thread that has been soaked in antiseptic.

Cleaning Wounds. When the bleeding has stopped, cut the hair from the edges of the wound and remove all dirt, clots of blood, splinters, and foreign bodies of every kind. This may be done by carefully syringing the parts with clean, warm water or a warm antiseptic solution. Foreign bodies may be removed with forceps or by pressing small pieces of cotton soaked in an antiseptic solution, gently over the surface of the wound. Punctured wounds (except those around joints) should be probed to ascertain if any foreign bodies are present.

Drainage. Drainage is necessary to provide for the escape of pus should the wound be infected. Drainage should be provided at the lowest part of the wound.

Dressings. Wounds should be dried carefully with gauze or cotton, treated with an antiseptic, covered with dry gauze or cotton, and a bandage applied; or cotton or gauze, soaked in antiseptic, may be placed over the wound and held in position by a bandage. If the location of the wound will not permit bandaging, the wound may be treated with an antiseptic and covered with a loose covering of cloth or burlap sacking on the inside of which is fastened a clean piece of gauze large enough to cover the wound. Bandaging a wound for too long a period of time may prevent the area from covering itself with skin, resulting in the formation of proud flesh. After a wound has begun to granulate (fill in with repair tissue), it will often heal much better if no dressing or bandage is placed in contact with it, provided it is not irritated by flies.

Rest and Restraint. This will depend entirely upon the nature and extent of the wound. If the injury is slight, the animal may continue to work; otherwise he may be kept in a box stall, crosstied, or subjected to some other form of restraint.

Aftercare. All wounds should be kept dry, and dressing should be changed only often enough to keep the wounds clean. As little washing as possible should be done, and the parts should be sopped instead of rubbed. After cleaning and drying, a new dressing should be applied if it seems advisable.

Flies. The healing of wounds that cannot be covered is sometimes retarded by the presence of flies. The edges of such wounds, and also the surface if not too moist, may be covered lightly with pine tar.

Maggots or Screwworms. Wounds sometimes get flyblown and maggots appear. Their presence is recognized by a thin, bloody discharge from the wound and the red, angry appearance of its edges. If the depths of the wound are carefully examined, movement of the maggots may be noted.

With the forceps, pick out the maggots that are visible and wipe out the cavity with a swab of cotton that has been saturated with tincture of iodine.

Excessive Granulations (Proud Flesh). In sluggish, slow-healing wounds, small, rounded, fleshy masses are often formed that protrude beyond the edges of the wound. These fleshy masses are called proud flesh. The growth may be kept down by removing with scissors to the level of the skin and treating with boric acid or tincture of iodine, or by searing to the level of the skin with a heated iron, care being taken to see that the surrounding skin is not burned.

CONTUSIONS *(Bruises).* A contusion is an injury of a part without a break in the overlying skin.

Causes. Blow from a blunt object. Being kicked by another animal is a common cause.

Symptoms. When over a muscle, they produce soreness and lameness. If severe, they may rupture a blood vessel, which will result in a fluctuating swelling caused by an accumulation of blood in a cavity usually just under the skin. Such injuries are most common on the thigh and buttocks. Contusions over a joint are often very painful and may be mistaken for a sprain of the joint. Bruises on any area where a bone is covered only with skin are often very painful and may result in thickening of the bone at the point of injury.

Nursing and First-Aid Treatment. Rest and general method of treatment as outlined for tendinitis on page 181. In bruises over a muscle, where a fluctuating swelling results that does not reduce in a week or ten days, the swelling may be opened with a knife at its lowest point to allow the fluid contents to escape. After opening, the external parts should be kept clean and the wound painted with iodine once daily.

PENETRATING FOOT WOUNDS *(Nail Pricks).*

Causes. Most penetrating wounds of the foot are caused by the animal stepping on nails or screws. At times, the sensitive tissue of the foot may be penetrated accidentally by a misdirected shoeing nail.

Prevention. Police corrals and roads for loose nails and screws. Exercise care in riding animals in the vicinity of wrecked buildings or new construction. In the field, many nails and screws are picked up in horses' feet near ammunition dumps or warehouses.

Symptoms. Most nail wounds occur in the frog at the juncture of the frog and bar. Lameness may not be present immediately following the infliction of the wound, unless the nail remains in the foot. If the nail does not remain in the wound, appreciable lameness may not appear for a day or more. Nail wounds should receive early treatment or pus may form under the horn and break out at the hair line at the heel. Lameness, heat in the foot, and tenderness are constant symptoms.

Nursing and First-Aid Treatment. If the nail is still imbedded in the horn, before removing it thoroughly clean all dirt from the bottom of the foot by washing with water and then with cresolis solution. Remove the nail or other object. With a knife, thin the horn over a fair-sized area surrounding the penetration and make final opening about one-eighth to one-fourth inch in diameter through the horn to the sensitive tissue. A good complete opening through the horn for drainage of wound secretions is essential. Saturate a rather small pledget of cotton with tincture of iodine and place it on the wound. Over this place a pad of oakum, covering part or all of the bottom of the hoof, hold it in place with strips of tin or light sheet metal of such length and width that their ends can be engaged between the hoof and the branches of the shoe. Do not probe the wound in the sensitive tissue and do not compress the dressing so tightly that the secretions are dammed back into the wound. Dress daily with iodine until the wound appears to be dry and healing, then apply a tar dressing under an oakum pack about every three days until no further dressing is necessary.

EYE INJURIES.

Causes. Eye injuries are usually due to blows, scratches, or punctures from brush or forage, and to small objects lodging on the front of the eyeball or under the lids.

Symptoms. Watery eye, flow of tears from the eye, reddened membranes, and partial or complete closing of the eye are symptoms of all forms of eye injury. If the cornea or clear part of the eyeball itself is injured, the cut or wound may be visible and the area surrounding it will become milk-white in color. Ordinarily, foreign matter merely lodged behind the lids does not cause the eyeball to become milky. The former condition is always more serious.

Nursing and First-Aid Treatment. If there is any foreign body under the lids, flood it out with clean water or remove by the careful use of a tightly rolled swab of cotton gauze. Then flood the eye several times daily with boric acid solution, which is prepared by dissolving two level mess-kit spoonfuls of boric acid in a mess-kit cupful of warm water. Cover the eye with a pad of cotton about eight inches square covered with gauze and held in position with strings tied about the head and to the halter, or sew the pad on the inside of an improvised head bandage (See page 164). In bad cases, soak the pad in boric acid solution before applying. Keep the animal in a darkened stall.

CORNS. A corn is a bruise or an inflammation of the sensitive structure tissues underlying the horn in the region of the heels.

Causes. Caused by external bruising, such as by overreaching, or by bruising due to concussion within the foot incident to the foot striking the ground while the animal is in motion. Conditions that increase the amount of concussion, or changes within the hoof that interfere with the efficiency of the normal shock absorbing mechanism of the foot and throw additional strain on certain structures, are conducive to corns. Fast or long-continued work on hard-surfaced roads, which increases the normal concussion, will cause corns or general foot soreness. Lack of frog pressure, dry feet, high or unduly low heels, leaving shoes on too long, and contracted heels are all possible causes of corns. Lack of normal frog pressure (difficult to secure in the shod foot) is the usual predisposing cause. Defective shoeing is at times a cause. Corns very rarely occur in the hind feet. Corns occur most often in horses with upright pasterns.

Prevention. Shoe for maximum frog pressure, avoid loss of horny frog due to thrush, maintain the normal moisture content and elasticity of the horn of the hoof, avoid unnecessary hard or fast work on unyielding surfaces, prevent contraction of the heels by proper hoof care and corrective shoeing, and avoid the unnecessary use of calked shoes.

Symptoms. Lameness in some degree is always a symptom. With mild corns in both forefeet, lameness may be evidenced only by a slight stiffness and shortness of gait in the forelegs. At times, lameness may be very marked. One or both forefeet may be affected, or only one heel of a foot. The affected heel and quarter will be hot, and possibly there will be soreness to pressure on the bulb of the heel. When the wall at the heel is tapped with a hammer or the buttress or both heels compressed with tongs, the animal will flinch. In light-colored feet, the horn of the wall at the heel will appear red; and the horn of the sole near the heel will be bloodstained. In neglected cases, the inflammation may become so severe that puss will form beneath the horn and break out at the bulb of the heel.

Nursing and First-Aid Treatment. Remove the shoe and reduce the inflammation by cold packs on the hoof or by standing in cold water. Rasping the entire wall thin over the quarters often affords great relief. Lower the wall at the buttress and quarter to relieve that part from bearing on the shoe. Shoe with a bar shoe and a pad to get increased frog pressure. Follow preventive suggestions. If pus has formed, the underrun horn should be removed and free drainage established. General treatment should be the same as for nail wounds, until dry, then apply tar and oakum dressing and shoe with a bar shoe.

TREADS AND OVERREACHING.

Causes. Treads are injuries, or wounds, in the coronet on the front or sides of the foot, and may be self-inflicted or caused by the shoes of other animals. They are frequent and serious among animals with calked shoes and are frequently caused when animals are crowding through doors, and during shipment. Overreaching wounds are self-inflicted injuries to the bulbs of the heel, pastern, or fetlock that are caused by the animal's hind foot striking the part. These injuries are frequently inflicted when landing after jumping an obstacle, at the fast trot, and at times at the gallop. Animals that have not acquired a natural balance while carrying a rider, and "leggy" animals, are particularly likely to be affected. Wounds similar to overreaching wounds are often caused on the heels of the hind feet by another horse crowding up on the animal from the rear.

Prevention. The nature of some of the causes suggests the means of prevention. Shoeing with rocker-toed shoes and high heels, which speed up the action of the forefeet, is often beneficial. Jumping horses, in which the injury cannot be prevented otherwise, should be jumped with bell boots.

Symptoms. Tread wounds are usually in the coronet and the skin, and often some of the horn at the top of the hoof is torn. There is usually heat and swelling in the part. Most overreaching wounds occur at the bulbs of the heel, and the skin above the horn is more bruised and scraped than cut. The horn at the heel is torn loose and may be separated from the sensitive tissues considerably below the hair line. Sometimes the horn does not separate until several days after the bruise occurs. Lameness is usually not pronounced unless dirt packs between the loose horn and sensitive tissue, or the wound becomes infected.

Nursing and First-Aid Treatment. Clip the hair around the wound and clean thoroughly with cresolis solution. Remove all foreign material. With scissors, cut off all loose flaps of skin or tissue; and with a hoof knife or rasp thin the horn in the region of the injury. Saturate a small pledget of cotton with iodine and bandage it tightly over the injury. Dress in this manner daily. When the wound appears dry and is healing, cover with tar and a small pad of oakum and bandage tightly.

INTERFERING WOUNDS. Interfering wounds are self-inflicted wounds made on some part of the inside of the leg, usually the fetlock, by being struck by the hoof or shoe of the opposite leg.

Causes. Defective conformation, such as toeing out, cow-hocked, and narrow-breasted. Fatigue is often a cause in animals that do not otherwise interfere. Defective shoeing is often a cause. Traveling over uneven footing may cause temporary interfering. Fatigued animals are more likely to interfere behind.

Prevention. Corrective shoeing. If not correctable, use leather or felt interfering boots, or pad the part with oakum held in place with a bandage.

Symptoms. The injury may vary from a slight roughing of the hair at the coronet, or inside of the fetlock, to a deep wound causing marked lameness. At the moment of interfering the animals will often carry the leg for a few steps without putting weight on it, then go very lame for a few steps and soon proceed without lameness.

Nursing and First-Aid Treatment. Treat the same as other wounds. Apply a thick, padded dressing to avoid further injury.

QUARTER CRACK.

Causes. Dryness of feet, lack of frog pressure, contracted heels, injuries or deformity of the coronary band, long toes, large nails, and nails driven too near the heel.

Symptoms. A crack in the wall of the hoof that follows the grain of the wall, occurring most frequently in the quarters. It may extend from the coronary band to the bearing surface of the wall, but as a rule the crack begins at the coronary band and extends downward only a short distance, increasing the length at the same rate as that of the growth of the wall. Only those cracks which extend through the entire thickness of the wall and cause bleeding or lameness are of consequence.

Nursing and First-Aid Treatment. The first step is to soften the horn of the wall by wet packs, bran poultices, or standing the animal in water for a few days. After this, clean out the crack and cut away the overlapping edges of the horn. For an inch or more on each side of the crack, and for one and one-half inches or more downward from the coronary band, rasp the wall as thin as possible without injuring the "quick" or drawing blood. Trim away the bearing surface of the wall from a point one-half inch in front of the crack back to and including the buttress so that the affected quarter does not come in contact with the shoe. Shoe with a bar shoe, with good frog pressure, over a leather pad with tar and oakum. Keep the wall soft by the daily application of tar, especially over the crack. A little tar rubbed vigorously into the coronary band once a week will stimulate the growth of horn.

EQUIPMENT-CAUSED INJURIES. Equipment-caused injuries, especially those caused by the saddle and the field equipment attached thereto, are extremely important, since in the field such injuries may be the cause of two-thirds or more of all animal disability. Generally the longer a mounted command is in the field, the greater will be the number of injuries of this type. When horses are worked hard and probably underfed, one of the first places to show muscle waste is the back. The whole shape of the back is altered and the thickness of the muscle padding overlying the bones will be so diminished in thickness that the likelihood of injury is greatly increased. This loss of muscle will render the once-well-fitted saddle almost hopelessly ill-fitting, and active measures must be taken to compensate as fully as possible for the loss. The injuries that are caused by equipment are almost always either abrasions (rubs) or contusions (bruises). Occasionally the back will scald, a condition in which the hair and outer layers of the skin may peel as if they had been blistered.

General Causes. All equipment-caused injuries are caused by either friction or pressure. Obviously there can be pressure without friction, but there cannot be friction without some degree of pressure. Pressure may be almost constant, as would result from a very tightly cinched saddle, or it may be intermittent (pounding or blows), as would result from a loose cantle roll or from the rider "pounding" the cantle of the saddle. The damage done to a back by constant pressure is the result of a diminution, or almost complete loss, of the blood supply to the skin and immediately underlying tissue because of compression of the blood vessels. Whether skin dies quickly or slowly depends upon the degree of compression of the blood vessels. If complete, the area under pressure may die in a few hours; if incomplete, it may take several days. The greater the weight on the back, the greater the pressure on the skin, and with every increase in pressure less blood is circulating through it. Pressure is never quite the same at any two points on the back, so that damage will probably appear only at the points of excessive pressure. However, the most perfectly fitting saddle it is possible to conceive will cause a pressure sore if worn long enough with no relief from pressure. The effect of pressure on the blood supply of the skin is well demonstrated by an examination of the sweat markings on the back when the saddle is removed. The hair will never be uniformly wet with sweat. It will be wettest on those areas which were covered by the blanket but which *did not* carry the weight of the saddle. The areas that were pressed upon by the bars will be drier, and if the pressure has been excessive at any point, the hair will be dry or practically dry. The character of the sweating is explained by the simple fact that pressure on the skin lessens the blood supply to

188

the sweat glands and the excretion of sweat is diminished or completely stopped. The damage done by intermittent pressure or blows is not due to a blood starvation in the part, but to direct tissue injury. The damage done by pressure is not evident immediately upon removal of the saddle, but usually manifests itself within an hour or so by a hot and painful swelling. A gradual diminution of the pressure will in no way lessen the damage that has been done nor will it lessen the severity of the tissue reaction. The sooner the offending pressure is relieved the less will be the damage. Friction causes abrasions of the skin. Some part of the saddle or equipment rubbing on the skin wears away the hair and upper layer of the skin more rapidly than the body can replace the lost tissue, and an abrasion results. Friction-caused injuries (abrasions) are more superficial and far less severe than pressure-caused injuries. An abrasion will usually scab over with a rather hard scab. If the animal is ridden and the affected area is not protected from pressure, even rather moderate pressure on this hard scab may cause the death of the deeper layers of the skin beneath the scab, and a so-called sit-fast is the result.

Predisposing Causes. There are many predisposing or contributing causes of sore backs. Even though all other things may be perfect, if the horse has not been conditioned properly and the skin of the back hardened and accustomed to carrying weight, saddle sores are certain to result when the horse is suddenly called upon to carry the weight of full field equipment. Excessively long hours under the saddle are sure to cause injuries even under the best of conditions. Excluding failure to condition the animals, nothing is more productive of sores than improperly assembled, fitted, or adjusted riding equipment, and yet no contributing cause should be more easy to remedy. Dirty equipment, particularly dirty saddle blankets, is inexcusably the cause of many abrasions and some pressure-caused injuries. A hard, sweat-caked blanket does little to pad the back or equalize areas of pressure. There can be no doubt that an improper seat and improper methods of riding, such as slouching or "pounding" in the saddle, have been the causes of many sore backs. However, it is probable that in many instances the cause would have been found elsewhere had the research been more diligent.

Prevention. Due to the fact that saddle sores do occur even under what appears to be the best of management, it is reasonable to ask whether they can be prevented to any great extent, or whether it is one of the penalties we must pay for having domesticated the horse. It is a common but not always a necessary penalty; and its frequency is greatly increased by indifference, ignorance, and lack of intelligence. If the causes of saddle sores are fully understood and active measures taken to locate and eliminate them, the number of injuries can be greatly reduced. First, the predisposing or contributing causes discussed on page   must be reduced in number or, if possible, eliminated. Next the specific cause must be found and overcome. Every injury is due to a certain definite cause, which if removed produces no further effect. The position or location and character of an injury are not accidental circumstances, but are the result of some definite abuse. If one is familiar with the various causes of such injuries, a glance at a saddle sore should immediately suggest its possible cause or causes and the means of prevention. The location of the injury will determine the offending position of the equipment, and

189

its character will indicate whether it has ben caused by pressure or friction. Remember that it is rare indeed that friction and constant excessive pressure are present at the same point. However, excessive pressure may be present at one point and friction at another not far distant. In fact, excessive bearing of the saddle at one point may lead to excessive friction at another. Thus equalized bearing (pressure) of the saddle is to be sought as the basic method of preventing both types of saddle-caused injuries. When a saddle is in proper position on the back and has its most even bearing, it should be cinched only tight enough to prevent turning when mounting or dismounting and to prevent undue movement when the horse is in motion. A cinch that is too tight not only interferes with breathing, but unnecessarily adds to the pressure on the back. The relief from constant pressure afforded by leading, loosening the cinch, and occasionally lifting and resetting the saddle during the day's march is of great value in decreasing the number of pressure-caused injuries.

10

The Horse in Motion

Every student of equitation should have at least a basic knowledge of the horse's gaits and the manner of locomotion. With this knowledge the rider perceives why a certain position of head, neck, body, and members facilitates the performance of the desired movements. It becomes clear that the aids of rein, leg, and weight, instead of being merely signals indiscriminately selected, are carefully selected means of assisting or retarding the action of certain parts so as to make the desired movement the most natural thing for the animal to do under the circumstances. In judging horses, a knowledge of the mechanics of locomotion is of great value in determining the beauties and defects of the gaits.

CENTER OF GRAVITY AND BASES OF SUPPORT. It seems impossible to determine exactly the center of gravity of an animal's body. Experiments have shown that the center of gravity of the average horse, in a normal standing posture, is a point approximately at the intersection of three planes passed through the body as follows: a perpendicular median plane dividing the body on its long axis, a perpendicular plane passed through the body at the girth, and a horizontal plane slightly below the level of the point of the shoulder. Obviously the conformation of an animal will vary this location. A long neck and heavily developed forequarters, with relatively light hindquarters, will place the center of gravity farther forward than in the average animal and result in an animal heavy on his forehand. Any displacement or movement of the head, neck, or legs will cause this center of gravity to vary its position within the mass. The extension of the head and neck displaces the center of gravity forward, and a turning of the head or neck displaces it laterally. Movement of the animal in any direction is usually preceded by a displacement of the center of gravity in the direction of movement; however, in

191

Center of Gravity *It has been assumed for years that the location is the thoracic area, shifting slightly according to speed and direction of movement. Recently authorities at Cornell University have developed a method of locating the center. A line is drawn through the shoulder (describing what is commonly known as the shoulder angle) and a second line is drawn through the hock and stifle. At the point of intersection a bisecting line is dropped to a point just below midway of the body. When the hind legs are drawn up under the body (collection) the shoulder angle decreases slightly and the center shifts to the rear. When the thrust of the hind legs is farther back (as in racing or jumping) the hock-stifle line becomes more horizontal, thus shifting the center of balance farther forward. [Ed.]*

highly collected gaits the center of gravity may be displaced considerably to the rear to gain lightness of the forehand, but lateral displacement is always in the direction of movement. The speed of the gait is to a considerable degree proportionate to the forward displacement of the center of gravity. When the animal is in motion, the body is moved in both the vertical and horizontal directions. The "daisy cutter" or horse with low action, and long, free stride moves his body a minimum in the vertical direction is pleasant to ride. Exaggeration of vertical movement greatly increases muscular fatigue, decreases the speed, and makes the gait rougher. If we could view in profile the path of movement of the center of gravity of a galloping horse, it would, no doubt, appear as an undulating line or series of waves, the summits of which would be separated by the length of one stride. The body of the horse in any leaped gait is at its maximum elevation above the ground during the period of suspension. The untrained horse at freedom develops a coordination of muscular movement and balance that we call "natural balance." He learns to juggle his center of gravity in such a way that he may perform many intricate movements. The degree of natural balance varies with the conformation and mental makeup of the horse. Certainly at play, the untrained horse at times performs spontaneously some of the higher schooling movements with a degree of brilliance and perfection that we might strive for years to attain under the saddle. When the horse is ridden, we try to place the center of gravity of the rider as nearly as possible directly over the center of gravity of the horse, but in any event we destroy his "natural balance." By training in mounted exercises, we assist the horse in developing a new and "acquired balance" while carrying a rider. The center of gravity of the combined mass of horse and rider is, of course, considerably farther above the ground than that of the horse alone, and stability is decreased. The rider presents to the horse a body with an independent center of gravity, and the horse can do little to control its position in relation to his own. The rider can very materially control the position of his center of gravity with relation to that of the horse. If he moves his center of gravity in the direction in which the horse is shifting his for a movement, he accelerates or aids the movement and "goes with his horse." If he moves in an opposite direction, he hinders the movement and tends to check the action. The racing jockey, with his high and forward seat, is assisting the horse in a forward displacement of the combined center of gravity, and consequently is increasing the speed. It is always better that the rider remain passive during the performance of a desired movement rather than for him to execute an ill-timed movement intended to assist, or perchance a contradictory movement.

At rest, in his normal position at attention, the *base of support* of the horse is an elongated rectangle, formed by lines connecting the feet. If we drop a perpendicular line from the center of gravity to the plane of the base of support, we will find that this line does not meet the rectangle in its exact center, where it should for maximum stability, but on the long axis of the figure nearer the end formed by the line joining the two forefeet. Thus forward and lateral movements are executed with the greatest ease, since the body is relatively unstable in these directions. The forefeet carry about thirteen percent more of the body weight than the hind; e.g., a thousand-pound horse might carry 565 pounds of his weight on his forefeet and 435 pounds on his hind feet. While the base of support at rest is a four-point base or a rectangle, we find that in motion the bases of support appear as triangles, lines, or a point and disappear entirely during suspension in leaped gaits. While the forelegs of the horse supply some impulse of propulsion, in the ordinary gaits their function seems to be support and cushioning of the body weight while the hind legs supply the main propulsive impulses.

STUDY OF GAITS. For at least two centuries horsemen have been studying in detail the rhythm and mechanics of the various gaits of the horse. In earlier studies the work was confined to the tale told by the tracks and direct observation with the eye. The latter is very difficult when we consider that the feet of a running or trotting horse, traveling thirty miles per hour, attain a velocity of at least sixty miles per hour. Later, various forms of simple pneumatically or electrically operated devices were developed to record the timing and order of movement of the feet. In 1879 instantaneous photographs made with a succession of separate cameras added new knowledge and disproved many former beliefs. The development of the high-speed motion-picture camera, and the resulting slow-motion capability in projection, opened the field for research study of the gaits in all their phases and, in addition, the reactions of the rider. While this method has been used to some extent, there is much work that might yet be done to deny or confirm our present knowledge, and to study unexplored phases.

NOTATION. For the purpose of placing on paper in a schematic form for the study of the timing and order of movement of the feet, the system known as the Notation of Marey was long ago developed and adopted. The system is comparable to music in that the symbols represent time intervals. Let us consider the notation of a man walking. We can let a line of a certain length and kind represent the period of time that the man's left foot is in contact with the ground, and a different line for the time his right foot is in contact. The intervals between the succeeding lines, representing successive contacts of the left foot, would represent the periods of time the foot was off the ground, and similarly for the right. The notation would look like this:

```
Left foot: - - - - - - - - - - - -     - - - - - - - - - - - -     - - - - - - - - - - - -
Right foot:        ************          ************          ************
```

We might place this on cross-section paper so that each subdivision of the ruling would represent, say, 1/128th of a second, and we could then readily see the duration of each movement as represented in the notation. To represent the notation for the horse we merely have to add two more symbols. Most of the notations shown hereafter differ from those shown in *The Exterior of the Horse* (Goubax and Barrier), in that the comparative time intervals of flight and contact of the members are absolute, since they are taken from original studies of slow-motion pictures of various gaits.

DEFINITIONS. To be able to discuss gaits we must have a clear conception of certain terms used in their description. The term *gaits* is applied to the various recognized means by which progression is usually accomplished by the play of the

194

members. We classify first as to whether they are *natural* or *acquired*. Some authorities list the walk, trot, gallop, and amble as natural gaits; however, the amble is not used naturally by more than a very small percentage of our American horses. In some of our Standardbred horses the amble and pace appear as natural gaits, and in some Saddlebred horses the special saddle gaits may be used as natural gaits. However, only the walk, trot, and gallop seem to be most nearly natural to all horses, irrespective of breed. *Acquired* gaits are those developed as a result of training or breeding, or both combined: the amble, pace, rack, and running walk. Most of the acquired gaits, except the pace, bear close resemblance in their manner of performance to either the walk or trot.

Gaits are further classified as *marched* or *leaped: marched* when one or more of the members is in contact with the ground throughout the complete stride; *leaped* when all of the members are clear of the ground during some stage of the complete stride. During the time the body is completely clear of the ground it is said to be in *suspension,* while *projection* is the measurement in time or space of movement during suspension. The gallop is always leaped and the walk marched.

Gaits are classified as *diagonal* or *lateral: diagonal,* if the diagonal members, left fore and right hind or right fore and left hind, are advanced and planted in unison or distinct succession—all of the natural gaits are diagonal; *lateral,* if lateral members are advanced and planted in unison or distinct succession. The pace is a distinct lateral gait.

The term *beat* is applied to the sound produced by a foot striking the ground, or sound of the simultaneous striking of two feet.

The term *time* is applied to the time interval between successive beats, or successive phases of the stride.

The *track* or *trail* is the succession of imprints of the feet upon the ground.

Stride is the distance between successive imprints of the same member. In moving the distance of one stride, the horse completes the cycle of movement of the members characteristic of the gait.

Step is the distance between two successive imprints of the two forefeet or the two hind feet; it usually is equal to one-half of the stride; however, in lameness the steps are of unequal length.

The term *contact* is applied to the meeting of the foot with the ground, and is measured in time. This time is frequently divided into halves, the dividing line being the instant the leg is vertical over the supporting foot.

The term *flight* is applied to the movement of a foot from a contact to a successive contact. We describe it in time, direction, and length, the latter being synonymous with stride of the member.

The gait is said to be *collected* when the length of the stride is shortened and the height of action is increased, with a displacement of the center of gravity to the rear of its usual position and with a consequent lightening of the forehand. When a horse is in any collected gait he is not strongly obligated to any established direction of movement, for he can check the movement considerably after its direction with a minimum of effort and without loss of balance or smoothness. Collection in place is brought about by a backward displacement of the center of gravity, and usually a shortening of the base of support. The horse is disposed as to

195

be in the best position to initiate a movement in any direction. This implies muscular and mental alertness in anticipation of movement.

The gait is said to be *extended* when the length of the stride is increased and the height of action or flight is diminished and there is a forward displacement of the center of gravity. The members are fully extended at the beginning and termination of contact. In general, *extension* may be the opposite of *collection*.

THE NATURAL GAITS.

Walk. The walk may be defined as a slow, four-beat, diagonal, marched gait in which diagonal members are advanced and grounded in succession. From a halt the movement may be begun by either a fore or a hind foot, but more frequently it is begun with the left fore. In such case the order of movement and grounding will be: LF - RH - RF - LH. With each grounding a beat is produced. The times between the beats are equal in the ordinary walk. The walk may vary in rate very considerably in the same or different animals; it may be as slow as two miles per hour, or some individuals may walk at six miles per hour or more. The cavalry service has established the rate of four miles per hour as the marching rate at the walk. The average horse, unless trained to the gait, may experience some difficulty in walking at this rate. The notation of the ordinary walk is:

Let us examine this notation in detail. First it appears that the time of flight of any member is only about one-half the time of contact. In the particular gait shown the ratio is 7:13, and, considering each character in the lines as representing a unit of time, the stride is complete in twenty units. Let us pick up the gait after it is established at the time when the LF goes into flight. We now find the horse has a two-point lateral base of support (RF-RH), which persists for two units of time. Next the LH contacts, giving the horse a three-point base of support (RF-RH-LH), a triangular base that persists three units of time. The three-point base of support ceases with the beginning of flight of the RH, and the horse has a two-point diagonal base of support (RF-LH), which persists for two units of time. Following this analysis through for a full stride, we find that during that period of time the horse has had eight distinct and different bases of support, alternating three-point and two-point bases. Represented diagrammatically, the successive bases of support in the one stride we have just considered would appear as follows:

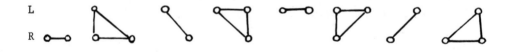

Now if we examine the track or trail we will find that it looks like this:

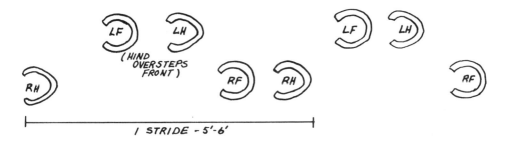

The capital letters F and H represent the imprints of the fore and hind feet respectively.

In all good walkers the imprint of the hind foot will be in advance of the imprint of the forefoot on the same side. If the rate is slower we may find the hind superimposed on the fore or in rear of it. The natural ordinary walk varies considerably in different horses but basically it remains the same. The walk may be either "collected" or "extended." In the collected walk, the spacing or time between the beats, instead of being equal, becomes irregular. The time between the beats of diagonals is decreased, while that between laterals is increased and the gait begins to take the nature of a slow marched trot. In the walk, the vertical displacements of the center of gravity are slight, hence it is the least fatiguing of the gaits.

Trot. The trot may be defined as a more or less fast two-beat, diagonal, leaped gait. The varieties of the trot are slow (short), ordinary, long, and racing. The slow or short trot, if not collected, is a marched gait and the imprint of the hind foot will be found in rear of its corresponding fore. There is a very fleeting period when all four members are in contact. In theory, the ordinary trot is a perfect two-beat gait in which the diagonal members are advanced and grounded absolutely in unison; but it appears that in the natural ordinary trot of most horses the beat of the hind very slightly precedes the beat of its diagonal (imperceptible to ear). In the racing trot the movement of the diagonals begins to be disassociated, with the beat of the hind preceding the fore, giving an irregular four-beat trot. The notation of the ordinary trot with perfect unison of movement of the diagonals would look like this:

This is of the same horse and drawn on the same time scale as the preceding notation for the walk. Examining this notation, we find that the stride is completed in sixteen time units and that the foot is in contact six time units and in flight ten time units, almost the exact reverse of what we had for the walk. The cadence of the trot in this instance is only one-quarter greater than at the walk, yet the speed is increased more than two times. Speed is increased by shorter and more powerful thrusts of the members and increased length of stride. Beginning our

197

examination of the stride with the termination of contact of the left diagonal, we find that the body is in suspension for a period of two time units, or until the right diagonal (RF-LH) is grounded. This two-point diagonal base of support (a line) persists for six time units; next, a period of suspension for two time units, followed by contacting of the left diagonal (LF-RH) for six time units, completing the stride. In each stride we have two different bases of support and two periods of suspension. Represented diagrammatically the bases of support would look like this:

The trail on the ground might look like this:

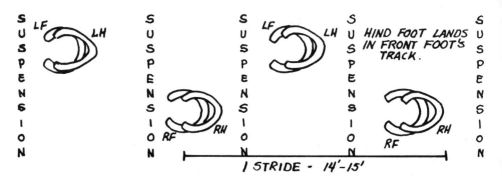

The average stride at the ordinary trot (eight to nine miles per hour) will be about that shown above. It will be noted that the imprint of the hind is slightly in advance of that of its fore on the same side. The horse is said to "overstep." The length of the "overstep" indicates the distance the body traveled while in suspension. The length of the overstep is often as much as six feet in the racing trot, when the length of the stride is nineteen or twenty feet. The speed of the trot may vary from five miles per hour to over thirty miles per hour. The rate of eight miles per hour has been accepted as the regulation marching rate.

Since the center of gravity is displaced considerably in a vertical direction at the trot, it is obvious that this gait is far more fatiguing than the walk. If the energy expended in walking a mile is one unit, it has been estimated that slightly more than two units will be expended in trotting a mile at eight miles per hour. The "collected" and "extended" trots will be considered later.

Gallop. The gallop may be defined as a fast, three-beat, diagonal, leaped gait in which the simultaneous beats of one diagonal (second-beat) occur between two *successive* beats of the opposite diagonal. The varieties of the gallop are slow gallop (canter), ordinary or natural gallop, full gallop, and racing gallop. This classification is based on rate of movement. Of course the timing of movement of the members varies with the variety. A horse is said to "gallop in the right (left) lead" when the right (left) forefoot is last to leave the ground before the period of suspension.

198

A horse is said to *gallop true* when he gallops on the right (left) lead when turning to the right (left). If the reverse is true, he is said to *gallop false*.

The natural gallop is *united;* that is, the horse gallops with the forefeet galloping in the same order as the hind, producing a diagonal gait. In the *disunited* gallop the fores gallop in reverse order to the hinds, a lateral gait.

The notation of the ordinary gallop (about twelve or fourteen miles per hour) on the left lead, of the same horse used above for the trot and walk, would look like this:

```
LF:        - - - -        - - - -        - - - -        - - - -
RF:      *****        *****        *****        *****
LH:    - - - -      - - - -      - - - -      - - - -
RH:  *****      *****      *****      *****
```

First, we note that the stride was completed in fifteen units of time; the LH was in contact five units of time and in flight ten units of time. The contact time of other members is less, about four and one-half units for the diagonal members and four units for the leading left fore. The contact time of the leading fore is slightly shortened, due to the increasing acceleration of the body while this member is in contact. Beginning the stride with the contact of the RH, we find the horse has a one-point base of support for about three units of time. The diagonals (LH-RF) contact, giving him a three-point base of support (RF-LH-RF) for two units of time. The right hind then goes into flight, and the horse has a two-point diagonal (RF-LH) base of support for one unit of time. The left fore is grounded next, and there is a three-point base of support (LH-RF-LH) for two units of time. The diagonals then pass into flight and there is a one-point base of support (LF), leading foot, for two units of time. This is followed by a period of projection for three units of time. In each stride there are five distinct and different bases of support and a period of suspension. The bases of support in a stride diagrammatically represented would look like this:

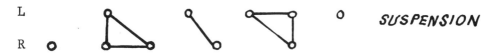

Of course, actually these triangular bases are so elongated as to appear almost as a line when the trail is examined. The trail would look something like this:

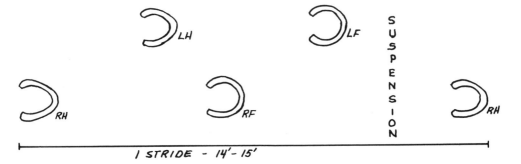

199

The speed of the gallop may vary from possibly as slow as six miles per hour to over forty miles per hour. The world's running record for a mile is 1:32 (Mopsus) over a straight course and 1:34 2/5 (Equipoise) over an oval course.* For military use the maneuvering gallop is at the rate of twelve to fourteen miles per hour, and the full gallop at about sixteen to eighteen miles per hour. If the gallop is slowed to around eight miles per hour (canter), the timing changes and the gait becomes a four-beat gait. The forefoot of the diagonal contacts before the hind so that the diagonal beats disassociate and the gait begins to take on the character of a lateral gait. If the horse was on the right lead, the beats would be produced in this order; first beat–LH; second beat–LF; third beat–RH; fourth beat–RF. At this gait the bases of support would appear as follows:

The length of the stride might be shortened to as little as five or six feet.

If the speed of the gallop is increased above that of the natural gallop, the beat of the diagonal begins to disassociate, but in this instance it is due to the hind foot of the diagonal grounding before the fore. The gait may, at thirty-five miles per hour, be a distinct four-beat gait with almost equal spacings between the beats. The length of the stride may be twenty-five feet or more.

The notation of the gait would look like this:

```
LF:         - - -         - - -          - - -          - - -
RF:    ***         ***          ***          ***
LH:  - - -        - - -         - - -          - - -
RH: ***        ***          ***          ***
```

The stride is accomplished in only thirteen units of time, each member being in flight more than three times as long as it is in contact. Contrast this with the walk. The three-point bases of support have disappeared. Diagrammatically represented the bases of support in each stride would look like this:

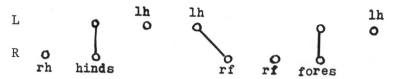

The gallop is the most fatiguing of gaits, and it has been estimated that it requires five to ten times as much energy as is required at the walk to cover a like distance. In the performance of this gait, the leading diagonal does much more work than the other diagonal pair of legs. For instance, the horse we have just considered is working his LF and RH more than the other diagonal. To equalize the work done, the horse must change leads. Racing horses almost always gallop true around the turns, but often change leads upon reaching the head of the stretches to rest the left diagonal, and then change to a true lead on reaching the next turn.

*As of 1935 (Ed.)

THE LEAP OR JUMP. The leap may be executed from a standing position in collection or from any of the natural gaits, but in the experienced jumper it is best performed from the gallop. Being the faster gait, it affords the horse the needed momentum to negotiate the obstacle, and, what is more important, the position of the members in the gallop are almost identical with the position necessary for jumping. However, in jumping, the usual locomotory order is reversed. Very low or narrow obstacles are often taken by merely an increase in the length of the projection of one stride of the gallop.

Assume that a horse at a gallop on the left lead is approaching an obstacle of moderate height. During the last stride or two before the leap, he will slightly diminish his speed, at which time he is estimating his obstacle, judging his point of takeoff, measuring his stride, and disposing his feet in preparation for the takeoff. In the last stride or two there is marked disassociation of the diagonal beat. The beat of the left hind more closely follows that of the right hind, and, of course, the hind feet are placed more closely together on the ground. The more closely together the hind feet are planted, the more effective will be their combined thrust in the leap. To obtain this effect the horse will speed up the action, but shorten the phase of flight of the left hind foot. In the last stride the base of support is somewhat elongated, and the horse appears to be crouching on the forehand with the forelegs forward receiving the shock. The forequarters are thrown upward off the forelegs, somewhat as a pole-vaulter using the vaulting pole. The forelegs give a powerful downward thrust. Coincident with this movement, the center of gravity within the body is shifted to the rear and the hindquarters are dropped, while the strongly flexed hind legs are advanced well under the mass and grounded. There is a short period of suspension that has been accomplished by the forelegs before the hind legs are grounded for the final thrust. The right hind foot will be grounded slightly in advance of the imprint of the left fore. The left hind imprint will be a short distance in advance of that of the right hind. The long axis of the body is now in the position that the powerful extension thrust of the hind legs will project the body (center of gravity) into the trajectory calculated to clear the obstacle. At this point it might be well to discuss the possibility of a change of lead that we so frequently observe in leaping. In most cases the change of lead, if one is to take place, is originated in the hind feet in this last contact before the thrust is given. Above, we have noted that to assure that the hind feet are planted close together the horse speeds the action of grounding of his left hind. If this action is sufficiently speeded, it would ground the left hind before the right hind is grounded, a change of lead with the hind members would be accomplished and the change in front completed before the forefeet are grounded on the other side of the obstacle. This change may possibly be explained by the supposition that the last hind foot to leave the ground (the leading hind foot) imparts to the body a slightly rotating action, and the diagonal forefoot is extended to contact first on landing. The horse we were previously considering has not made this change of lead with his hind legs, and so does not change leads, but lands, as would be expected, on his right forefoot followed by his left fore. Again the horse springs off his forelegs and the hinds pass under the mass and contact the ground in a position in advance of the imprints of the fores, and then the fores are grounded quite the same as in the usual galloping stride.

201

The height of the obstacle, or rather the apparent height of the obstacle, as measured against the jumping ability of the horse, influences the probability of a change of leads. The higher or more difficult the obstacle, the more likely is a horse to change. The horse of average jumping ability will change leads more than fifty percent of the time over obstacles three feet six inches to four feet in height. Clever and experienced jumping horses change leads much more frequently than do horses of moderate experience. Experienced horses will change seventy-five to ninety percent of the time over the obstacles above four feet three inches in height. Many horses prefer to approach the obstacle on the right lead and may perform better from this lead. This is explained by the fact that most training and show jumping is done to the right hand, giving the horse more experience on this diagonal.

When the body, after the takeoff, passes into the trajectory of its flight, its movement along this trajectory must follow, in general, the laws of movement of a projected body; however, the horse can and very often does modify the movement to some extent by alternation of the position of his members while in flight. As a general rule, low and broad obstacles are covered by a long and flat trajectory, while obstacles of height are taken with a short and arching trajectory. Occasionally, over obstacles of considerable breadth and sometimes over those of height, the legs will execute galloping movements while the body is in flight. Rotation of the body, and especially a rotation of the hindquarters, is often resorted to by the horse to place the members in a better position to clear the obstacle than would be possible by flexion of the legs alone. The world's high-jump record for a horse with a rider is eight feet and 13/16 inches. Obstacles of more than thirty-two feet in breadth have been cleared by a horse with a rider.

SCHOOLING OR TRAINING MOVEMENTS. For the purpose of giving the horse an "acquired balance" with a rider, for discipline, and for muscular development, the horse in training is given training exercises known as schooling movements. These movements are not gaits in themselves but merely modifications of the natural gaits that, when performed under the restrictions imposed, tend to promote proper muscular development, coordination, and suppleness. The execution of these movements is not to be considered an accomplished end *per se,* but rather a step toward the development of a horse best fitted to perform the work for which he is to be used. The training movements might be likened in their purpose to the finger exercises of the pianist.

ACQUIRED GAITS.

Pace. The pace may be defined as a fairly fast, two-beat, lateral, leaped gait in which lateral pairs of legs are advanced and grounded in unison. Pacing is a natural gait for some Standardbred horses. The slow pace, or amble, is at times a marched gait. The pace at either extreme of speed is usually a four-beat gait. The pace is primarily a gait for harness horses, and it is not used as a military gait because of the difficulty of changing to the gallop from the pace. The pace is much less stable than the trot, since the bases of support are always lateral. The maximum speed of the pace slightly exceeds that of the trot.

Rack. The rack is an acquired saddle gait. Slow-motion pictures of the saddle gaits

202

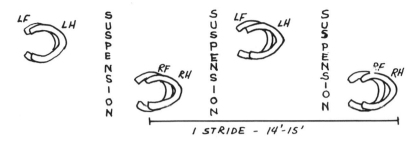

| STRIDE - 14'-15'

Although not a gait employed by the Cavalry, and therefore not included in its manual, this diagram of the pace will be of interest if only to compare it with that of the trot. [Ed.]

have not been available for study; therefore, reference is made to what has been written on the subject. The rack and the singlefoot are apparently the same gait; at least the latter is one variety of the former. The gait has been described as a modified trot and also as a modified pace. At times it partakes of the nature of the trot, and at other times the pace, and when a true singlefoot, it is exactly between the two gaits. The action of the hind foot precedes the fore, whether the gait approaches the lateral or the diagonal character. It is always a collected gait as the horse is driven strongly forward with the legs against a restraining curb. The rack, after the walk, trot, and canter, is the fourth required show gait of the five-gaited American Saddle Horse. The speed of the gait varies between five and twenty miles per hour, but in the show ring it more often approaches the higher rate, at least twelve miles per hour being required by most judges.

In addition to the four saddle gaits already mentioned, the five-gaited horse is expected to show one of the "slow gaits" listed in the following paragraphs.

Fox-Trot. The fox-trot is a slow, marched trot in which there is a disassociation of the diagonal beats, the action of the forefoot preceding that of the hind. The rate of this gait is about five or six miles per hour and is always performed on a loose rein and with a low carriage of the head.

Running Walk. The running walk has been described as a slow, marched trot with disassociation of the diagonal beat, the beat of the hind slightly preceding that of its diagonal fore. By others the gait has been described as an accelerated walk. The latter is probably more nearly correct. The head is carried higher, the rein is tighter, and the speed is greater than in the preceding gait.

Slow Pace. The slow pace is a slow, marched pace with a slight disassociation of the beat of the lateral members, (broken amble).

ADVANCED SCHOOLING MOVEMENTS

Dressage. The word *dressage* is a French world meaning "training" as applied to the training of a horse. A "dressage exhibition" or an "individual dressage" means the exhibition of a highly trained horse or a competition in which the so-called high school movements are required.

The meaning of "high school movements" can be more clearly understood by first considering the higher training of the horse and its purpose. Beudant states, in substance, "The high school is the quest for complete control of the forces of the horse so that the rider may dispose of them as he wills." Thus we may conclude that high school movements are those requiring impulsion, balance, and lightness. Such movements, however, are as a rule artificial, as contrasted with the three natural gaits, the walk, the trot, and the gallop. High school movements are quite unnecessary for basic training, but they are the best means by which to arrive at the perfection of such training. This advanced training has a similar effect on the horse that a high school or college education has on human beings. The horse's mentality becomes more highly developed, he acquires greater muscular development, and because of his increasing lightness, he becomes easier to manage and submits more and more to the will of the rider. Gustave le Bon, a French psychologist who studied riding and horses, says, "The high school is the *basis* not the crown of intelligent riding."

DESCRIPTION OF MOVEMENTS. The following descriptive rules have been published by the International Equestrian Federation (F.E.I.).

In Hand. The horse must be "in hand" either at the walk or while working. A horse is "in hand" when his hocks are in place, head and neck more or less extended according to the rapidity of the gait, head steady and jaw relaxed, and he offers no resistance to his rider.

The Halt. When halted the horse stands squarely on his four legs and is immobile, but must be ready to move forward at the lightest pressure of the legs.

The Ordinary Walk. Free, regular, and long. The horses walks lightly but calmly with an even, deliberate step, marking clearly four beats equally spaced and very distinct. The rider keeps constant and soft contact with the horse's mouth.

When these four beats cease to be regular, the horse is disunited.

The disunited walk must not be confused with the amble.

The amble is a gait in which the horse displaces his members by lateral bipeds simultaneously.

The Extended Walk. The horse covers ground as rapidly as possible, but without rushing or becoming disunited. The hind feet extend beyond the forefeet in flight.

The rider gives plenty of freedom to the head and neck without losing contact. He can thus always change the gait of the horse, or his speed or direction.

The Collected Walk. The horse moves freely to the front. His neck is raised and arched. His face approaches the vertical. His hindquarters engage. The gait remains a walk with a regular succession of beats. Each step covers less ground but is higher, since the joints articulate more. The mobility is greater.

The Ordinary Trot. The ordinary trot (natural or average) is an intermediate gait between the extended trot and collected trot. The horse, going forward frankly and straight with no tendency to cross, engages his hocks, which remain very active, and softly stretches his reins, in an attitude balanced and relaxed. The strides must be as even as possible, the hind feet exactly following the front feet.*

The ordinary trot should not be confused with the Mitteltrab, *which is a more elevated, more rapid, and more brilliant gait. (Ed.)*

The Extended Trot. The horse extends his action; the head and neck stretch out; energetically urged by the haunches, the shoulders gain ground to the front without being noticeably raised.

The Collected Trot. The raised head and neck permit the shoulders to act with more liberty in every direction; the hocks, brought further under the mass, maintain the energy of impulsion, in spite of reduced speed. The horse takes shorter strides, but is lighter and more mobile.

At the ordinary and extended trot, the rider generally rises to the trot by posting. At the collected trot and half collected trot he sits in the saddle.

The Ordinary Gallop. An intermediate gait between the extended gallop and the collected gallop. The horse moves freely in his natural balance, keeping perfectly straight from head to tail.

The Extended Gallop. The neck extends; the muzzle is carried more or less forward; and the horse increases the length of his strides without losing any of his calmness or lightness.

The Collected Gallop. The shoulders, well relaxed, are free and mobile; the haunches are active and alive; the rate of forward movement decreases, but impulsion is not diminished.

The Half-Collected Trot and the Half-Collected Gallop. The gait is less active and the cadence slower than the ordinary trot and the ordinary gallop. The haunches are higher and less active than in the collected trot and the collected gallop. (Translator's note: These are the gaits of a horse "in hand" in the early stages of his training.)

Change of Lead. The horse changes leads "in the air" in one single stride and while advancing. The change of lead is said to be "in the air" when it is executed during the short time of suspension that follows each stride of the gallop. The horse should remain straight, calm, and light.

The Back. The retrograde movement of the horse; it is correct when the diagonally placed legs are raised and grounded almost simultaneously, the horse remaining straight. The horse moves to the rear step by step, constantly ready, upon the demand of the rider, to halt or to move forward without stopping.

All Gaits. A light mobility of the jaw, without nervousness, is a guarantee of the obedience of the horse and of the harmonious distribution of his forces.

The grinding of teeth is a form of resistance on the part of the horse. The judges should take this into account in their scoring.

Changes of Gait and of Speed. These should always be distinct and rapid, yet without abruptness; the previous cadence is maintained up to the moment that the horse is required to take the new gait, or comes to the halt.

On passing from backing to forward movement, the horse should not show any sign of halting.

The Changes of Direction. According to the school, the horse may remain either straight or slightly bent on the arc of the circle which he describes.

Serpentine. To execute the serpentine, the rider commences his first loop by progressively gaining distance (moving away) from the short side. He terminates his last loop by progressively nearing the short side in the opposite end.

The Two Track. In the two track, the horse moves on two tracks, the head, neck, and shoulders always preceding the haunches. A very light bend, permitting the horse to look in the direction in which he is moving, adds to his grace and helps to free the shoulder on the outside. The outside legs cross those on the inside. Any slowing of the gait must not be tolerated. The inside legs must be in agreement with those on the outside, and vice versa.

The two track may be demanded:

On the diagonals. In this case, it is customary that the horse be held roughly parallel to the long side of the hall or ring.

By haunches in (head obliquely to the wall).

By haunches out (haunches to the wall—inverted).

These two movements may be executed on a straight line, on a circle, on or during the turn.

The Counterchanges of Hand (Broken Lines). The rider leaves his original direction by an oblique and moves either to the quarter line, the center line, or the far side; then he returns by an oblique to the line that he was following at the beginning of the movement.

The Counterchanges of Hand, Holding the Haunches (Zigzag). The attention of the judges is directed on the attitude of the horse, the crossing of his legs, the precision, suppleness, and regularity of his movements. At the gallop the number of strides executed is taken strictly into account.

Any abrupt movement at the moment of changing direction is a fault.

The Half-Pirouette. The half turn on the haunches. At the walk, the inside rear foot may turn in place without leaving the ground. Describing a semicircle about the haunches, the shoulders commence their movement, *without any period of rest,* at the instant that the inside rear ceases to advance, and then resume the forward movement, *without a break,* when the turn is ended.

The Pirouette. The pirouette is a volte on two tracks, the haunches in, with a radius equal to the length of the horse, and in which the forehand describes a circle about the hindquarters.

Whatever the gait at which the pirouette is executed, the horse must turn without briskness, conserving throughout the cadence of the gait and the regularity in the movement of his members that it requires.

The two front legs and the outside hind turn around the inside hind, which forms a pivot and which should return to the same place each time that it is raised.

The Passage. A curtailed and shortened trot, very elevated and very cadenced. It is characterized by the more accentuated flexion of the knees and hocks, and by the graceful elasticity of the movements. Each diagonal, very evenly, is alternately elevated and put down in the same cadence, gaining little ground to the front and prolonging the suspension.

The toe of the front foot in suspension should normally be elevated to the height of the middle of the cannon bone of the front in support. The toe of the hind foot in suspension should be elevated only a little above the fetlock joint of the hind in support.

The same passage cannot be demanded of every horse. According to their conformation and temperament, and also according to the energy of their impulsion, some horses have the gasture more rounded and wider, other quicker and shorter, but the rocking of one hip on the other is considered a fault.

The Piaffer. The passage in place, the members in suspension elevating a little higher than in the passage.*

All movements should be obtained without perceptible effort on the part of the rider, who should be sitting upright, the loins and hips supple, thighs and legs fixed, and the upper part of the body easy, free, and erect.

The use of the voice, no matter how, and single or repeated clucking, are strictly forbidden; they are considered a very serious fault, and should result in a cut of at least four points in the mark awarded for the movement during which they have been employed.

Riding with two hands is required, except in the movements where it is specifically stated that the reins should be held in a single hand.

NOTE: *The notation and discussions of the natural gaits and the leap included in this chapter resulted from the study of slow-motion picture films owned by the Cavalry School, and those very kindly loaned by individuals.* [Ed.]

The horse must remain absolutely in place. Even if he advances only a few centimeters at each placing of his feet, with a cadence that is well marked, regular and brilliant, his piaffer can be considered "satisfactory" and no more. [Ed.]

11

Origin and Characteristics of Breeds
of Horses and Mules

BREED DEFINED. A breed is a group or race of animals related by descent that have distinctive characteristics that are not commonly possessed by other individuals or groups of the same species, and that are sufficiently well fixed to be uniformly well transmitted. Breeds have been developed by man, either intentionally or unintentionally, and require his restraining influence to prevent mixture with other races, and consequent loss of distinctive characteristics. The distinctive characteristics or features of a breed determine its economic importance. Curiously enough, there is not a breed that does not possess at least one distinctive characteristic in which it surpasses all other breeds. The possibilities that may be developed from any one breed are as definitely determined as the character of a horse's get is fixed by his ancestry. The three factors determining breed characteristics and, through them, the economic importance of the different breeds are:

The origin in blood that constitutes the hereditary force with which the breed is endowed.

The environment by which these bloodlines have been molded.

The purpose for which they have been bred; in other words, the ideal toward which the breeders have aimed.

The study of breeds, therefore, resolves itself into a consideration of the following essentials:

Origin.
   In blood.
   Geographical.
Development.
   Men.
   Methods.
History.
   Men.
   Events.
   Dates.
Characteristics.
   Breed types.
Economic importance.

FOUNDATION STOCK. The origin in blood is of greatest historical interest. It is one of the most important factors determining breed characters. The modern breeds are more or less composite in their origin. They were all derived in some degree from breeds or stocks that had already attained distinction on account of merit. In some cases, the combination of bloodlines was intentional, but it was more often incidental or even accidental. These historic horses can in turn be traced to a more limited group of common ancestors, and so on until the bloodlines focus in but a very few basic stocks. Darwin believed that all races had descended from one common ancestry. He attributed the extreme differences noted between modern breeds to environment.

While various authors differ somewhat in their conceptions of the origin of the domestic horse, they seem to agree in substance that he has been derived from several wild types that, with the exception of the Przhevalski horse of Mongolia, have since become extinct as wild species. Since each of the recognized wild types are known to have lived in more or less definite geographical areas, it might be safe to assume, as Darwin has suggested, that all of these types traced to a common ancestry and that their differences were due to the effect of environment. Most probably these types were preceded by others which in turn trace back to the small (cat size) "dawn horse," Eohippus, of the Lower Eocene Period.*

At least three types of the wild horse are recognized as progenitors of breeds of the domestic horse. Asia, Europe, and Africa each produced one more or less definite type. One was the so-called steppe horse of Asia, a descendant of which still exists in a wild state as the Przhevalski horse of northwestern Mongolia. The horses of Europe were of the "forest" type. Under the more favorable conditions of central and southern Europe they were smaller and have been referred to as the "Celtic pony" and the "Norseman's horse." The present pony breeds probably trace directly to the Celtic pony. The "desert" type was a product of Northern Africa and is known as the Libyan or Barb horse. The desert or Libyan horse has played the most important role in the development of the light breeds of horses.

*Probably 225,000,000 years ago. [Ed.]

Classification of breeds by type. Breeds may be classified according to the type to which their representatives conform, as:

Draft Type. Percheron, Belgian, Clydesdale, Shire, and Suffolk.

Heavy Harness Type. Hackney, Yorkshire Coach, Cleveland Bay, French Coach, German Coach, and Russian Orloff.

Light Harness Type. American Standardbred or American Trotting Horse.

Saddle or Riding Type. Thoroughbred, American Saddle Horse, Arab, and Morgan.

Ponies. Shetland, Welsh, and Hackney.

New Strains of Horses. During the last ten to twenty years, several new strains of horses have been published through the formation of registry associations by groups of breeders and through classifications provided for them by some livestock and horse-show association. It is doubtful if any of these rather recently developed strains are sufficiently fixed in their characteristics to merit being designated as a separate and distinct breed under the accepted definition of a breed. All of these strains are of riding type.*

American Quarter Horse. This strain received its name from its ability to run fast for a short distance. It probably first originated in Virginia but is now most widely raised in Texas. The horse is much prized by ranchers as a cow horse. He is a compact, short-backed, deep- and round-bodied, heavily muscled horse with a rather short neck. His average height is about fifteen hands and his average weight about 1,150 pounds. The foundation stock has been largely of the Thoroughbred breed.

Tennessee Walking Horse. This strain was developed in Tennessee largely from American Trotting Horse and American Saddle Horse foundation stock. His distinguishing characteristic is a fast, walking gait.

Palomino. At present the name Palomino, as applied to horses, indicates that the horse belongs to a group classed together largely on the basis of color. The typical color is a golden yellow, with white or silvery mane and tail, so the horse is sometimes known as the "Golden Horse." The strain first gained prominence in California, where its ancestors are said to be the horses of the early Spanish explorers.

Appaloosa. This strain originated in Oregon and its distinguishing characteristic is a white croup flecked with small spots of the prevailing body color, which may be any commonly found horse color.

In the four decades that have elapsed since these breed types were classified, much progress has been made by American Quarter Horse owners to establish the strain as a breed. The type is well fixed today, and it is now widely recognized as a true breed, versatilely employed for stock handling, polo, hunting, eventing, and hacking. On a much smaller scale the Tennessee Walking Horse is now considered by many authorities to have evolved into a true breed, since its distinctive characteristics have become fixed through sufficient generations of selective and controlled breeding. [Ed.]

American Quarter Horse *Courtesy American Quarter Horse Association.*

Tennessee Walking Horse Stallion Ebony Masterpiece *Courtesy Tennessee Walking Horse Breeders and Exhibitors Association.*

Albino. As the name indicates, this strain is pure white, the skin is pinkish or flesh color, and the eyes are usually of a bluish color.

American Spotted Horse. This strain has been little developed and the only characteristic is a spotted coat, which is described variously as pinto, paint, piebald, or calico.

THE ARAB.

Origin. No race of horses has enjoyed a more sentimental popularity or has had its history more obscured by myth and tradition than the Arab. In a general way, Arabs have been erroneously considered as the original source of the best blood. There is every reason to believe that horses similar to the best Arabs were in Northern Africa more than a thousand years before horses were known in Arabia. Their introduction was apparently from Africa, and took place some time between the first and the sixth centuries. The number of good horses in Arabia is much smaller than is generally supposed, and these horses are chiefly in the hands of certain families or tribes in the interior desert. The Arab proper, a descendant and not an ancestor of the original Libyan horse, is known as the Kohl breed, so named on account of the peculiar blue-black or antimony tint that characterizes the skin of the body.

The breed is composed of five strains that are believed by the Bedouins to be derived from a single mare named Keheilet Ajuz. Hehelian, the name of the most prominent strain, is derived from her name. The Darley Arabian, the greatest foundation sire of the Thoroughbred, was of this strain. Collectively, the strains are termed Al Khamseh, and they extensively interbred.

Characteristics. The principal colors of the true Arab are bay, brown, chestnut, gray, and flea-bitten gray. Black is a very rare color; dun is practically unknown. A dark mane and tail on a chestnut Arab is an undoubted sign of blood. The most characteristic physical points about the true Arab are his size and the peculiar and beautiful way he carries his tail.

He seldom exceeds 14/2 or 14/3 in height and weighs from 850 to 950 pounds. The tail is set on very high, well elevated, and carried to one side. The Arab has a handsome, intelligent head; broad forehead; large, kind eyes; straight or concave line of face; large nostrils; well-carried ears; and lean, wide jaw. The head and neck are well united but are carried a little high. The shoulders are well sloped, but the withers may err on the side of thickness due to the excessive muscling. He has capital forelegs with long, strong pasterns and a small hoof of tough, dense horn. The loin is flat, broad, and powerful; the barrel is roomy, the back ribs are long; and the croup is level. The hocks of the Arab constitute his weak points in that they are small and deficient in bone. Many individuals are inclined to be calf-kneed.

Economic Importance. Despite the fact that Arabs do not shine as racers, hunters, or polo ponies, they are of value for producing light cavalry horses. Their courage, docility, great ability for enduring long fatigue, and ability to subsist on rough herbage are qualities of preeminent importance.

Arabian Stallion El Paso *Courtesy Mary Jean LaCroix.*

THE THOROUGHBRED.

Origin and Development. Thoroughbred is the proper name of the English running, racehorse breed. Any other application of the term to horses is incorrect. It should neither be confused nor used synoymously with purebred, the adjective employed to denote the absence of any alien blood in the ancestry. In view of our knowledge of the history of horses in Great Britain, it is not probable that the origin of the Thoroughbred was from Oriental blood exclusively, although their lineage has been carefully guarded for so long that all trace of the common stock of the country has long since been bred out. They are, therefore, truly purebred. In discussing the development of the Thoroughbred, the reign of Charles II may be used as an important landmark, inasmuch as the modern Thoroughbred may be said to have been invented during his time on the throne.

The Romans brought over a large body of cavalry horses, many of which were crossed with the native stock. William the Conqueror, Roger de Boulegne, and the Earl of Shrewsbury introduced many Spanish horses during the Conquest. The first Eastern horse to be brought in was an Arabian presented to the Church of St. Andrew by Alexander I, King of Scotland. Edward III, who was an owner of running horses and interested in obtaining a lighter cavalry type, imported fifty Spanish horses because he believed that their blood would materially improve the native stock. During the reign of Henry VIII, some of his noblemen imported

213

Thoroughbred Stallion Secretariat. *Courtesy Meadow Farm.*

several Spanish stallions and mares, and James I caused a half dozen Barbs to be imported. Among these was the Markham Arabian, concerning which several interesting facts are known. The English horse at this time was able to perform quite notably on the track, but was coarse and ponderous compared to the imported Spanish and Barb horses.

The Helmsly Turk, whose name appears in the stud book, was imported during the time of Charles I. After the execution of Charles I, Cromwell continued the improvement of horses and maintained a stud and also a racing stable. The White Turk was added to the stud by his studmaster, Mr. Place. At this time, the English horse was able to hold its own with Eastern importations and must have been a rather creditable animal. This brings us to the reign of Charles II, to whom we owe the foundation of our present race of Thoroughbreds. He commissioned his Master of the Horse to go abroad and bring back some mares of the best blood he could find. He returned with six or eight Barb mares, which were added to the Royal stud and become known as the Royal mares. During this period, the three sires generally credited as the foundation sires of the breed were brought into the country and mated with the Royal mares and with native, or part native and part Barb, mares. These sires were the Darley Arabian, a pure Anazah, imported in 1706; the Byerly Turk, imported in 1689; and the Godolphin Arabian, brought from Paris in 1724. There are prominent families in the Thoroughbred and derived breeds that can be traced directly to each of these sires. Eclipse, the most conspicuous individual in the history of the English turf; Blaze, the foundation sire of the Hackney; and Messenger, the progenitor of the American Standardbred, were respectively four, three, and six generations removed from the Darley Arabian. King Herod, a great racehorse, was a line descendant of the Byerly Turk; and Matchem, a noted racehorse and sire, was a grandson of Godolphin Arabian.

Although the real era of Thoroughbred breeding is usually considered to have begun with the importation of the Royal mares by Charles II, horse racing of a primitive character was reported in the latter half of the twelfth century. Henry VIII was the first king to maintain a racing stable of his own, and English sovereigns since that time have been enthusiastic patrons of the turf. Through these centuries of breeding, the most rigid selection has been practiced, turf performances alone being the standard. Customs of conducting races and types of horses that could win, however, have undergone considerable modification within recent generations.

Thoroughbreds were introduced into this country by the English colonists in The Old Dominion, in which section the Thoroughbred is still strong, especially in Virginia. The first Thoroughbred of note to be imported was Diomed, the winner of the first English Derby. He was brought over in 1779. In a straight line descent from Diomed came Sir Archy, the first truly American Thoroughbred; Boston, his grandson, conceded to have been one of the greatest American racehorses, and his son Lexington, a scarcely less remarkable performer than Boston and a most influential sire, figuring in the American Standardbred and Saddle families as well as in the Thoroughbred.

Characteristics. Most characteristic are the extreme refinement; the small proportioned head; clearly defined features; straight face line; near ear; fine throttle; long, sloping shoulders; well-made withers; long, lean neck well attached; muscular thighs and quarters; straight hind legs; large heart girth; strong, sloping pasterns; and a rather small foot of dense horn.

Economic Importance. The Thoroughbred is the foundation of our hunting stock. His blood is represented in our hacks, polo ponies, and nearly all our harness horses, not to mention the remounts for the cavalry.

One of the objects of racing is to improve the breed of horses. By having a good stamp of blood horse, we improve nearly every particular hunter, hack, polo pony, cavalry horse, and harness horse, in their several types, whatever may be the case on the turf.

THE STANDARDBRED OR AMERICAN TROTTING HORSE. An American breed of horses whose members excel at trotting or pacing. To be eligible for registry an animal must be the get of a registered Standard mare and a registered Standard stallion. At one time qualification for registration was based on performance alone; that is one mile in 2:30 or better trotting, 2:25 or better pacing.

Origin. The foundation bloodlines of the breed were laid in Orange County, New York, the original seat of the breed. The chief interest in trotters centered about

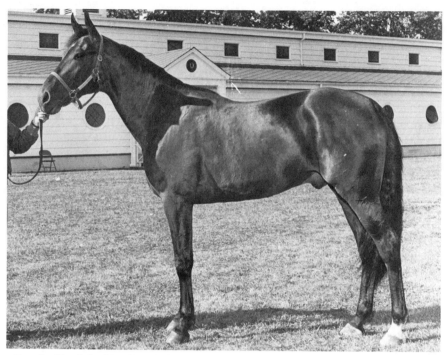

Standardbred Stallion Nevele Pride. *Courtesy United States Trotting Association.*

New York City, where the improvement in the construction of roads gave a great stimulus to road driving. Later, the seat of the breed moved to Kentucky and eventually covered all of the states in general and California in particular.

The two most notable foundation sires were Messenger and Justin Morgan. Messenger was a gray Thoroughbred, six generations removed from the Darley Arabian, and was imported from England as an eight-year-old in 1788. He stood most of his life about New York and Philadelphia. His sire was Mambrino, the progenitor of some of the finest Coaching horses in England. The most famous son of Messenger was Mambrino, named after his paternal grandsire. Mambrino, the son, was never raced but was a successful sire. His son, Abdallah, was sire of Hambletonian 10, or Rysdyk's Hambletonian, the most conspicuous sire of the Standardbred. The latter's dam was by Imp. Bellfounder of Norfolk blood.

It has been suggested that the facts that the horse stock about New York was descended from horses brought over by the Dutch, and that a family of trotters were native to Friesland, would account for so many of Messenger's get being trotters. Messenger and other Thoroughbreds imparted the speed and stamina, while their get derived their instinct to trot from their Dutch-bred dams.

Hambletonian 10 was foaled in Orange county in 1849 and sired 1,321 colts before he died in 1866. He is described as a bay horse of excellent structure but very plain, the large head and Roman face especially rendering him objectionable to the eye.

The important early families of trotters were the Hambletonians, Mambrino Chiefs, Clays, Morgans, Bashaws, and Pilots.

The greatest brood mare in the foundation of the Standardbred was Green Mountain Maid, the dam of Electioneer.

Characteristics. Standardbred horses are of all shapes, colors, and sizes. Compared with the Thoroughbred, there is a marked absence of the greyhound type, the Standardbred being round barreled and well ribbed up. The pasterns are shorter; the shoulders heavier and straighter; and the withers are lower. The hocks are generally very large and strong, and the quarters are well muscled. The neck is shorter and is attached to the shoulders so that it is carried higher than that of the Thoroughbred.

Economic Importance. With a wide range of adaptability to almost any kind of service, the Standardbred is the best exponent of the light harness horse. Many hunters are part Standardbred, and some of the champion saddle horses have been of this breeding. Except for racing and very limited use for pleasure driving, the breed is of little economic importance today. Prior to the use of the automobile, horses of this breed, or containing some of the blood of this breed, were to be found on nearly every farm, where they were used as buggy horses and for lighter farm work. They were also used extensively in towns and cities for light delivery work and for utility and pleasure driving. Horses of this breed or horses containing the blood of this breed made up the bulk of riding and lighter artillery horses used by the Army during World War I. The breed is now little used for the production of riding type horses. The utility driving horse of preautomobile days is now almost extinct.

THE MORGAN HORSE. The Morgan is an American breed of horses developed largely in the state of Vermont. The original Morgans were considered harness horses, but after the development of the Standard or American trotting horse their popularity as road horses was considerably diminished. The breed played an important part in the development of the Standardbred and the American Saddle Horse. The purebred Morgan of today is generally considered a riding type of horse, rather than a harness horse. Like the Standardbred horse, horses of Morgan blood have been used in the New England states and elsewhere for all manner of work from riding to light draft.

Origin. The Morgans are perhaps our oldest trotting family. They are descended in the paternal line from Justin Morgan, a remarkable individual that was foaled at Springfield, Massachusetts, in 1789 and lived thirty-two years. He was a small horse, about 14/2 in height and 950 pounds weight. He was noted for his wonderful performances of endurance, speed, pulling power, and intelligence. His individuality was no more striking than the prepotency with which he impressed his get. His breeding has never been satisfactorily established. Colonel Joseph Buttell has given the sire as a Thoroughbred called Beautiful Bay, and the dam as a member of the Wildair family of Thoroughbreds. A Dutch origin, similar to that of the Norfolk trotter, has been suggested and does not sound unreasonable. The Thoroughbred ancestry, however, is the one usually accepted. The three most notable sons of Justin Morgan were: Bullrush Morgan, Woodbury Morgan, and Sherman Morgan,

Morgan Stallion Bennfield's Ace *Unlike the original concept of a muscular, blocky, utility-type horse, this animal typifies the present-day trend toward developing a breed similar to the American Saddlebred. [Ed.] Courtesy American Morgan Horse Association.*

from whom came the three greatest horses of the breed in their day. Morgan mares were mated with sons and grandsons of Hambletonian, and later those of Denmark, to such an extent that for years the breed in its original purity and type was threatened with extinction. The blood was spent mainly in developing the Standardbred and American Saddle Horse.

Characteristics. Bay, brown, and black colors prevail outside the Lambert family, in which chestnut predominates. The Morgan stands about fifteen hands; is very compactly made with a short, strong back; deep ribs; broad loins, strong coupling, a breedy head, proudly carried; rather short, heavy neck, with prominent chest; short legs well set on each corner and of unusual substance; and an airy, busy, but not high way of going.

Economic Importance. The advent of the automobile was a great setback to the breeding of Morgan horses. Except as a riding horse, the Morgan breed is at present of little economic importance. The number of purebred Morgan horses is relatively small and the breed has never enjoyed wide popularity other than in some of the New England states. There are a considerable number of Morgan horses in California. In certain cattle-ranching sections of the country, Morgan stallions have been used for mating with native ranch mares to produce a sturdy type of cow horse.

THE AMERICAN SADDLE HORSE. The development of this breed has been parallel in many respects with that of the Standardbred. Both are the result of a top cross on what might be termed a native mare foundation. In each case, the descendants of one individual have constituted a family that has dominated the breed. Their respective histories are also more or less contemporaneous. Denmark, the Thoroughbred whose progeny founded the Saddle breed, was foaled in 1839, while Messenger reached this country in 1788, and his great grandson Hambletonian was foaled in 1849.

Origin. The original American Saddle Horse was born, of necessity, on the frontier, where, because of the lack of good roads and suitable vehicles, the horse's back afforded the chief means of transportation. The easy, lateral, ambling gait was cultivated, and those horses which showed the greatest aptitude in this direction were selected for breeding. Selection has been based not only on performance but on ideals in type, conformation, and quality as well. These have been sought and are clearly marked in the prepotency of the foundation family. The list of foundation sires is headed by Denmark, a Thoroughbred by Imported Hedgeford. Three other Thoroughbreds, one Morgan, and two Canadian sires are listed among the total of ten accepted by the American Saddle Horses Association as foundation sires. Denmark had numerous progeny, the most notable of which was Gaines Denmark. His dam, the Stevenson mare, was a great ambler. She represented the

American Saddlebred Stallion King's Sport *Courtesy American Saddle Horse Breeders Association.*

219

common stock of the country and was believed by some to be of greater foundation importance than Denmark himself. The two important families of this breed are the Denmark strain, which produced Rex McDonald, the sire of Rex Peavine; and the Chief strain, which produced Harrison Chief and Bourbon King. The chief centers of breeding are Kentucky and the region about Columbia and Mexico, Missouri. The Civil War and the increased popularity of the Standardbred subsequent to that period, proved a serious setback to Saddle Horse breeding, but it has been gradually regaining its popularity.

Characteristics. The Saddle Horse is rather upstanding, and possesses a beautifully molded head and neck. The neck is attached high, the low withers merging into the neck. The barrel is rather round and lacks depth at the heart, the croup is level. He has a flashy way of going with head and tail carried high. He is often deficient in substance, due to being bred so finely for show purposes. The colors are not confined within any limit, although certain families are very uniform in transmission of color. Chestnut is a very common color.

THE HACKNEY. Preeminently a show harness horse today, and more generally criticized as deficient in stamina than in any other one respect. The Hackney was originally a road horse of unusual endurance.

Origin. Early Hackney history is set in Norfolk and adjacent counties where, as early as the latter part of the eighteenth century, there existed a remarkable family of distance trotters. This was in the primitive days of vehicles and roads, and these Norfolk trotters, as they were called, were used chiefly under the saddle. The fact that this was the first line of trotters is significant. This trotting instinct in the prototype of the modern Hackney has been accounted for in many ways. Since these horses were originally stoutly made, blocky, and heavy-fronted, and have remained so until comparatively recent times, it is reasonable to suppose that they carried, in addition to the Thoroughbred blood that predominated at that time, some degree of cold blood. The speed, courage, and stamina of the Thoroughbred, coupled with the natural inclination of the colder-blooded Dutch horse to trot, resulted in the square-gaited, fast, enduring, and rather high-going Norfolk trotter. The real beginning of the Hackney breed is fixed at the original Shales Horse, foaled in 1760, by Blaze, a Thoroughbred race horse three generations removed from the Darley Arabian and out of a stout, common, hunting mare of Norfolk. With improvement in roads and vehicles, Hackneys were used more in harness, and their naturally high, trappy action was cultivated. They have become the harness horse par excellence in England and America.

Characteristics. Typical Hackneys are comparatively short-legged animals, rarely standing over 15/3. Their weight is greater than their stature would indicate. Their heads are square in outline, deep in jaw; necks well crested but frequently heavy, lacking finish at the throttle, and giving a heavy forhand. Naturally high flexion of the hocks and knees is the most distinguishing feature. Chestnut color with flashy white markings all around has been most common, although bays, browns, blacks, and roans are acceptable.

The Hackney pony is a representative Hackney under 14/2, eligible to the same registration, and frequently bred along similar lines on one side as the full-sized Hackneys.

THE FRENCH COACH. The name French Coach is of American origin, since the breed is known in France as Demisang.

Origin. Since the seventeenth century, when the government studs were established, the French have been breeding horses for army service. Their method up to 1840 was to mate Thoroughbred stallions with the native French mares of Normandy. Horses so bred were called, most appropriately, Demisang (half blood). Since 1840 the halfbreds have been interbred. One of the stallions, Young Rattler, brought to France in 1820, gave rise to a side line of coach horses. There are really three types of Demisang; viz., the cavalry horse, the trotter, and the so-called coacher.

Characteristics. The correct type is a good-sized, rather upstanding individual, close and full made, but quite bloodlike in head, neck, withers, feet, and legs. He is not drafty and lacks the style of action typical of the Hackney. Bays, browns, and chestnuts, with occasional blacks and roans, are the usual colors. They have never been successful in the stud of this country.

THE GERMAN COACH.

Origin. The different states of Germany have been producing big, stout horses for the German cavalry for so long that their origin is obscure. Some Thoroughbred and Oriental crosses have been made, no doubt, but as a rule the German horse shows no refinement, and cold blood predominates in his veins. Each state has been a law unto itself and has developed a type somewhat distinctive. The type of German Coacher that was formerly imported into this country came from Oldenburg and East Friesland.

Characteristics. The German Coach is the largest of any of the heavy harness breeds, weighing 1,500 pounds in some cases. If not too drafty, it has an ideal harness form but is lacking in finish, quality, style, pace, and action; in short, it is too cold. Individuals are bay, brown, or black with little if any white.

THE CLEVELAND BAY AND YORKSHIRE COACH. The original Cleveland Bay was an old-fashioned coach horse. He could qualify neither as a harness nor as a saddle horse. As a result, the mares were bred to Thoroughbred sires. In turn, the best halfbreds were interbred or remated with the Thoroughbred, and produced either good hunters or good carriage horses. The Cleveland Bay takes its name from the Vale of Cleveland in Yorkshire. Early importations were used in this country for the production of utility horses. In recent years, they have been used in a limited way for crossing with Thoroughbred mares to produce a heavyweight riding horse.

The Yorkshire Coach horse is the result of the same breeding as the Cleveland Bay and derives its name from the county in which it was developed.

THE PERCHERON.

Origin. The foundation of the Percheron was composed of the Norman descendants

Percheron Stallion *Courtesy Percheron Horse Association of America.*

of the original Flemish stock, mated with Oriental stallions. These crosses were either incidental to current events or were made with a definite purpose in view. They had a most important influence in determining the type of horse into which the Percheron was to develop.

The Percheron first attained distinction as a stagecoach horse in the days before railroads were built. It was work that required a draft animal capable of rapid speed; the ordinary road horse could not stand the pace. The breeders of La Perche specialized in this type of horse, and their success marked the beginning of Percheron popularity.

The railroads replaced the stage coach in the nineteenth century. The French breeders foresaw this crisis, and perceived for agriculture a new era that would require a different stamp of horse. The true draft horse was to supersede the "diligence" type. Even in their efforts to meet the demand for a horse of greater weight and power, however, the La Perche breeders did not lose sight of the desirable characteristics of hot blood derivation, which were retained in so far as they were consistent with the increase in size and power.

Characteristics. The Percheron may weigh as much as a ton and still possess a refinement of head and neck, a general suppleness of form, a texture of bone and hoof, a degree of quality and finish throughout, together with an energetic, yet

222

perfectly tractable disposition that is not equaled in any of the other draft breeds. Stallions vary from 16/0 to 16/3 and weigh 1,900 to 2,100 pounds. Mares are some two inches less in height. He is not quite so large as the Shire or the Belgian; has a somewhat more upstanding, less blocky form than the Belgian; head of good proportions, finished in crest and throttle; full, bright eyes; bone of good texture, but in some cases too fine; fetlocks of the very best texture; and hoofs of dark brown. His way of going manifests a snap and boldness not displayed by draft horses as a rule. Gray and black are the most common colors, although bay, brown, roan, and chestnut are encountered.

Economic Importance. In this country Percherons outnumber all other draft breeds combined. There are over 33,000 Percherons on farms.* Since being introduced in Ohio in 1851, they have been popular with the farmers of the Middle West. The fact that most native American mares have some hot blood may account for the fact they have always nicked well with the Percherons.

THE BELGIAN.

Origin. Belgium is included in the original territory to which the old Flemish horse was indigenous. Since the history of the breed records no other stock, we conclude that this breed is directly and exclusively descended from the old Flemish stock. The long hair and black color of the Flemish horse have been bred out by selection. There were originally three types in as many different regions, but these have been amalgamated into the present Belgian cart horse.

Characteristics. The Belgian is a massive, drafty chunk with short legs; a compact body; wide, muscular ends; and deep, wide, spreading ribs. The head is square and medium-sized; the neck short and heavy-crested. The hoof is too small, the bone is inclined to be round, and there is a general lack of refinement. He is an easy-keeper, ships well, and is popular with feeders for these reasons. He is rather sluggish, and his immense width causes him to roll or paddle a little at the walk. Chestnut and roan are the predominating colors. The first importation was in 1866.

THE CLYDESDALE.

Origin. The name Clydesdale is taken from the Clyde River in Scotland, in the valley of which the breed has been developed. The earliest history of horses in Britain describes a horse akin to the Scandinavian ponies. After the importance of size was impressed upon the Britons by the Roman conquest, the size was systematically increased by royal edict. The blood of all the British draft breeds was derived essentially from Flemish sources. It is a matter of record that as many as a hundred Flemish stallions were imported at one time. The conditions of life surrounding these breeds during their formative period, and especially the variance in the notion of what constitutes a draft horse, as expressed by the Scotsman and Englishman, are ample to account for whatever differences in type there may be between the Clydesdale, the Shire, and the Suffolk. The Scotsman attaches especial importance to the legs, feet, pasterns, manner of going, and a free, springy stride.

*As of 1935. [Ed.]

223

As a consequence of the inevitable law of correlation, there has come to be associated with this character of stride more length of leg and back but less width and massiveness.

Characteristics. The Clydesdale stands over more ground than any other draft breed, and has well-directed legs viewed from either way. The quality of bone is ideal, the slope of pasterns and shoulders are excellent, and the feet excel in size and shape. The fetlock has a large feather of fine quality hair. The action is true, straight, and springy. The barrel is small, the head plain, and the back is low. Bay and brown colors predominate, with occasional blacks, chestnuts, and roans. White markings on the face and usually on all four legs are characteristics.

THE SHIRE.

Origin. The Shire was developed by the Englishman along the lines he desired for a draft breed. The foundation was the same as that of the Clydesdale, and only by selective breeding did the two distinct types emerge. The low-lying fen country of Cambridge and Lincolnshire is more conductive to massiveness than are the uplands of Scotland.

Characteristics. The typical Shire weighs more than any other breed, although he is not so stocky as the Belgian. There is a marked absence of quality in the head, texture of hair, bone, and hoof. The fetlock has a large, coarse feather. His temperament is extremely phlegmatic. The range of color is greater than in any other breed, and he may be found in any shade from black to roan and gray. His popularity in this country has been restricted, but a percentage of Shire blood in dams from which market geldings are produced is acknowledged to be a valuable asset.

THE SUFFOLK.

Origin. Characterized as being of the purest lineage and of most uniform color, the Suffolks are bred more exclusively for farm work than are any of the other draft breeds. This stamp of horse is known to have been bred in Suffolk for over two centuries. Practically all purebred representatives trace back to a common ancestor, the Crisp Horse of Ufford, foaled in 1760. They are produced almost exclusively in Suffolk and Essex for farming purposes.

Characteristics. By virtue of their good dispositions, ease of control in the harness, and easy-keeping qualities, the Suffolks are especially adaptable to farm work. They are invariably a chestnut color of varying shades with little, if any, white, They are smaller than other draft breeds and have a smooth, rotund form, and a clean leg devoid of feather.

MULES. A mule is the product of a jackass (male ass) and a mare; a hinny is the product of a stallion and a female ass or jennet. Mules and hinnies are hybrids and are almost invariably sterile. Horse and zebra hybrids have been successfully produced.

The Jack. The so-called American or "Mammoth" jackass or jack, although but a few generations removed from imported stock, has the reputation of getting a higher class of mules than the imported jacks. Of such imported breeds as the Catalonian, Poitou, Maltese, Andalusian, Majorcan, and Italian, the Catalonian is the most popular. The jack most desired for mule breeding is at least sixteen hands high. The more weight and substance he has the better. He is long and wide in form, having good-sized, well-shaped head and ears; straight legs of ample bone; and well-shaped feet of good size and texture. Black with light points is the color most favored.

The Mare. The mule is believed to take after the sire in matter of head, ears, bone, and foot, while its stature and form of body, especially, are derived chiefly from the dam. Mares of good size and shape, with a dash of hot blood, are best adapted to the production of mules.

The Advantages of the Mule. The mule has some distinct advantages over the horse for some kinds of work. They may be enumerated as follows:

He stands hot weather better and is less susceptible to digestive disorders and laminitis.

A mule takes better care of himself in the hands of an incompetent driver than a horse does.

Due to its structure, the foot of a mule is less subject to disorders.

Mules are invariably good walkers.

Age and infirmities seem to count less against a mule than a horse.

Classes of Mules. There is an extended classification of mules, but they are bred for essentially two purposes: viz., work in the fields and in the mines. Farm, sugar, and cotton mules are bred chiefly from well-bred mares of hot blood and are, therefore, rangy, fine, and snappy movers. The mine demand, which is for a draftier, bigger-boned mule, is met by mating the smaller, smoother class of draft mares with big-boned jacks.

12

Transportation of Horses

This chapter in the original edition dealt largely with rail and water transportation, now obsolete practices not discussed in this revision. Discussion of air transportation has not been introduced herein because of the complexity of government regulations and the relatively small number of horsemen who patronize this form of transcontinental and intercontinental transportation. [Ed.]

When it is desired to place horses at a point more than a few hours distant by marching, and where the horse is not needed as a transport animal enroute, some form of transportation is usually used. This is especially true where the rapidity of movement is a controlling factor or where the condition of the horse before, during, or after the movement is of prime importance. Every person concerned with the transportation of animals should have a good working knowledge of the means of transportation, facilities available, and management of animals being transported.

HIGHWAY TRANSPORTATION. The highway transportation of horses followed the development of the automobile and the motor truck, and more especially the advent of the high-speed pneumatic-tired truck designed for use on our modern surfaced roads. Because of their cumbersome size and very considerable weight when loaded it seems that the movement of any motor-actuated road vehicles for transporting horses, unless it be light-weight, low-capacity trailers, must necessarily be very largely restricted to improved roads.

Types of Vehicles. The commercial types of vehicles may be classified as follows:

> *Motor Trucks:*
> Enclosed horse vans (truck chassis).
> Stake body cargo trucks.
> General cargo trucks.

Semitrailers:

Semitrailer truck tractor unit.

Trailers:	Van or open
Truck drawn.	stockbody type
Passenger car drawn.	

Horse Vans. The horse van mounted on a truck chassis is a very satisfactory type of vehicle for highway transportation of horses. It was the first type of refined vehicle developed for this purpose. It has been, in large measure, superseded by the vanlike tractor-trailer units, which have many advantages. Horse vans are practically all custom made. Manufacturers use some standard motor truck chassis, increasing the wheelbase if necessary, and build the van body to suit the desires of the purchaser. These vans vary in capacity; by far the greater number of six-horse capacity. They are equipped with stalls, lights, ventilating windows, floor mats, padding, equipment compartments—in fact, everything that can be designed for the deluxe transportation of horses. Over muddy or unimproved roads the movement of such a vehicle would be very difficult. In many parts of the country such vans are in service as common carriers and are used for shipping racehorses, show horses, hunters, and polo ponies. Horses shipped in vans, under good conditions, seem to ship quite as well as those shipped by railroad express in horse baggage cars.

Standard Stake or Slat-Body Trucks. Standard commercial trucks with high-side stake or slat bodies are quite extensively used for transporting ordinary livestock such as cattle or horses. Horses may be transported in such a truck by tying one or more horses or, if loaded to capacity, the horses are loaded free. This type of truck is without stalls or stanchion bars to separate the horses, and as a rule the bed is quite high above the ground. Because of the sway, pitch, and inclination of the truck, horses are often thrown or crowded against each other and maintain their balance with difficulty. This method of travel for a horse is quite hazardous and very fatiguing. From the standpoint of freedom from injury, exposure, and fatigue, this method of shipping is not as satisfactory as rail shipment in an ordinary stock car.

Semitrailers and Trailers. The more recent trend in the development of highway vehicles for transporting horses has been in the direction of semitrailer truck tractor units. The semitrailer section of the unit is usually of the closed van type with side entrance. They are equipped as described for horse vans in the second preceding paragraph above. Some are made with an open top, slatted livestock body, and with permanent or removable stanchion bars to provide stalls. They are usually of six- or eight-horse capacity. Semitrailers of this general type are far more satisfactory than ordinary truck vans. The absence of driving mechanism makes it possible to set the bed or floor much lower; this results in greater stability and increased ease in loading. The truck tractor, or prime mover, is a standard or especially designed truck that carries much of the forward weight of the semitrailer.*

The portee cavalry, developed at the beginning of World War II, transported complete squads (eight horses, eight men, and their tack, weapons, rations and equipment) in a six-ton combination animal and cargo semitrailer with a rear opening. The horses were loaded four abreast, all facing forward. [Ed.]

Light two-horse, two-wheel trailers, of both the van and slat-body types, have proved quite satisfactory, and standard models are now produced commercially by manufacturers. They are designed for use with passenger automobiles or light trucks and are expensively used by owners of small stables for both long and short hauls of show horses, hunters, and racehorses. The better commercial bodies are of the van or closed-body type and are completely equipped.

PREPARATION OF HORSES FOR SHIPMENT.

Health. Only horses in perfect health should be shipped. When practicable, temperature readings taken just prior to loading will frequently detect animals in the early stages of a sickness that might otherwise not be discovered.

Feeding. When the shipment is going to be of two or more days duration, the feed, especially the grain, should be reduced for two or three days in advance, and bran fed dry or in mashes to soften the dung and assist in preventing the constipation, which is usually incident to shipment. Do not give physics.

Condition. As a general rule the harder the condition of the horse the better he will withstand the hardships of long shipment. However, horses in hard condition should be slightly let down for long shipments. Unconditioned or green horses stand shipment very poorly, especially if they are in poor flesh or fatigued; they are then easy prey for the communicable diseases.

Clipping. All horses for water transportation in tropical climates should be clipped before loading. Clipping is not necessary for other forms of shipment. Recently clipped horses should not be shipped in cold weather.

Shoes. For all forms of shipment where horses are shipped loose, the hind shoes at least should be removed, preferably all shoes. Under no circumstances should calked shoes be permitted in a shipment. Horses shipped by truck or trailer are usually intended for use very shortly after unloading and are usually shipped shod. Bell boots afford the greatest measure of protection from self-inflicted shoe injuries and from treads of the adjacent horse. Because of the considerable amount of sway and jolt of highway vehicles, too much attention cannot be paid to the prevention of injuries from shoes. Injuries above the region protected by bell boots are not common, and bandaging the legs affords little protection.

Bandaging. Rest bandages afford some degree of protection to the lower legs and, in severe weather, serve as clothing. Bandages should never be used on horses in shipment unless the attendant can reset the bandage every day at least. A horse entangled in a loose bandage may become frantic and injure himself far more severely than any injury the bandage was intended to prevent. If bandages are used be sure the attendant knows how to reset them properly. Bandaging tails to prevent hair rub is a dangerous practice unless done very expertly. A well-padded haunch bar is better. A special felt-padded shipping halter with a heavy felt roll at the poll will protect the head from external injury and abrasions from the halter.

Health Certificates, Tests, and Quarantine. Practically every state requires that animals shipped into the state shall be accompanied by a health certificate, issued by a veterinarian in the state of origin of the shipment, stating that the animals are free of communicable disease as determined by a physical examination made just prior to shipment. Some states further require evidence that the animals have reacted negatively to biological tests for certain diseases. Animals being shipped into the United States from a foreign country must be tested and quarantined in accordance with such rules and regulations of the United States Department of Agriculture as may be applicable in each case.*

Inspection of Vehicles. All trucks, trailers, cars, ships, or aircraft should be carefully inspected shortly before loading. Examine for anything that may injure animals such as projecting nails, sharp corners or edges, broken slats in cars, rotten or broken floors, head room, stoutness of stalls, methods of restraining the animal, and ease with which the animal may be removed in case of emergency. When shipping by truck or trailer do not forget to check on the mechanical part of the vehicle and its supply of gas, oil, and water. Check the feed and implements for care of the animals. Commercial transportation facilities should be checked for disinfection, which should be accomplished immediately after unloading the last public shipment; if in doubt, require another disinfection before loading.

Care of Animals During and After Shipment. Horses should not be confined in trucks or trailers for more than about ten to twelve hours without unloading. More animals have become sick during or after shipment because of improper ventilation and heat than have been injured by wind or exposure to cold. Plenty of fresh air is always needed, but direct drafts must be avoided. Light covers may protect the body from draft, and from chafe or abrasion; they should be well fastened.

Horses are fatigued after shipment and, when unloaded, should be given rest and light feeding. It is well to allow only hay for several hours. Water at freedom should not be given until at least two hours after unloading unless the animals have been watered within the previous six hours. Horses should not be turned loose in large corrals after unloading because, in their exuberance at being released, they will run and play too much, and frequently "founder" themselves. It is best to stable or confine in small enclosures until they have recuperated. After a horse has been shipped it takes at least the equivalent of the time consumed by the journey to get him back in as good condition as he was at the time of shipment. Do not hurry the process; the capabilities of recently shipped horses are frequently overestimated.

Diseases of Horses Following Shipment. Seasoned animals seldom develop contagious diseases as a result of shipment. Green horses, or those not having been previously associated with large groups of animals, or that have not been previously shipped, almost always contract some form of shipping disease. Colds (page 174), influenza (page 175), strangles (page 175), and ringworm (page 180) are communicable diseases that often occur among unseasoned horses following shipment. While it seems to be the lot of most horses that are shipped about to any extent to

---

The military quarantined newly arrived horses for a twenty-one-day period. Normally a working quarantine, this was found to be an effective means of protecting the older horses from any communicable disease brought in by the newcomers. [Ed.]

contract diseases sooner or later, everything possible should be done to prevent them. The horses should be in the best possible condition to resist infection, and possibly they will escape contracting disease.

Index

231